ALSO BY DAVID WOOLDRIDGE:

*Conductor's World*　(*1970*)

# CHARLES IVES

11/6/81

# →CHARLES  IVES: A Portrait

## by
## David Wooldridge

## FABER  AND  FABER
### 3 Queen Square
### London

56950

c\s8

First published in England in 1975
by Faber and Faber Limited
3 Queen Square London WC1

ISBN 0 571 10687 0

Originally published as *From the Steeples and Mountains*

Mr. Wooldridge wishes to acknowledge the grant of a fellowship from
Chapelbrook Foundation to do this book.

Grateful acknowledgment is made to Warner Bros. Music for permission
to reprint three lines of lyrics from "Ballad of a Thin Man," by Bob
Dylan, copyright © 1965 by M. Witmark & Sons, All Rights Reserved;
to City Lights for permission to reprint an excerpt from *Call Me Ishmael*,
by Charles Olson, copyright 1947 by Charles Olson; and to Harcourt
Brace Jovanovich, Inc., for permission to reprint a paragraph from *The
Making of Americans*, by Gertrude Stein, copyright 1934 by Harcourt,
Brace & Co., Inc., and copyright 1962 by Alice B. Toklas.

Extracts from Charles Ives, *Essays Before a Sonata* (edited by Howard
Boatwright), and from the *Memos* (edited by John Kirkpatrick) are
quoted by kind permission of the copyright owners, W. W. Norton &
Co., Inc., New York.

*Printed in Great Britain by*
*Whitstable Litho, Straker Brothers Ltd*

*To Julius Herford, Abbey Simon and Hans Tischler*

There are many that I know and they know it.
They are all of them repeating and I hear it. I love it
and I tell it. I love it and now I will write it.
This is now a history of my love of it. I hear it
and I love it and I write it. They repeat it.
They live it and I see it and I hear it. They live it
and I hear it and I see it and I love it
and now and always I will write it.
There are many kinds of men and women
and I know it. They repeat it and I hear it
and I love it. This is now a history of the way they do it.
This is now a history of the way I love it.

GERTRUDE STEIN: *The Making of Americans*

# Contents

# Illustrations

*(following page 178)*

Uncle Isaac and Aunt Emily Ives outside the family house, Danbury.
*(Scott-Fanton Museum, Danbury, Conn)*

The room where Charles Ives was born.
*(Scott-Fanton Museum)*

Centre Church, New Haven.
*(New Haven Historical Society)*

The Ives family piano.
*(Scott-Fanton Museum)*

Ives at Yale, with roommate Mandeville Mullaly.
*(Scott-Fanton Museum)*

59th Street, looking towards Columbus Circle, 1898.
*(Byron Collection, Museum of the City of New York)*

Broadway, from Liberty Street, a turn-of-the-century view.
*(Byron Collection)*

Wedding picture of Charles and Harmony Ives, June 9 1908,
with the Twichell family.
*(Ives family collection)*

Charles and Harmony at Umpawaug Road, West Redding, 1929.
*(Ives family collection)*

The Housatonic at Stockbridge.
*(Charles Elliott)*

Elk Lake, from Pell Jones's.
*(David Wooldridge)*

The old Methodist Church, Hartsdale Road.
*(J. LeViness)*

Keene Valley Plateau—"Universe Symphony."
*(Keene Valley Historical Society, Keene Valley, N Y)*

Charles Ives and adopted daughter Edith, July 1924.
*(Scott-Fanton Museum)*

# FROM THE STEEPLES
# AND MOUNTAINS

# Prologue: Music's Ishmael

I take SPACE to be the central fact to man born in
America, from Folsom Cave to now. I spell it large
because it comes large here. Large, and without
mercy.

Some men ride on such space, others have to
fasten themselves like a tent stake to survive. As
I see it Poe dug in and Melville mounted. They are
the alternatives.

CHARLES OLSON: *Call Me Ishmael*

Charles Ives has this dimension. Other composers—those that survived—dug in, by necessity or choice. Ives mounted. His music
rides on such space. The man, his life, the whole pattern of his thinking are witness to it. A sense of space, a use of space, an understanding of space that transcended metered time. Sidereal.

A Connecticut Yankee—like Mark Twain/by adoption, like
Melville, nearly—, schooled in the Puritan decencies (and the pro-
prieties, which he shed; he " 'most never went to church" after he
married Joe Twichell's daughter), yet more of the Old Dispensa-
tion: an Old Testament prophet crying a New Mythology in the
American wilderness, along with his insurance tracts and political
nostrums. Like Thoreau—Alcott's words—"he of all men seemed
the native New Englander, as much so as the oak, the granite ledge;
our best sample of an indigenous American, untouched by the old
country . . ." Like Melville—Olson's words—"*a comprehension
of* PAST, *his marriage of spirit to source*"; and, "*a confirmation of*
FUTURE."

In later life he grew himself the nice familiar beard, clasped
a cane against his advancing infirmities, wore, now AGGRESSIVELY, the
old Danbury felt hat he'd worn at Battery Park in 1915, and played

the recluse at his Redding homestead. It had not been like this in former years. A passport photograph taken in 1924, when he was nearly 50 and his last major works 7 years behind him, shows Ives with his adopted daughter Edith: face still clean shaven, powerful athletic frame neatly attired in a tailored business suit.

Tall, very shy—as tall men tend to be, as Hawthorne was—Ives enjoyed the daily round of selling insurance in New York City for over 30 years because it brought him in touch with living people. For the musical establishment he had no time: they were cop-outs, smelled to him of formaldehyde. Yet during the first 19 of those years, from 1898 to 1917, he wrote more music, of greater stature, than most composers in a lifetime. Then he stopped, abruptly, in early middle age. He lived till 1954, age of 79.

In his life were TWO MAJOR FORCES:

(1) His father, George Edward Ives, born in Danbury/Conn, 1845. Conductor of the local orchestra, the town band, church choirs and choral societies in the area, in his youth a Union Army bandmaster. He invested his son with a thorough working knowledge of a variety of musical instruments and a literature that ranged from Bach and Beethoven and Brahms to Stephen Foster and the musical "happenings" of the Camp Meetings.

(2) His wife, Harmony Twichell, daughter of the Rev Joseph Hopkins Twichell of Hartford, close friend of Mark Twain. She married him in 1908, when Ives was 33, she just turned 32.

Uniting these two forces, as SPIRIT and CONSUMMATION:

(3) His absolute commitment to the group of mid 19th century writers and thinkers known as the New England Transcendentalists. One of his major works—the *Concord* Sonata (and the companion *Essays Before A Sonata*)—deals specifically with the transcendentalists of Concord. But transcendental propositions underlie almost the entire gamut of his music.

Dividing them, as the INHIBITING FACTOR:

(4) 4 years of formal musical study under Horatio Parker at Yale University. After his graduation in 1898, Ives turned his back on professional music-making and became an actuarial clerk for Mutual Life Insurance at

$5 a week. It took him several years to slough off academic influences in his composition, but his contempt for institutional musicians—"all those lily-pad Doctors of Music"—remained cordial and lifelong.

Ives had a comprehension of America's seers and poets that would have been remarkable for a composer or a businessman. For one who was both it was marvelous. Among these: enormous respect for Emerson, enormous admiration for Hawthorne, enormous affection for Alcott, total identification with Thoreau—these were his favorites. Of Melville, no mention. Yet more than any other it is Melville who foreshadows Ives in the use of an extended rhetoric that is specifically American: this thing of SPACE—fact central to American man. The progressions of Ives's music, like Melville's prose, are borne on a living speech rhythm, not on someone else's verse. But with Ives, a Yankee speech rhythm. A collage of musical vernacular transfigured.

It took a special intelligence to break with the verse conventions of Western music, nearly 2,000 years of musical history. It took the faculty of mind that could hear things as they really were, and apart from the way it had been taught to hear them. It took the integrity of spirit to hold on through infinite care and trouble to the exact sounds it wanted. And it took an impatience born of too much patience, and the honesty that impatience breeds—the kind of honesty Melville wished of Shakespeare,

> that the muzzle which all men wore over their souls in the Elizabethan day might not have intercepted Shakespeare's free articulations; for I hold it a verity, that even Shakespeare was not a frank man to the uttermòst. And, indeed, who in this intolerant universe is, or can be ? But the Declaration of Independence makes a difference . . .

It was an idea close to the root of American transcendentalist thought. Thoreau wrote of Alcott:

> This man is the independent of independents—is, indeed, the sole signer of the Declaration, and a Revolution in himself—a more than '76—having gone beyond the signing to the doing it out fully . . .

Of himself, he said:

> To whatever corner of the world I may wander, I shall deem it good fortune that I hail from Concord North Bridge . . .

And Emerson called the Revolution

> the overflowing of natural right in every clear and active spirit of
> the period . . .

Things went wrong, of course. The overflow got out of hand. New
social inequities crowded out the old social injustices. Politically, the
clear and active minds were canceled out by those less clear, inactive:
Democracy & all that. Inalienable Right got betrayed some. But for
the writers and artists of the next age the Declaration meant the opportunity to pursue their craft honestly—Independence, not so much
from English and European and Classical cultures, as from the peer-
pressure of tradition, conformity, parrot-fashion imitation. Only
music malingered dismally, generation over generation of American
composers making the pilgrimage to Europe, like dowagers to a spa,
to fetch back the irrelevant seed of a foreign culture for the continuing delight of the little old ladies.

Ives saw that gawking, cap in hand, at Europe offered NO WAY.
A musical transplant simply could not work. American soil was as
fertile as any, but if the seed were foreign the growth must be
foreign, and in an alien musical climate would neither prosper nor
endure—outside a hothouse. But if the seed was native, original,
prime, the thing might work—and any seed would do for a start,
from a Gospel Hymn to *Old Black Joe.* Given the soil—this seed—
careful husbandry, at aboriginal hands, was all. The essence of culture.

In *Essays Before A Sonata,* Ives has:

> It has seemed to the writer that Emerson is greater—his identity
> more complete, perhaps—in the realms of revelation—natural dis-
> closure—than in those of poetry, philosophy, or prophecy. Although
> a great poet and prophet, he is greater, possibly, as an invader of the
> unknown—America's deepest explorer of the spiritual immensities—
> a seer painting his discoveries in masses and with any color that may
> lie at hand—cosmic, religious, human, even sensuous . . .

It was Emerson started him off. Emerson and Thoreau. Emerson, who said:

> Let me admonish you, first of all, to go alone; to refuse the good
> models, even those which are sacred to the imaginations of men . . .

who said:

> And why need we copy the Doric and the Gothic models ? Beauty,
> convenience, grandeur of thought and quaintness of expression are
> as near to us as to any . . .

who said:

> We have listened too long to the courtly muses of Europe . . .

And Thoreau, who said:

> English literature, from the days of the minstrels to the Lake Poets
> —Chaucer and Spenser and Milton, and even Shakespeare, included
> —breathes no quite fresh and, in this sense, wild strain. It is an
> essentially tame and civilized literature, reflecting Greece and Rome.
> I do not know of any poetry to quote which adequately expresses
> this yearning after the Wild. I do not know where to find it in any
> poetry, ancient or modern, any account which satisfies me of that
> Nature with which even I am acquainted. You will perceive that
> I demand something which no Augustan nor Elizabethan age, which
> no CULTURE, in short, can give. Mythology comes nearer to it than
> anything.
>      Perchance, when, in the course of ages, American liberty has
> become a fiction of the past—as it is to some extent a fiction of the
> present—the poets of the world will be inspired by American myth-
> ology . . .

They started him off because Ives was his father's son, tuned from
the first to their wavelength, reared from the first to be "an original,
aboriginal; a beginner." Not as William Billings was a beginner, a
pioneer, who thought it best "that every Composer should be his own
Carver"—whose vision then went forfeit to the competent. But as
Emerson was a beginner, a revealer—America's deepest explorer
of the AURAL immensities, with a perspective of AURAL space that
America also gives. A musician's perspective, if he has the gumption
to use it.

Thoreau's prophecy was fulfilled even before he uttered it, by
Melville. His Ahab rides on such space and is prisoner of it, destroyed by it, devoured by an obsession. The fiction of liberty becomes
the myth. Ives's mythologies derive from other fictions of liberty—

the once popular songs, the hymn tunes, the national hymns, his allegories of America's wars fought in the name of Liberty. "A comprehension of PAST" through "his marriage of spirit to source"—a transcendental spirit to a vernacular source. And, "a confirmation of FUTURE"—a future to which, who shall say are the rightful inheritors ? Today's audiences, little old ladies and all ?

Thoreau's apperception went to the core, his use of the word CULTURE synonymous with the little old ladies in a thousand different guises that all added up, sooner or later, to the same thing: THE SYSTEM. Cultural, social, or political. You ride it or it rides you. Either way it turns you soft—"emasculates" was Ives's term. Or you get off, like Henry David. If you're Charles Ives you probably don't get on the g—d—— thing in the first place . . .

But Charles Ives did. Twice. The 2 big enigmas about his life were:

(1) Horatio Parker and the musical establishment; and

(2) 30 years with Insurance—THE SYSTEM with a vengeance.

Enigma Number 2 is simpler than Enigma Number 1, so take it first.

A lot of pious nonsense has been written, in Ives's extenuation, about the insurance business being more idealistic 75 years ago. Insurance meant big money and big money turns men into monsters once they get a smell of it—any time, any place, and that's a fact (as men say). Wall Street 1898/1929 wasn't any different. Then came the financial panic and some people woke up to the fact and a lot more didn't, ever again. But that's another story and Ives was out of it by then anyway. But at the time he joined Mutual Life in 1898, big business was more corrupt if anything, not less. Less hypocritical, perhaps. Bigger, too. Just look at the lower Manhattan skyline and figure when all that was built. Built to last, more elegant (in a way), more leisurely, both more ostentatious and more subtle. Wealth with stealth. None of the rat race, the fast buck to be made—not in the open, anyway. In pre World War I America, as in Europe, people could still be relied upon to "know their place"—know which side their bread had the butter on. And if they forgot, there was always the Wall Street banker standing beside them on the elevated train to remind them.

Whether Ives admired this aspect of THE SYSTEM, he could live

with it. Making money at any job—outside music or in—meant being
a huckster, compromising one's integrity. Ives chose to dirty his hands
in business, not in his beloved music. And he respected men who had
come by their wealth with brainpower and imagination. He survived
—and prospered, to the tune of nearly $2 million—because making
a lot of money was a natural by-product of his own executive imagination, not an end. And making a lot of money didn't get in the way
of his proper job—writing music. Not that he didn't work hard in
business. But he looked on his 5-days-a-week commitment in the city
as a creative diversion that gave renewed stimulus to his real work
—composition. Unlike Wallace Stevens, he had no ambition to become president of his insurance company, the only Emperor of Ice
Cream.

That was why Ives's proposed Constitutional Amendment, limiting all private incomes to $20,000 a year, got nil response. A man
who didn't take money-making seriously wasn't yet a criminal, but
he had to be a crank. If Ives had been into making money heart &
soul he'd have realized that—either been totally corrupted himself
by then, or seen the folly of it all. Capitalism worked on capital—
large amounts of private capital made corporate. Limit that and
the whole system went under.

Ives's mention of Wordsworth, Shakespeare, Charles Lamb, in
"The Amount to Carry"—the guide he had put out in 1912 for insurance salesmen ?  Did it bring "tone" to the insurance business,
as some have claimed ?  Dear hearts, none of the salesmen had ever
heard of Wordsworth and Charles Lamb. And if they'd heard of
Shakespeare, it was as a figure of fun.

A LAST FACT. Late in 1913, Ives wrote a *Matthew Arnold*
Overture, as 3rd of a projected series on "Men Of Literature." The
music is lost, but seems to have been based on Arnold's Sonnet "West
London," a poem full of mawkish Victorian condescension towards
"the working classes": an expression of the immutable *status quo*,
with never a hint that their lot might be bettered, only heavy moraliz-
ing on how they "pointed an example" to the "unheeding rich." The
man's heart was in the right place, but it never occurred to Arnold
how his own comparative prosperity had fed on their poverty. Nor to
Charles Ives. Had he lived in England in the early years of the 20th
century he'd have been a Fabian socialist, like George Bernard

Shaw, attacking social & political ills from a position of financial security. Which is about what he did anyway . . .

. . . back to

## Enigma No 1

and A FIRST FACT. Yale—still a Liberal Arts College in Ives's day—presented the milder aspect of THE SYSTEM: the Academic aspect, wholly benevolent in purpose, largely benign in effect, with all the advantages and few of the disadvantages of most other Institutions of Higher Learning. Ives enrolled there in all wide-eyed innocence, his courses with H W Parker only one part of the normal academic curriculum. Parker himself was totally unaware that MUSIC had all the disadvantages, few of the advantages . . .

To get to the root of the problem—what Ives was up against, eventually overcame—you have to go back a century and more, get out your horse & buggy and follow the Post Road to Boston and its environs. Boston, perennial problem child, starting with the Boston Tea Party and problems for the British. T S Eliot's Boston, the "quite refined, but refined beyond the point of civilization." Tea parties, removed, since the first, to the genteel sanctuary of the Boston parlor. The Boston drawl, "more English than the English," that sends Englishmen into silent hysterics. And, put another nickel in, MEW-SICK, MEWSICK, MEWSICK . . .

Yet Boston bred musical visionaries back in Colonial days. Benjamin Franklin was one—born in 1706, 21 years after J S Bach, composer, music critic, inventor of musical instruments, author, philosopher, and statesman. He brought insight:

> I have sometimes, at a concert, attended by a common audience, placed myself so as to see all their faces, and observed no signs of pleasure on them during the performance of a great part that was admired by the performers themselves; while a plain old Scotch tune, which they disdained, and could scarcely be prevailed upon to play, gave manifest and general delight . . .

William Billings another—born in 1746, 10 years before Mozart. He added the craft:

> Perhaps it may be expected by some, that I should say somewhat concerning Rules for Composition; to these I answer that Nature

is the best Dictator, for all the hard, dry, studied Rules that ever
were prescribed, will not enable a person to form an air . . .

After 1776 it took the American creative artist a little while to comprehend that he was on his own now. The first musical voice was
Lowell Mason's. Mason, born in Medfield/Mass in 1792, from 1827
(the year of Beethoven's death) a resident of Boston. Music educator
and composer of very many hymn tunes, some used by Charles Ives.
Editor, since 1821, of *The Boston Handel & Haydn Society Collection
of Church Music;* first clue to the impending musical crisis, a review
of its tenth impression, in 1831, by the New Haven *Chronicle:*

> . . . A book so valuable must become the standard of music in our
> churches, since its harmony and style are fixed on the immovable
> basis of science and good taste . . .

In 1838, AN ACHIEVEMENT: Mason's introduction, against bitter op-
position, of musical appreciation into the general curricula of
Boston's public schools—nearly a century before anything the like
in Europe. And, in 1838, AN ADMONITION: Emerson's address, on
Literary Ethics, to the graduating class of Dartmouth College, New
Hampshire:

> Men looked, when all feudal straps and bondages were snapped
> asunder, that Nature, too long the mother of dwarfs, should re-
> imburse herself with a brood of Titans, who should laugh and leap
> in the continent, and run up the mountains of the West with the
> errand of genius and love. But the mark of American merit in
> painting, in sculpture, in poetry, in fiction, in eloquence, seems to
> be a certain grace without grandeur, as itself not new, but derivative,
> a vase of fair outline, but empty . . .

Emerson neglects mention of music, maybe sensed that American
merit in music already was a lost cause. Immediate history consented.
11 years later, Lowell Mason's son William led off the musical
exodus to Europe, as music's reply to the European political exodus
to America the previous year. The musical chess game developed like
this:

> *1849:* William Mason, 20, arrives at the Leipzig Conservatory
> to study piano with Moscheles and composition with
> Moritz Hauptmann.

*1854:* Mason moves to Weimar to study piano with Franz Liszt.

*1857 :* John Knowles Paine, 18, from Portland/Maine, arrives in Berlin to study organ with Carl Haupt at the Royal Institute of Church Music.

Arthur Sullivan, from England, arrives at Leipzig Conservatory to study composition with Hauptmann.

Mason returns to Boston via Paris and London.

*1858:* Dudley Buck, 19, from Hartford/Conn, arrives at Leipzig Conservatory to study with Moscheles and Hauptmann. Animosity between Sullivan and Buck.    Check.

*1859:* Buck castles out of check to Weimar, fails to get to study with Liszt who has gone to Rome, and moves to Dresden to study organ with Johann Gottlob Schneider, teacher of Liszt, Mendelssohn & Schumann.

Paine moves to Frankfurt to study composition with Joachim Raff at the Hoch Conservatory.

*1861:* Paine returns to America a week after the South fires on Ft Sumter, settles in Boston/Cambridge.

END OF OPENING GAME. Moratorium on study in Europe during Civil War lasts coincidentally till the end of Reconstruction. Meanwhile, in Boston/Cambridge:

*1862:* Paine, aged 23, appointed Harvard's first Instructor of Music.

*1867:* returns to Germany to conduct his Mass in D with the Berlin Singakademie.

*1869:* receives Harvard M A, *honoris causa.*

*1870:* music becomes an elective study at Harvard.

*1873:* Paine promoted Assistant Professor of Music.

*1874:* Arthur Foote his first student to graduate. Removes himself from the chessboard by not going to Europe at all. Charles Ives born.

*1875:* Paine promoted full Professor of Music.

START OF MIDDLE GAME

*1876:* Henry Theophilus Finck graduates *summa cum laude* from Harvard. Goes to Munich to study composition with Rheinberger at the Royal Conservatory.

*1877:* Edward MacDowell, 16, from New York City, arrives at the Paris Conservatory to study piano with Marmontel. Debussy a fellow student.

George Whitefield Chadwick, 22, from Boston, arrives in Berlin to study organ with Carl Haupt at the Royal Institute of Church Music.

*1878:* Chadwick moves to the Leipzig Conservatory to study theory with Salomon Jadassohn, Rheinberger's former teacher.

*1879:* Chadwick moves to Munich to study with Rheinberger. Meets Finck, who is now studying ethnomusicology.

((Back in Boston, Theodor Thomas's performance of Paine's 2nd Symphony evokes scenes of the wildest enthusiasm. John S Dwight, editor of *Dwight's Music Journal* and hallowed arbiter of Boston's musical taste, stands on his chair and waves his umbrella in the air, opening and shutting it in a frenzy of uncontrollable emotion.))

*1880:* MacDowell, 19, moves to Frankfurt to study with Joachim Raff at the Hoch Conservatory.

*1881:* Parker arrives in Munich to study with Rheinberger.

*1882:* Philip Hale, from Boston, arrives in Munich to study with Rheinberger.

MacDowell, 21, appointed piano instructor at the Hoch Conservatory, Frankfurt.

*1885:* Parker returns to Boston. Further study with Chadwick.

*1888:* MacDowell returns to America and settles in Boston.

END GAME

*1891:* Dvorak appointed head of the National Conservatory of Music in New York. His faculty includes Parker (theory) and Finck (ethnomusicology).

*1892:* Frederick Shepherd Converse graduates *summa cum laude* from Harvard. Goes to Munich to study with Rheinberger.

*1893:* Parker adopts recent English translation of Jadassohn's *Harmonienlehre* for his theory class at the National Conservatory. Composes the oratorio *Hora novissima*. Philip Hale, in the Boston *Daily Advertiser*, wrote later: "It is a

work to which any European composer would be happy
to sign his name . . . "

*1894:* Dvorak returns to his native Czechoslovakia, bitterly
disillusioned with New York's climate of persistent musical antagonism to his ideas. It had been different in the
Midwest.

Parker, 31, appointed Yale's first Instructor of
Music.

Edward Burlingame Hill graduates *summa cum
laude* from Harvard. Goes to Paris to study organ with
Charles Widor. A fellow student is 10-yr-old Nadia
Boulanger . . .

GAME ABANDONED . . .

It never should have begun. Would any American *writer* have
gone to Europe—to study ? Even advanced study ? Even seriously
thought of going, to learn his job ? Would Emerson have gone ?
Would Hawthorne ? Would Thoreau ? Or Melville ? Or Whitman ? Gone to Europe *to learn to write* ? Of course they wouldn't.

Why not? Because 1776 and Independence along with it gave,
not the RIGHT of being independent, but the RESPONSIBILITY of being.
No rights without responsibility. And the responsibility right here at
home, not over there in Europe. The responsibility for molding an indigenous thing, not just from scratch, but indigenous top to bottom
and all the way through. As indigenous as Alcott's/Thoreau's "the
oak, the granite ledge." As indigenous as the Indian and the Negro.
But not *copying* them, any more than copying Europe. Not derivative.
Not the "vase of fair outline, but empty."

Of course they went to Europe, most of them, later on. And a few
of them stayed, like Henry James, to count the cats in Mansfield
Square. But they didn't go there to master their craft—technique,
style, command of language, call it what you will. They'd mastered
that before they went, "back home in the U S A."

So why was MUSIC so special ? It wasn't. It was only a meek
little old lady, soft, emasculated, barren. Or that's what it became.
Not by composers going to Europe. It could have been China or
Timbuktu, for all that matter. By their NOT staying at home. Not
right. Not responsible. "Not responsible"—the catchphrase of THE

SYSTEM. Music—and Boston—never got beyond Paul Revere. 1776 took their balls off.

This isn't putting Europe down. No one's denying the magnitude of its achievements in the arts. But they had been fought for, won, defended, proven, and that's why Europe had a cultural heritage. No one taught them how. Certainly no one taught their composers how. The American composer had to fight, win, defend, and prove himself on his home ground—not pilfer Europe's victories. The first American composer who had the guts to do that on the grand scale was Charles Ives. But no one had the guts to listen.

One post 1776 composer who didn't come from the Establishment, has therefore been overlooked, was Stephen Collins Foster— a name the Establishment still balks at, always did. Foster was 25 when the Fugitive Slave Law was enacted. The following year, four things happened:

> *1852:* Foster writes to E P Christy of his resolve "to pursue the Ethiopian business without fear or shame"—"the Ethiopian business" begun nine years earlier with the first appearance, at the Bowery Amphitheater/N Y, of "the novel, grotesque, original and surpassingly melodious Ethiopian Band, entitled, The Virginia Minstrels."

((The origin of the word Ethiopian is nebulous in this context, but the dark-skinned Ethiopian race provided an acceptable metaphor for white-skinned minstrels who wore burned cork on their faces. Ethiopian minstrelsy became big business, spreading quickly to the West Coast and to Europe. Its slapstick combined a genuine pathos that drew wide attention to the plight of the Negro, brought musical emphasis to the Abolitionist cause.))

> *1852:* Mr Thomas Hastings, a prolific and highly respectable composer of hymn tunes, writes an indignant letter to *The Musical Review & Choral Advocate,* deploring the fact that "Boston Sunday School children are being exposed to the depravities of 'Ethiopian minstrelsy' under the guise of *Old Folks at Home.*" Lowell Mason, sometime organist of Dr Lyman Beecher's church on Hanover Street, learns "with gravest dismay" that the only tunes the children of Boston's public schools are being taught—

or want to be—are Foster's. John S Dwight, of *Dwight's Music Journal,* dismisses Foster's songs as "cheap trash."

*1852:* Lyman Beecher's daughter, Harriet Beecher Stowe, publishes *Uncle Tom's Cabin*—suspect today for its Uncle Tom sentiments, earlier a valuable document in the Abolitionist cause.

*1852:* earlier in the year, 26-yr-old Stephen Foster made his first visit at the South, saw first hand the Negroes' own minstrel shows and attended their Camp Meetings. On his return, he wrote his letter to Christy. In his own way he wanted to be part of the Abolitionist movement—not for social/political reasons, but because he saw the slave culture and its struggle for emancipation as being musically viable. Musically viable, because its motive sentiment was viable, had direct reference to the human predicament.

*Addenda:*

(1)  The following Fourth of July, Ives's father, age 7, absents himself from the family picnic . . .

(2)  *1861:* Ives Sr, age 16, finds Foster outside a Harlem bar, late at night, a derelict, penniless alcoholic. No one knew what he was doing so far from his rooming house on the Bowery. George Ives helped him to a nearby house and never saw him again. Foster died in Bellevue Hospital, January 13, 1864, age 37. By then, George Ives was a Union Army bandmaster.

There is a lot of Abolitionist sentiment in the music of Charles Ives. A lot of Civil War sentiment, inherited direct from his father. A lot of Revolutionary War sentiment, his national heritage. And a lot of Evangelical Christianity—part Puritan, part Revivalist, part Humanist: Unitarian *and* Renaissance. All these mixed up together, digested and regurgitated as a New Mythology—expressed, mechanically speaking, as a collage of musical vernacular.

The clue is in a line from Ives's piece on Hawthorne, in *Essays Before A Sonata:*

. . . not something that happens, but the way something happens . . .

Something that happens is AN EVENT. An event, with Ives as with other composers, THE BORROWING OF MUSICAL MATERIALS. The borrowing of musical materials, in 16th century musical parlance, PARODY. The etymology of parody, from the Greek, MUSICAL SATIRE.

I use the word PARODY consistently for Ives's borrowing of musical materials—the words "quote" and "quotation" are entirely too narrow, too literal. But PARODY implies—should imply, used to—no sense of caricature. Nor does—should, did—SATIRE. Both words, in their precise sense, are didactic in their intent. If you want to construe them as burlesque you can, but you run the risk of missing the point. And the boat. Parody and satire, at their most dangerous, move swift as lightning—too fast for some.

The 16th century "Parody Mass" has a precise sense that falls outside the present argument. But 16th century parody in general was musical shoplifting, openly practiced, with no trace of embarrassment—lifting a well-known tune and using it in a piece of your own, expressly designed for the purpose. The way you used it—the music you constructed to go around it—was what counted. Used with discrimination · and imagination, its materials in proper juxtaposition, parody could evoke an association of ideas, tell a story, infer a moral, invite a conflict of opinion. It was introduced at a moment of history when music outstripped language as a means of communication: language in a state of turmoil, the educated speaking Latin, the uneducated a babel of different tongues and dialects, no one really listening to or understanding anyone else. Music their common ground, for listening *and* understanding.

Ives's use of PARODY, then, the "something that happens." *How* he used it, "the way something happens." Here the element of satire —poignant, pungent, dry, sentimental, grotesque, even with a sense of overpowering tragedy at times. But never malicious. He knew these old tunes too well, trusted and familiar friends in all their endearing guises. Knew, too, that in their "literal" state, many of them would invite nice smiles, provoke laughter, the knowing sneer. But he never could hear them in their "literal" state. His reason recognized a "literal" state, for academic purposes, but his imagination would not acknowledge one. His ear was preconditioned to hear these tunes with all their attendant overtones, all the remembered and half-remembered associations they had held for all the people who ever listened to them, or half listened, or did not listen at all. Not of his ear's own documentary knowledge. But as a poet's ear listens and hears and remembers. Of its imagining.

Any audience not moribund must react to Ives's music in some way. The bald familiar parody may surprise delight, provoke a spontaneous guffaw, an embarrassed smirk. The Rollos congratulate themselves on their celebrated national composer's "great sense of humor."

Any audience not moribund should be a little wary. Ives's music seldom is what it seems to be—never *only* what it seems to be. The delight was precipitate, perhaps—missed a point of stupendous humor somewhere else. The guffaw contrived—coarsened another instant of sublime comedy. The smirk no more than Ives expected—no less than he intended. Rollo stays away next time.

But "national"—yes: suddenly at twilight, hour of the autumn concert-series. And universal suddenly at midnight, the witching hour of Hawthorne's phantoms. At all other times personal—a New Englander's personal & private property. Posted: NO TRESPASSING—except at your own risk & take the consequences.

And "sense of humor"—yes: Ives's own personal & private brand. An impish sense of humor—pokes fun at plastic icons. At all other times the humor of a supreme intelligence, vast ingenuity, once termed wit.

# PRELUDE

# Danbury I

*Danbury. City, Fairfield co., SW Connecticut,
35 m. NW of New Haven, 25 m. E of
Hudson River; mean elev. 450 ft, max. 1,050
ft; situated on Still River, NE of Pine Mt,
S of L. Candlewood, in foothills of Berkshire
Mts; pop. 1,509 (1756), 3,180 (1800),
11,666 (1880) . . .*

The colonial-style clapboard frame house used to stand some 40 yds back from the dirt road of Main Street, one of the many new houses built after the British burned the town in 1777: its first oc-cupant Thomas Tucker, Deacon of the 1st Congregational Church, who opened a schoolhouse there in 1793; a sign outside the door declared "Hops for Sale" and sometimes announced "room for a few students" when he had put other pupils to work on the land because they hadn't paid their school fees. And when old Mr Tucker died, in 1829, the house was bought by Isaac Ives, great-grandfather of the composer. Sometime after 1851—the year they built the Danbury railroad, the year Isaac's widow died—tramlines were laid in the new cobblestone road, and horse-drawn street-cars began to ply back and forth in front of the house on their way to the station.

> *. . . original Pahquioque land purchased*
> *from Indian owners in 1684; settled in 1687*
> *and renamed Danbury by seven families from*
> *Norwalk and one from Stratford; town*
> *rights granted inhabitants by Act of General*
> *Assembly 1702; becomes borough in 1822;*
> *incorp. as city 1889; est. pop. 18,000 . . .*

A plain gravel footpath led from the sidewalk on Main Street, straight across the wide open lawn and up to the four stone steps of the pedimented front porch. The strap-hinged front door, in heavy paneled oak with a huge lock, polished brass doorknob and knocker, was topped by a Victorian beehive fanlight; set into the front wall on either side of the door a pair of single sash-windows. The forward aspect showed only this single tier of four windows, surmounted by a high gambrel roof with single central chimney stack. But a second gravel path led past the left-hand side of the house, disclosing a side elevation with Victorian sun-trap, two second-story windows with louvered shutters, and a small attic window just below the eaves.

> *. . . selected by Commissioners of American*
> *Army in latter half of 1776 as a military*
> *depot for large quantities of stores, provisions*
> *and munitions; raided by 2,000 British troops*
> *led by Gen Tryon, Governor of New York,*
> *April 26 1777; nineteen dwellings, the*
> *meeting-house, twenty-two stores and numerous*
> *barns and warehouses sacked; Gen David*
> *Wooster, leading Danbury forces, dies of*
> *wounds received in engagement . . .*

With the birth of Isaac's grandchildren—the youngest, George Edward, was born in 1845, the year old Isaac died—the house was enlarged to the rear in the form of a two-storied L, the sun-trap extended along its side as a flat-roofed open porch. Sometime after 1904 three dormer windows were let into the gambrel roofing at the front of the house, to lighten the declining years of George Edward's widowed sister Sarah Amelia, who lived alone with her maiden sister-in-law and companion, Lucy Cornelia Parmelee. After Sarah Amelia died in 1918, Lucy Cornelia was joined by her sister,

George's widow. And when the Danbury Savings Bank acquired the site of the house in 1923, and it was loaded onto an oversize truck and shipped bodily up to Chapel Place, the two old ladies remained inside throughout the move. A poignant picture.

> *. . . Landmarks: Wooster cemetery, burial*
> *place of Gen Wooster; Public Library,*
> *containing archives of* Danbury News, *founded*
> *in 1845 by James M. Bailey; theater, ambience*
> *of minstrel shows since 1841; fairground site*
> *of annual livestock fairs since 1821, held*
> *first Saturday & Monday in October; Isaac Ives*
> *House, built 1780, scene of meeting April 8*
> *1833 to establish library of mechanics . . .*

Charles Ives paid for the removal of the family house to Chapel Place in 1923. But when, in 1966, that site was also acquired by the Savings Bank—for a parking lot—the composer was dead and the house threatened with dismemberment. It was accorded a last-minute reprieve and moved by private subscription to the meadow of Rogers Park as an adjunct to the Scott-Fanton Museum, which houses many of the Ives family heirlooms, including the original Stobart, Worcester & Dunham piano.

This was bought by Isaac's only son, George White Ives, in 1849, the year he became founding secretary and treasurer of the Danbury Savings Bank, and its six-octave keyboard addressed with varying felicity by his four surviving children—a fifth had died in infancy. At that time the front entrance led into a hallway: on its right the parlor, where the piano was seated against the rear wall; on its left the dining-room, where a large wooden chest became the Savings Bank's first "office." A single tier of stairs led up to the two front bedrooms, a rear bedroom and three more at the side, and the bathroom. About the time of the composer's birth an imported porcelain bath of latest French design was installed—some measure of the relative affluence of this 2nd generation of Ives family at 167/169 Main Street.

Charles Ives was a 9th generation American, his ancestor William Ives an immigrant to the New World in 1635. William's forebears are conjectural, though there is evidence that his father was Thomas Ives, squire of Swatham, Norfolk. According to the Public

Records Office, London, Thomas Ives died in 1634, leaving his estate in this wise:

> "To *my eldeste Sonne* John
>   *my yongeste Sonne* Ralph
>   &  *my Onlie daughter* Elizabeth"

*"my eldeste"* and *"my yongeste"* suggesting the intervening factor of a third son in between. A further legatee of the will was a local farmer and intimate of the squire's, Ralph Tomkins, after whom *"my yongeste"* had been named.

On the midday tide of September 15 1635, "Master: Jo Gibbs, and the men, Having taken the Oathes of Allegiance & Supremacy," *Truelove,* a well-found ship of 105 tons, sailed out of the Port of London for the second time in three months, bound again for Boston, with 65 passengers aboard. Among these:

> *Labouring man* Thomas Burchard,
>   *his* wife & 6 children;
> *Husbandman* Edward Howe,
>   *his* wife, and five children;
> *Husbandman* Ralph Tomkins,
>   *his* wife, and three children;
> Richard Hawes, *Uxor,* and 3 children;
> Wm Bentley, *Uxor,* and two children;
> 59-yr-old Wm Bartley, and his 15-yr-old
>   bride, Alice, "heavie with childe"; and
> *Capt* Wm Ives, *late Kings Man,* 28, bachelor.

The presence in the same vessel of *Capt* Wm Ives and *Husbandman* Ralph Tomkins—native of Swatham and legatee of Thomas Ives's estate—could hardly be fortuitous. What is strange is that no William appears in Thomas Ives's will. But in the archives of Norwich Town Hall is a report of a *Capt Yves* being cashiered the Duke of Norfolk's regiment in 1634, "that he was importunate with my Colonels mistresse"—the nature and extent of importunity undisclosed. If the charge referred to William Ives—if Thomas Ives was in fact his father—it would account for his being cut off with a shilling. Apart from the stain on the family scutcheon—of being cashiered—Norfolk in the 1630s was a hotbed of Puritanism, and any shadow of social misconduct rigorously condemned. Certainly there would have been every reason for a bachelor of 28, dismissed from his regiment and disowned by his father, throwing in his lot with a family friend and setting his hopes on the New World.

Last evidence of William's conjectural paternity is the fragment of a letter dated May 22, 1639, at *Quinnipiac, in the Colony of Connecticut,* and addressed to John Ives Esquire, of Swatham. Quinnipiac was renamed New Haven in 1640, William Ives among its first settlers in 1638. Nothing is known of William's subsequent history except that he married soon after settling in New Haven, and that a son John— a common enough name, in all consciousness, but further slight support for a brother named John—was born in 1640.

John Ives married Hannah Merriam of New Haven and moved to a settlement 10 miles up the Quinnipiac River, where their first child—also John—was born November 16, 1669. In 1670 the settlement was named Wallingford, after the English Berkshire village, and gained a reputation for the excellence of its silver and nickelwork.

On December 3 1693, John Ives Jr married Mary Gilbert, a great-grandchild of Sir Humphrey Gilbert, and moved five miles further north to the village of Meriden, settled in 1661. This lies near the source of the Quinnipiac, and the area then yielded silver and nickel in profusion; Meriden, like Wallingford, became famous for its work in silver and nickel. In Meriden, too, the name Ives now flowers on every second tombstone in the churchyard—among them, the headstone of "Elam Ives, of Hartford," author of *American Psalmody* and *The Musical Spelling Book,* sometime collaborator with Lowell Mason of Boston, who retired to Meriden and "departed this life the fourth day of December 1864, in the sixty-second year of his age."

On September 28 1694 a third John Ives was born, and in the fullness of time married Hannah Royce. Their first child—John again—was born July 4 1729, married Mary Hall, daughter of the Meriden pastor Isaac Hall, and served as ADC to General Washington in the Independence War.

John and Mary had three daughters and two sons—Isaac and Othniel. Isaac, born January 13 1764, graduated from Yale University in 1785, moved to Danbury, and went into the hatting business for which the town became famous. He married twice: (1) in 1793, 20-yr-old Jerusha Benedict, daughter of Zadock Benedict; and after she died in childbed of a stillborn child three years later, (2) 25-yr-old Sarah Amelia White, daughter of Joseph Moss White, a newly prominent Danbury citizen. Her brother Ephraim had married Thomas Tucker's daughter Charity.

> *. . . Danbury hat-trade originates 1780 when Zadock Benedict opens first American beaver-hat factory in small shop on north side of Main Street, near where later was the railroad station; 56 hat-shops in Danbury by 1808, of which 37 owned by Benedict family, each employing three to six workers and producing nine to 15 hats a day; demand for hats in beaver, felt, and Australian fur spreads to Eastern cities and the South; demand for hat-boxes leads to local manufacture of box-making machinery and paper; hatpins and brooches also locally worked, in silver and nickel fetched from Quinnipiac River . . .*

In 1797 the Benedict hatters opened a branch in New York City and Isaac Ives was sent there as its manager. His only child, George White, was born in New York February 28 1799, trained as a mechanical engineer (as his father had done at Yale), worked for a while at Leary & Co hatters in New York, and in 1831 married Sarah Hotchkiss Wilcox from Brookfield, who was teaching infant school in Danbury: an enthusiast of Emerson, confidante of Margaret Fuller, and something of a bluestocking. Isaac and Amelia had moved back to Danbury in 1829 and bought the house on Main Street; and after their son's marriage, he and his bride came to live there too. Their eldest son, Joseph Moss, was born in 1832, Isaac Wilcox in 1835, Sarah Amelia in 1837, Sarane Elizabeth in 1843 (she died 10 months later), and George Edward on August 3 1845.

> *. . . first railroad from Danbury to S. Norwalk opens 1851; connects with Hartford & New Haven RR, now extending N to Springfield with connections for Boston, and SW to New York City which it enters over tracks of NY & Harlem*

*RR; New York, New Haven & Hartford RR
Co. founded by interstate merger 1871;
Danbury becomes jc. for four lines of NY, NH
& H RR: N to New Milford, joining the
Housatonic RR to Pittsfield, Mass.; S through
E. Danbury, Bethel, W. Redding (forRedding),
along the Norwalk River to Norwalk and S.
Norwalk; E through Hawleyville, Sandy Hook,
Naugatuck and all stations to Hartford; and
W to Putnam Jc. on the NY Central RR . . .*

Perhaps Joseph Moss took the train to New Haven when he was sent up to Yale in 1851—only to be sent down again at the start of his sophomore year for climbing the bell-tower and muffling the morning bell, which made everyone late for class. ((His nephew Charles inherited this compulsive interest in bells, though he put it to more constructive use.)) But Joseph's father was not amused by his eldest son's alpine propensities, and he was put to work in a branch of Benedict's hatters in Boston. By 1856 he had gone into business on his own account; the Boston directory for that year has the entry:

Ives (*Joseph M.*) & Tuthill (*George*), hatters.

1856 was the year he met Emerson at the Lowells' house in Cambridge; and after his father's death, in 1862, took Emerson home to Danbury to meet his mother. His father, ever since hearing Andrews Norton's attack on transcendentalism, had never quite trusted Emerson's radicalism; but his mother had been at Emerson's Danbury lecture in 1850, and was thrilled to meet the great man in person.

1856 was also the year Joseph met his second-cousin, Amelia White Merritt, who was 21; he fell in love at first sight, courted her three years, and married her in 1859. But like his grandfather's first wife, she died in childbirth only three years later, leaving him to care for an infant son, Howard Merritt. Joseph returned home to Danbury broken-hearted, and the news that his father was dying.

With his father's death and his brother's recent bereavement, Isaac Wilcox, the second brother, decided to leave home and seek his fortune in New York City; the North and the South were at war, and speculation on Wall Street was running high. Isaac married Emily

Keeler in 1863, had one son, George Forrester, who became a Chicago antique dealer, and made and lost his fortune several times over.

But his sister Sarah Amelia had neither his speculative imagination nor Joseph's transcendental bravado. Nor was she much blessed of originality, for ever since Joseph married his second-cousin, in 1856, Sarah Amelia was determined to marry *her* second-cousin, Amelia Merritt's brother Jacob. She kept up the campaign for 12 years, and it was only when Jacob Merritt married quite another Sarah, in 1867, that Sarah Amelia—30, and in terror of becoming an old maid—married Lyman Brewster, the pampered son of a rich and forceful Danbury widow, and went to live with him at her house. In 1871 Jacob Merritt died, aged 34. Four years later Joseph Ives, once married to Jacob's sister, now married his widow.

When Lyman Brewster's mother died, in 1878, her house was sold. Sarah Amelia decided that she and her husband, though childless, should move into the house on Main Street and look after her aging mother, and her two brothers and their families should move out. Joseph's son Howard was 16 and away to school, so he and his second wife took a house at 368 Main Street. George, his wife, and their two small children moved to 16 Stevens Street.

George Edward had turned out to be the only musical member of the family. When the elder children had shown little talent for music, their father—kindly but firm, and rather unimaginative—decided not to waste money on piano lessons for his youngest son. But he changed his mind when, in 1853, 7-yr-old George Edward absented himself from the 4th of July family picnic. Diligent enquiry among the elder children discovered three things: (1) that George was not there because he was off somewhere trying to earn some money to buy a flute; (2) that he had harbored a secret passion for music almost since infancy; and (3) that his parents were constantly punishing him for being found at the piano when he should, they decided, have been somewhere else. This was why young George wanted a flute. He might still be punished for coming in late to meals, but in the meantime he could practice undiscovered and undisturbed in the barn up the road, or somewhere. Happily, his parents were amenable to the idea of George studying music, and from then on he had regular lessons—a remarkable instance of mid 19th century enlightenment, American *or* European.

In September 1860, George, now 16, was sent to study piano, theory, and German with Carl Foeppl, an Austrian musician of his mother's New York acquaintance who lived on a small farm in Morrisania, lower Westchester County—now the Bronx. Work with Foeppl took up five days of the week, and on Saturday mornings George used to take the train down to Manhattan for cornet lessons with Franz Schreiber, who played in the New York Philharmonic— now in its 19th season. On Saturday evenings, Schreiber used to smuggle him into the Philharmonic concerts, conducted alternately by Bergmann and Eisfeld. And late one Saturday night, when he had missed the last train and was walking back to the Bronx, George had the honor of helping an incapacitated Stephen Foster home from a neighborhood bar—or home, so he thought—and wrote his parents in a state of great excitement.

George's notebooks for the next two years show a complete grounding in harmony, counterpoint, & fugue; many workings of Bach chorales (including *Es ist genug*) with figured basses added; and two movements of *Jesu, meine Freude*, opera scenes from Gluck and Mozart, parts of baroque Masses, marches and dances, all transcribed from full-score in George's hand. ((Also five cryptic references to an "Emma Stout, Morrisania, N Y," suggesting that his life had its moments of feminine diversion.))

In August 1862 a cousin of his grandfather's, Col Nelson White, anxious to divert him from his father's recent death, suggested that George form a band for his regiment, the First Connecticut Heavy Artillery. The band, composed mainly of German musicians, was recruited in Connecticut and enlisted in September—George Ives, at 17, the youngest bandmaster in the Union (or Confederate) Army. Family documents contain a number of official communications, and the deference they show a boy still in his teens is remarkable. For George, apart from his extraordinary musicianship, had a natural ease of authority and won the respect and admiration of his musicians and superiors both. The story is told—and apt to be told, with variations, of any popular figure with a famously tin ear—of General Grant's remark to President Lincoln when they heard the band playing at Richmond: "It's the best band in the Army, they tell me. But I couldn't say. I only know two tunes. One of them's *Yankee Doodle* and the other isn't . . ."

On June 26 1865, George wrote his mother from Drury's Bluff, just below Richmond, where the regimental band was quartered:

> I've got a little Darkie working for me "as is a Dark." I'ld like to bring him home with me if you could use him. He's a good worker and honest . . .

((In 1932, his son Charles wrote:

> Father taught this boy how to write (both English and music), brought him home with him. Grandmother took him in, brought him up and sent him to school in Danbury. She and Grandfather would take anybody and everybody in, and give them their last cent and last cookie, if their sense of injustice was stirred . . . ))

In September 1865 Georges Ives was discharged and sent on one year's sick leave—the first manifestation of an illness that was to strike him down, suddenly, in his fiftieth year. The entry in his journal for March 11 1868, just after he returned to Danbury:

> A space of three years servitude—& one year sick—from Sept '62 to Sept '66. In New York on last date. Took three lessons of Mr F at 17 Christy Street in or about Dec '66 into '67. Been boarding at Mr F's on 91st Street since June '67 . . .

((Carl Foeppl had sold his farm in the Bronx and moved down to Manhattan, where he owned a boarding-house for musicians on West 91st Street, and gave private lessons at his home on Christy Street.))

On March 7 1868 George received his bounty and came home. Grew restless and returned to New York City. Became restless there and returned to Danbury for good. Here he quickly became the center of the community's musical life, conducting choirs, bands, orchestras, and Camp Meeting concerts throughout Fairfield county —all *gratis*, needless to mention. An announcement in the *Danbury News* the following year:

> Geo. E. Ives'
> POPULAR CONCERT
> at Concert Hall
> Friday ev'ng, July 2.

*The following artistes will appear:*
Miss L Smith, Prof C A Foeppl,
Mr Franz Schreiber.

*Chorus of 40 voices, with Orchestra*

George Ives raised the standard of the local community orchestra to such a level that the committee—like many another since—began to have ideas above their station, and wanted to engage a "professional" from New York. They even persuaded Theodor Eisfeld to come up to Danbury and hear the orchestra. George Ives, aged 25, took them through a rehearsal of the Mozart G minor Symphony, K550. Eisfeld assured the committee that the orchestra was in excellent hands, spoke briefly with its conductor, and left within the hour—to the dismay of Danbury hostesses who had just arrived, and were expecting him to stay and entertain them.

Unlike his son Charles, for whom Haydn and Mozart remained "ladies' music—pretty little sugar-plum sounds" to the end of his life, George Ives's concerts show a constant preoccupation with Mozart at strategic points in his programs, in part as a leavening of the dreadfully facile crud he was obliged to fill the rest with. No reflection on the musical taste of the Danbury audience: it was as bad, and worse, in New York and Chicago; worse still in Leipzig —*vide* Hans von Bülow's letters to his mother only a few years earlier. The program of a concert given in 1871 in Brewster/N Y, 10 miles west of Danbury:

MUSICAL SOIREE
by Mr. Ives,
for the Purchase of an Organ
for
ST. JOHN'S CHURCH,
AT BREWSTER'S HALL,
On Wednesday Ev'ng, June 25.

PROGRAMME
PART I

1. OVERTURE—Gazza Ladra.   2 Pianos, 8 Hands     Rossini
2. MORCEAUX, Agreeable.         "          "         Chwatal

    3. CHRISTMAS CHANT, arr. with Chorus (responsive)    Ives

    4. MARTHA DE FLOTO—Variations.   1 Piano,
      4 Hands                                    Oesten

    5. FANTASIA—Vesper Hymn.   Solo.        Wallace

    6. OVER THE WAVES WE FLOAT.   Vocal Duett.    Glover

    7. GRAND MARCH.    2 Pianos, 4 Hands     Kalkbrenner

    8. WEDDING MARCH.     ”    8   ”     Mendelssohn

    9. THE HEATHER BELLS.   Vocal Duett.     Wurzell

  10. FANTASIA.   Solo.                  Schwing

  11. ANVIL CHORUS—Il Trovatore.   2 Pianos, 8 Hands   Verdi

  12. CHORUS—Gloria.   From Twelfth Mass.     Mozart

Part II of the program also has 12 items; also begins with a Rossini Overture—*Tancredi* (2 Pianos, 8 Hands)—and ends with the *Dona nobis pacem* from the same Mozart Mass, here preceded by Meyerbeer's *Coronation March* (2 Pianos, 8 Hands). At the foot of the announcement:

      "Tickets 25 cents: Soiree to commence at 8 o'clock."

    The program tells many things. No "artistes" are mentioned, since this was a benefit concert "for the purchase of an organ"— St John's was the new Episcopal Church in the neighboring village of South Salem. George Ives had a choral society in Brewster, and the concert was held in the town's only public hall. The Kalkbrenner *Grand March* (2 Pianos, *four* Hands—one solo player to each piano, that is to say) offered a *moment critique*, envisioning a brace of blushing maidens resolved to DO THEIR BEST. Or damnedest. A purist might quibble about placing two such rumbustious war-horses as *The Anvil Chorus* and *The Coronation March* right before the Mozart *Gloria* and *Dona nobis pacem*. But the concert was, after all, to raise money for a new church organ, and the native exuberance of the Verdi and Meyerbeer was calculated to put the audience in a just frame of mind to listen to Mozart—and leave the concert to go and drum up more donations, many of them.* Then again, the two

* The audience at Brewster's Hall did not know, George Ives did not know, no one in America or Europe knew, in 1871, that "Mozart's Twelfth Mass" was spurious. It enjoyed great popularity during the 19th century, was performed at a number of important European festivals on the centenary of Mozart's death, and not until the early years of this century exposed as the fraudulent work of a composer called Zulehner, a minor contemporary of Beethoven. Why, how,

overtures—though perhaps not so familiar to a New England audience in the 1870s. But Rossini is a skillful and engaging showman. So was George Ives.

What came between, in both halves, is mostly long forgotten—mostly better forgotten perhaps. But that does not mean its ordering was not done without every care, without an intimate knowledge of all the music to be played, without a discerning ear for the audience's tolerance and response. Even the most trivial music might have a function in a just context, and George Ives understood that as few others.

Then there were his own pieces: *Christmas Chant* in Part I, and in Part II *The Wood Horn* ("responsive") with cornet obbligato (clearly played by the composer), and an anthem, *Hosanna*, also "responsive." Charles Ives spoke little about his father as a composer: writing of his Yale experience he says "Father was not a composer, and Parker was," and Ives aficionados generally discount it. But if George Ives thought well enough of these three pieces to include them in a program that also included Mozart—and do a *Christmas Chant* in June, no less—they must have had more than occasional merit.

Since his return to Danbury in 1868 George had been living at home with his mother, his eldest brother Joseph, and Joseph's son Howard—"Howdie." Henry Anderson Brooks, the Negro boy George brought home with him in 1865, had returned to Virginia in 1869 and now was living with his mother in Chesterfield/S Carolina.

It was a compact enough little family, but there was a dearth of womenfolk. George was nearly 26, still a bachelor, and likely to remain one if he went on giving all his time to music. Joseph was nearing 40, in ten years had not remarried, and yearly grew more isolated and morose. Howard was 10, and in need of a mother. His grandmother had been more than a mother to him, but now she was 63 and feeling the strain of a high-spirited 10-yr-old. Next year Howard was sent away to school.

In the fall of 1872 George met Mary Elizabeth Parmelee, the elder daughter of Noah David Parmelee, a farmer from the neigh-

it took so long for intelligent and distinguished musical minds to uncover the hoax is another story, one central to CI's later animadversion to blind reverence for names, labels, &c.

boring village of Bethel, where P T Barnum was born. Her mother's home town was Weston/Conn, where she had sung in the church choir as a girl; now she sang in the choir of St Thomas's, Bethel, which George sometimes directed. Her second daughter was Lucy Cornelia, the same who came to live with Sarah Amelia at the family house on Main Street in 1904. There were two sons—and there had been a third, George's exact contemporary, killed at the battle of Chancellorsville. George was quickly made to feel at home, and on New Year's Day 1874 he and Mary Elizabeth were married. Ten months later, Mary Ives gave birth to her first child . . .

# Danbury II

You ask of my Companions. Hills, sir—and the
Sundown, and a Dog large as myself, that my
Father bought me— They are better than Beings
—because they know—but do not tell—
EMILY DICKINSON: *letter to Col Higginson*

Charles Edward Ives was born in Danbury/Connecticut, October 20
1874, just over a month after the birth of Arnold Schoenberg in a sub-
urb of Vienna/Austria, Imperial vintage. In May, Verdi's *Requiem*
had received its first performance in San Marco cathedral, Milan. During the summer, 34-yr-old Tschaikowsky had finished his first piano
concerto, premiered October the following year by Hans von Bülow,
in Boston. In September, 41-yr-old Brahms discarded the penultimate
draft of his first symphony, conceived nearly 20 years earlier. By
October, at Wahnfried, Wagner was putting the final touches to the
full-score of *Die Götterdämmerung.* Dvorak was 33, Elgar 17,
Mahler 14, Debussy and Delius 12. The American Civil War had
been over for nine uneasy years.

A happy event, 10 composers, and a lingering canker. The event
turns out to be another composer. Because of him, our perspective
of 10 other composers is fractionally/radically altered. The canker
lingered on.

But for Charles's parents, in October 1874, only present joy over
a firstborn son. The following year George Ives did express interest
in going to Boston to hear von Bülow at the start of his pan-American
concert tour; but it meant canceling lessons and rehearsals that could

not be made up—and besides, his brother Joseph was getting married again. And 20 years later he wrote to his son, anxious to have a detailed history of the New York performance of *Die Götterdämmerung* he had been to hear. By then, Brahms was an established favorite, Dvorak head of the National Conservatory in New York, Debussy known to New York audiences for *L'après-midi d'un faune,* Delius for his *Florida* Suite, written on an orange plantation near Jacksonville; Elgar, at 37, still unrecognized, even in his own country.

Mary Ives's second son, Joseph Moss, was born on February 5 1876, destined for a more illustrious career during his lifetime than his now more distinguished brother. The following November, Rutherford Hayes won a disputed Presidential victory over his Democratic rival. Local control returned to the South, eight years' Civil War Reconstruction was considered formally at an end, the basic Abolitionist ideal—George Ives said, and many agreed with him— treasonably betrayed. But there were lessons to the children of the townsfolk to be given, the Saturday morning rehearsal with the community orchestra prepared, music for the Sunday service looked over, the Thanksgiving services now only three weeks distant organized. A man with a job of work to do could not afford to let his emotions run away with him; the most George could do was vent his feelings to his mother, and trust her to convey them to their former Negro protégé, Henry Anderson Brooks, away in South Carolina. His reply—December 28 1876—was laconic: right before Christmas, the house in Chesterfield where his mother was living had been burned down. Burning Cross territory.

A fragment of family history and a particle of soul-food for thought—minor but essential ingredients that impart a fleeting bitterness to the flavor of Charles Ives's works.

## Two Interpolations

Charles Ives did not know No 1. Somewhere along the line he must have been aware of No 2. *Add* to his preoccupation with social/political injustice and "the war-mongers":

## Interpolation 1

> *1565:* Hawkins makes the first of three voyages round the
> world collecting slaves for the Spanish Americas.

*1604:* Virginia Plantation founded under Royal Patent from James I—"Nowhere else in Our Realm shall Tobacco be grown." Slave-labor.

*Industrial Revolution:* has its own native slave-labor to employ. Despite strenuous minority protests from Quakers, poets, and statesmen, Europe as a whole unconcerned about black slavery—except where fortunes are to be made. Elsewhere the Black Man, like the American Indian, is exotic decoration—e.g. Maria Theresa's black page-boy in *Der Rosenkavalier* (18th century Austria).

*American Civil War:* for Europe as a whole, a private squabble between the North & South—subject to the above financial proviso. British captains of industry support the Confederacy.

This is putting an emphasis Ives himself didn't—consciously— on the Civil War as *musical catharsis.* Cutting out the glory: *The Red Badge Of Courage, Gone With The Wind* were its glory, if it had one; Ives's *Elegy To Stephen Foster, The Black March (St Gaudens)* its catharsis. Ives was fairly immediate post Civil War generation. He was too close, hadn't the conscious perspective. At Danbury Academy he had been fed the kind of pap in *Altemus' Historical Series:*

. . . of the various subjects forming portions of the history of a nation, none has been so generally acceptable to young people as the record of its WARS . . .

When America entered World War I he joined the "we'll get the sneaking Kaiser" ballyhoo, wanted to drive a volunteer ambulance in France, forgot his job. Forgot the intuitive perspective accorded him by his father, inherited direct from Stephen Foster, bypassing the Civil War social/political faction.

Around the time of Charles's marriage in 1908, his mother recalled an incident from his childhood to her grandchildren—Moss's children. Charles never had an expressed remembrance of it, though it became the outward pattern of his life for more than 30 years . . .

*1878:* A SMALL BRICK BOOTH. By the sidewalk on Main Street, in back of the old elm tree that stood to the right of the house as you looked out of the window, PEOPLE were

building a SMALL BRICK BOOTH. 4-yr-old Charles would
stop examining the cracks between the piano keys and
clamber down from the piano stool and go to the front
window and stand there on tiptoe, watching them. Or
run out the parlor and across the hallway and into the
dining-room—you could see them better from the window
in the dining-room. Then race out the front door and
over the lawn, dragging me after him, to inspect and
supervise the work. N. T. BULKLEY, it said, when they
put the notice up. N. T. BULKLEY of WOOSTER CEMETERY.
"INSURANCE AGENT." "Mossie, let's play INSURANCE
AGENT, Mossie . . . I'll be the AGENT . . ."

That was before Charles and his parents and his baby brother
moved to 16 Stevens Street, early in 1879. He was having regular
music lessons from his father by then:

My father had the belief that everyone was born with at least
one germ of musical talent, and that an early application of great
music (and not trivial music) would help it grow. He started both
the children in the family—and most of the children in the town,
for that matter—on Bach and Stephen Foster. Quite shortly after
they were born—always regardless of whether they had or would
have or wouldn't have any musical gifts or sense, &c . . .

Music lessons covered nearly every aspect of music-making:
violin, piano, organ, woodwinds, brass, harmony, counterpoint &
fugue, sight-singing & ear-training—especially ear-training. George
Ives was no more than an adequate violinist, more interested in
mastering its sound effects, natural & artificial harmonics, differing
timbres of sound at differing parts of the bow and different points of
the string, than conventional string techniques. When he had taught
his son what he could, Charles was sent to John Starr, cousin Howard's teacher, in the nearby village of Brookfield. For lessons on
snare-drum he went to young Mr Slier, the local barber, who had
been first drummer-boy in his father's regimental band—his barber
shop inherited from "Judge" Homer Peters, the Negro barber and
town fiddler.

In the summer of 1880, when he was 5, Charles made his first
attempts at letter-writing, to his grandmother and to Aunt Amelia—

"Millie"—who were staying at Westbrook, a holiday resort on Long Island Sound, near the mouth of the Connecticut River:

> Danbuy comn
> july 15
>
> grandma it is time to right to you. it is hot today. I wish next time I could go to Westbrwok with you
>
> good by
> Charlie Ives

and to Aunt Amelia, on the notepaper of the law partners, "Lyman D Brewster, Samuel Tweedy, Howard B Scott":

> Aunt milliie i have worte to you for hhe fun fo it. I have a sour toe. how it clams. I have nothing out of my garden. my nane was in the paper for I wroked for the school. my head aches. I must leave you now.
>
> good by
> Charlie Ives

The manner of "school-wrok" was not disclosed—Charles did not spend his first day at the New Street School till April 12 1881. By July 1, his spelling had evidently improved—he received 100 for Spelling and for Reading in his Examination Report, 96 for Writing, and ranked 2 in a class of 15: "Eudora Osborne    Teacher."

In June 1881, on his 21st birthday, cousin Howard had married 24-yr-old Anna Wood Miner. Their three children followed headlong —the youngest, a daughter, born Christmas Eve 1884, named Amelia Merritt for the mother Howard had never seen. Charles now 10, music fast becoming his obsession. When they got back from infant Amelia's baptism, "Eddy" was summoned to the front parlor. Charles knew, when his father called him by his middle name, he had something important to say. The pith:

> A man can keep his interest in music stronger, cleaner, bigger, and freer if he doesn't try to make a living out of it. Assuming he lives by himself and has no dependents, no one to feed but himself, and is willing to live as simply as Thoreau, he may write music which no one would play, or publish, or listen to, or buy. But if he has a nice wife and some nice children, how can he let his children starve on his dissonances ?—answer me that, Eddy! So he has to weaken—

and as a man *should* weaken for his children—but his music does more than weaken: it goes "ta ta" for money—bad for him, bad for his music, but good for his boys!

By the summer of 1886, Charles had realized his ambition to go to Westbrook, where the family now had a regular summer place at the beach. Aunt Amelia had taken her mother down there in May, and a letter to her from Charles in Danbury says that he and Moss have been over to the family house on Main Street and are staying to supper with Uncle Lyman:

P S.   The chickens are all right.

Then, in July, from Westbrook, Charles's first letter to his father:

Westbrook 18 of July—86

Dear Papa

Mama received your letter last night. I am very sorry you could not come Saturday and stay Sunday . . . I am glad the concert at Patterson was a success . . . I go in bathing every day . . . we expect to come home this week. George Miner ( (Howard's brother-in-law) ) is here over Sunday . . . Mama is going to write to you tomorrow . . . Come down some day this week. I must close now . . .

and, with the great formality that marks all his letters to his father, the closure:

Yours Truly
Charlie

His next letter, 10 days later, just before they returned from Westbrook, mentions that he is "reading a very interesty book, named Huckleberry Finn," and contains the injunction to his father: "Please live to Grama's till I come." ( (George Ives was staying in the family house—"fixing most all the doors & the blinds in the house so they will work easier.") ) By mid-September, Uncle Lyman had gone down to Westbrook to join Amelia, and George and his family were looking after the Main Street house:

Dear Auntie

I have just returned from the chicken coop & have closed up

the chickens for the night . . . Mama has pickled some pears yesterday up home & little Amelia came over to see her. Mama has canned & pickled some peaches down here too. Tell Grandma there was a meeting of the Children's Home here last evening before last . . . I am going to cut the back lawn & give some of the grass to the chickens. Moss has watered the plants tonight . . . Did you tell me to empty the swill pail every day ? Annie said that you did. I have given the leaves of the corn to the chickens. Our orchestra have got to play again. We expect to have some new members: Ned Tweedy 2nd Violin & Harry Biddiscome piano instead of Fannie Blarderd. How many baths do you take ? Please tell Uncle Lyman to take a bath for me because I have to work, study ect. . . .

The letter is written on headed notepaper:

IVES BROS
GROCERIES
167/169 MAIN STREET DANBURY

One of the childhood games Charles and Moss used to play was "Grocery Store," adopting at first the name of the local grocers, Abbotts Bros. Later they had their father paint them a sign "Ives Bros, 167/169 Main Street"—the original numbering of the family house before it became 210 Main Street. Printed letterheads followed. Charles always regarded the family house as "Grandma's," and Aunt Amelia and Uncle Lyman as interlopers. Knowing Aunt Amelia's distaste for "tradespeople"—she always refused to acknowledge her second cousin, a Danbury florist, as being any relation at all—this was 11-yr-old Charles's way of annoying her. Plus his continual references to her chickens: he probably thought of her as an old hen. A letter to Uncle Lyman a week later is signed:

Your Humble chicken waterer. C. I.

SOME LOCAL COLOR. The outdoor Camp Meetings were still a vital feature of New England life during the 1880s—Charles's boyhood years. The center for Fairfield County was by the village of Redding, 8 miles south of Danbury, encompassed by heavily wooded, rock-strewn hills. Farmers and their families would come from all over the county, by wain or on foot. The meetings were like the old Revivalist

services of the South, with an admixture of stern Puritan fervor, something of the fervor of the Burned-Over District of western New York
state, to the singing of Gospel Hymns by thousands of "let-out" souls:

> Father led the singing, sometimes with his cornet or his voice,
> sometimes with both his cornet and his arms, and sometimes in the
> quieter hymns with a French horn or violin. He always encouraged
> the people to sing their own way—most of them knew the words
> (theirs) and the music (theirs) by heart, and if they threw the
> poet or the composer about a bit, so much the better for the poetry
> and the music . . .

PLUS A LOCAL TALENT

> *Aug 19 1888:* letter from Moss to his grandmother in West-
> brook—"Charlie is to play the organ in church today."
> Charles was 13.
>
> *Aug 26 1888:* letter from Charles to his cousin Anna—"Played
> the organ in church last Sunday and today."
>
> *Feb 10 1889:* aged 14, first Sunday as regular organist of West
> Street Congregational church.
>
> *Aug 22 1889:* letter from Charles in Westbrook—

Dear Papa,

  I received a letter from Miss Hollister this morning asking me
if I would be home Sunday—if I wasn't I could get Miss Mamie
Moore to play—the folks say I can stay over here till Monday.
Will you please see or find Miss Moore or write to her and see if
she will play—if she can't you can send me word . . . There will
be only 3 hymns and only a morning service. You might play cornet.
                    Yours Truly
                    C E Ives
P S.   Aunt Millie would like to have you ask Mr General Telephone
Smith to burn the worms off the big pear tree. If he hasn't done it.

> *Oct 19 1889:* first Sunday as regular organist of the Danbury
> Baptist Church.
>
> *Oct 20 1889:* the *Danbury News*, on his 15th birthday—

Charles Ives presided at the organ of the Baptist Church yesterday. He is the youngest organist in the State.

> *May 1893—Sept 1894:* aged 18/19, regular organist of St
> Thomas's Episcopal Church, New Haven.
> *Sept 1894—June 1898:* aged 19/23, regular organist of Centre
> Church, New Haven.
> *June 1898—Dec 1899:* aged 23/25, regular organist of 1st
> Presbyterian Church, Bloomfield/N Y.
> *Apr 1900—June 1902:* aged 25/27, regular organist and choir-
> master, Central Presbyterian Church, New York City.

EQUALS:

(1) 14 years' experience of organ-playing and hymn-singing;
(2) the proliferation of Hymn parodies throughout his compositions; &
(3) an IMPATIENCE:

> I've heard the same hymns played by nice celebrated
> organists and sung by highly-known singers in beautifully
> upholstered churches, and in the process everything in the
> music was emasculated—precise (usually too fast) even
> time—"ta ta" down/left/right/up pretty voices, &c. They
> take a mountain and make a spongecake out of it, and
> sometimes, as a result, one of these commercial travelers
> gets a nice job at the Metropolitan . . .

Charles Ives was 13 when he finished his first orchestral piece—
*Holiday Quickstep*—on Christmas Day 1887. It was performed three
weeks later by his father's orchestra at Taylor's Opera House—an
emporium built by the Danbury citizen and creator of "Taylor-made
Hats"—which made Taylor. A year later George Ives arranged the
piece for piccolo, 2 trumpets, 2 violins, and piano—played Christmas
Day 1888 by the Young People's Orchestra of Danbury at the
Methodist Sunday School, Moss playing piccolo, Charles directing
from the piano.

When he was 15—May 9 1889—the family left the home on
Stevens Street they had lived in for 10 years and moved to 10 Chapel
Place, next door to the future site of the family house, which was
brought up from Main Street in 1923. On May 23 Charles began
organ lessons with James R. Hall, organist of St James's Episcopal
Church—today moved from its original site on Main Street to West
Street.

April 18 1889 had been a milestone in Danbury's history. With a population exceeding 18,000, it was incorporated as a City. The civic celebrations had been planned by Lyman Brewster and James Montgomery Bailey, but they fell flat. It was decided to do them over on June 20. They started at 10 AM and lasted through the day, culminating promptly at 8 PM inside Taylor's Opera House with a George Ives Spectacular, *A Musical Trip To Coney Island*, a musical three-ring circus of P T Barnum proportions. In the *Danbury Evening News* next day, "A Card from Mr Ives":

> What was intended in the first place as an instrumental concert grew to such magnitude, both vocal and instrumental—through the kindness of many friends—that the concert was more than one man could manage without some shortcomings being apparent . . .

But no shortcomings apparent in the opinion of the accompanying review by the Danbury Newsman:

> Such an aggregation of musical talent was never seen on the Opera House Stage before . . . a musical presentation of the Danbury & Coney Island Railway . . . chorus, band and orchestra appropriately sang ((?)) *Auld Lang Syne* . . . the Greylark Quartette followed . . . *Serenade* by Van der Stucken . . . F Seymour's novel solos on glasses, sticks, bars and bottles . . . Trinity Church boy choir rendered *Peasant's Wedding March* by Sodermann . . . *Ave Maria* sung by Mrs Carrie Allen Baker . . . as an encore, *Rock Me To Sleep, Mother* . . . Master Gilmore sang *Daddy* . . . Mr Pierpoint picked the banjo, Mr Belden the guitar, rendered old airs . . . *Home, Sweet Home* was sung by the excursionists . . . The music then imitated the brass band at Paul Bauer's, while the one and only Levy rendered a cornet solo ((played by George Ives)). The representations of the German and Scotch bands were unusually true to nature . . . But it was the *William Tell* Overture that was the great feature . . . The whole entertainment concluded with the singing of *America* . . . The fireworks were a surprise . . .

The concert/spectacular had 3 consequences for Charles Ives:

> (1) Direct—he included two of its items in his first major organ recital, part of a concert given in the Baptist church on June 28 the following year:

Overture: *William Tell*      Rossini, arr. Rheinberger
*March Pontificale*      Lemmen, arr. Dudley Buck
*Home, Sweet Home*      J H Payne/Sir Henry Rowley,
     arr. Dudley Buck
Toccata in C major      J S Bach
Sonata in F minor      Mendelssohn

(2) Indirect—the effect of *America*, with massed chorus, or-chestra, and band, the audience joining in ((maybe the fireworks as well)), started him working on the *America* Variations, for Organ; first performance in Danbury in 1891, second performance in Brewster/N Y, February 17, 1892:

> One variation was the theme in canon, put in three keys together, B♭–E♭–A♭, and backwards, A♭–E♭–B♭—but this was not played at the church concerts as it made the boys rough and noisy . . .

((The variation has been lost . . . ))

> In the MS at the bottom of p 8 there are two rhythms made by off-accents ((4 ♫'s against 3 ♫♫'s)). In some of these passages, the lower pedal rhythm keep-ing the regular ¾ is omitted—this is often done in jazz today ((1932)). Also short Interludes between variations (right hand starting Hymn in F, left hand Hymn in D♭, as a kind of canon together). These only lasted five or six measures, but Father would not let me play them at the Brewster concert, as they made the boys laugh out loud . . .

((These Interludes are lost . . . ))

(3) Synapse. The success of the Opera House concert led George Ives to make the concert arrangement, *A Rale Ould Irish Medley*, played at Wooster House bandstand 10 weeks later, August 31 1889. As a surprise encore, he introduced his son's Overture, *The American Woods*, written during the same period of 10 weeks.

If one moment can be isolated as discovering the beginning of transcendental workings in a 14-yr-old's mind, it is this piece. The score no longer exists—only some MS fragments of a violin & piano arrangement. Page 1 of the full-score of the 2nd Symphony has:

> The second theme of the last movement is partly from an early short piece called *The American Woods* (Brookfield). The part suggesting a Steve Foster tune (while over it the old farmers fiddle a barn dance with all its jigs, reels and gallops), was played in Danbury on the old Wooster House Bandstand in 1889 . . .

while the marginalia on one MS fragment—added between 1894 and 1898—have:

> *above:* for Piano & Vio. from Am. Woods Overture
> score lost
> *down RH margin:* get cornet part Billy Hicks played, Arthur Clark trombone part, in "Steve Foster & John Starr Overture Columbia": send to 76 So. Middle, New Haven Ct . . .

Collate this:

(1) John Starr. Violinist. Charles's teacher. Cousin Howard's teacher. The following year—September 23 1890—his obituary appeared in the *Danbury Evening News:*

> Mr Starr was a well-known musician, being a skillful violinist, and was from his youth up identified with orchestral music at sociables and other entertainments in Danbury and the neighboring towns. Mr Starr was a native of Brookfield and died in the house where he was born. He was 48 years old.

Brookfield associated with (1) violins & violinists, country fiddlers, and (2) heavily wooded terrain—Thoreau-type country.

(2) Stephen Foster. The "Steve Foster" tune is *Camptown Races.* As it appears in Ives's 2nd Symphony, it is commonly identified with the dominant French horn figure in Dvorak's *New World* Symphony, premiered in New York, December 16 1893—i.e. before Ives started work on his 2nd Symphony. Its use in *The American Woods* antedates the *New World* Symphony by four years. As 14-yr-old Charles Ives used the tune, it was simply one from Foster's corpus of songs, apt in the context of country fiddlers

racing to a photo-finish, the whole Foster/Thoreau/musico-
political-catharsis bit too radically embedded in his musical heritage for him to be consciously aware.

(3)  Columbia—otherwise *The Red, White & Blue*, "O Columbia, the gem of the ocean . . . " Appears in the 1st, 4th
& 5th movements of the 2nd Symphony, and is a parody
that constantly invades Ives's later compositions—especially in music that has reference to Hawthorne . . .
*The American Woods* is its first appearance.

Two days after his 15th birthday, Charles started organ lessons
with Alexander Gibson, organist of St Luke's, Norwalk. He was now
giving more and more time to composition, and experimenting with
"interval series," as they are called—a device once thought to origi-
nate with Bartok and Berg, then aged 8 and 4 respectively. The MS
of an organ *Burlesque Cadenza* has the marginalia:

I played for Mr Gibson—it made him laugh!

Early in 1890 he began to sketch his first extended choral work,
the *Communion Service*, and to experiment with tonal resources. The
pages of MSS have the following headings:

*Kyrie* in F ( . . . E♭ . . . D maj. 1890 Jan 8)
*Sanctus* in E♭ ( . . . D♭ ), *Sursum corda* in D♭
*Credo* in D ( . . . in D♭ )
*Benedictus* in F
*Agnus Dei* in F, *Sanctus* in c & C
*Kyrie* in D

A footnote to the voice parts of *Kyrie II, Sursum corda, Sanctus II,*
and *Benedictus* reads:

copied by Father & sung in Episcopal Church Danbury Nov 1890

On Easter Sunday 1892, the Episcopal church performed his
*Gloria,* Charles guest organist for the entire service. For Evensong he
returned to the organ bench of the Baptist church for a performance
of his *Easter Carol.* The previous February he had played the
*America* Variations at St Thomas's, Brewster, in March enrolled at
the Danbury Academy. Now he was working on the *Intercollegiate
March* for large band—first performed by his father's band the following October at Danbury Fair. ((It was played in 1897 by the

Washington Marine Band for President McKinley's inauguration—by
the New Haven town band for the same occasion . . . ) )

Pieces for band are among Charles's earliest compositions: his
father's 1st Connecticut Regimental Band had been the finest in the
Army, the Danbury Band certainly the finest in New England. A slip
of paper identifies his Opus 1:

> Schoolboy March D/F.   Op 1
> Arr. Band    Sept 1886    C. Ives

C Ives aged 12. Certainly arranged with his father's help. The score
lost.

In 1886 or 7, a *Slow March* to the cantus firmus "Adeste
fidelis." Played on Decoration Day 1886 or 7 by the Danbury and
Carmel/N Y bands. The score lost. ((The "Adeste fidelis" section
incorporated into *Decoration Day*, second of *4 New England Holidays*, in 1912.))

In 1887, a 13-yr-old's *Circus Parade*—according to a list of
band pieces jotted down on the back of an Ives & Myrick calendar
40 years later. The score lost. Probable prototype for the 1894
sketch for theater orchestra & chorus, *The Circus Band*—to Charles's
own words—arranged the same year for voice & piano, included in
1922 as no 56 of *114 Songs*.

In 1888 or 9—before the move from Stevens Street to Chapel
Place—a 14-yr-old's *Fantasia on "Jerusalem the Golden."* The
score lost.

After leaving Danbury, one band arrangement of an 1892
March for piano.

Early in 1893, Charles Ives went to Hopkins Grammar School,
New Haven, to prepare for entry to Yale College. At his Danbury
schools he had shown great athletic prowess, a star player on their
football and baseball teams, team photos of "The Alerts" in the *Danbury Evening News*, &c, &c. A faculty more acceptable than music—
his or anyone's serious—to the "all-swing-together" confraternity he
was about to enter.

## Interpolation 2

. . . It is good to know of Alcott, the benign idealist, that when
the Rev Thomas Wentworth Higginson (later a Colonel in the

Northern Army), leading the rush on the United States Court House in Boston to rescue a fugitive slave . . .

E W Emerson: *Thoreau, as Remembered by a Young Friend*

. . . The Rev Thomas Wentworth Higginson has resigned his commission to become Colonel of the 1st South Carolina Volunteer Regiment of Black Contrabands . . .

Springfield *Daily Republican,* "Miscellaneous War News," February 23 1863

. . . Col Higginson, during a recent expedition into the interior of South Carolina, was injured by the concussion of an exploding shell, but at last accounts was doing well . . .

*Ibid.,* July 24 1863

# FIRST FUGUE

# New Haven I

I had a terror since September—I could tell to none—and so I sing, as the Boy does by the Burying Ground, because I am afraid—
EMILY DICKINSON: *letter to Col Higginson*

212 Orange Street

Mr Geo E Ives:

Dear Sir,

I was pleased to receive your letter of Mch 1st, giving your consent and sanction to your Son's desire, to come and play the organ for us at St Thomas's Church.

I think it will be unnecessary to write out any formal agreement. We certainly understand each other, in each and every particular, and as we have agreed, there seems to be no occasion for anything further. Hoping and believing this to be the beginning of very pleasant relations, I am, dear Sir,

Yours very truly,

Charles Bonney

New Haven     Mch 2     1893

P S   I shall communicate with your son in a day or two, and send him the music promised.   C B

And on March 6:

My dear Mr Ives:

I send you by Express to day the music taken from the

Organist's cabinet at the Church. You may keep it of course until you come to take your position, when you may restore it to its proper place. I hope you will read carefully the Psalter Preface, for therein lies the whole secret of my plan of chanting, and if you get a clear idea of that Preface, you will have no difficulty in accompanying that particular kind of work. I think it would be a good plan for you to hear the choir, as soon as you can now, either at a Sunday Service or Friday evening rehearsal. Much would be clear to you that is now very vague. Of course our music is now very plain it being the Lenten season, but you could see the order of things just as well. I want to urge you most strongly to study the Prayer Book thoroughly too. That is after all the rule and guide for every thing and everybody in the Episcopal Church, and if there are matters you don't understand write me and I will try to help you. Many questions may arise as to various matters from time to time, and I shall be more than glad to assist you all I can. Write to me at your convenience.

Very truly yours,
Charles Bonney

So the first link was cast. From a small industrial town in western Connecticut to a fishing town on Long Island Sound—not, in 1893, substantially larger than Danbury, but famous for its seat of learning that had brought immortality to its first modest benefactor, Elihu Yale. Still dominant, in 1893, the clerical robes of the Divinity School, which had served since the College's inception to redress an imbalance caused by radical non-conformist elements at Harvard Divinity School. Still the dominant confession of respectability, the Episcopal Church. Its choirmaster, for the town of New Haven, Mr Charles Bonney.

Charles Ives took up his duties as regular organist of St Thomas's on May 5—the Friday evening rehearsal. Whether or not he went to any of the intervening services or rehearsals, he was back in Danbury on April 16 for a performance of his *Song For Harvest Season* at the dedication of the 2nd Baptist Church there:

This piece was played when the new Baptist Church in Danbury was opened. Father played cornet, Mrs Smyth tried to sing, and I played the lower parts (on the organ) . . .

Two days later he wrote his father a postcard from New Haven:

Yours rec'd this noon. I gave the key to the organ to Mrs Smyth before I came away. Please send the excuse for the music lessons so I can use it by Thursday. I am pretty well fixed up in my room only I could do with a few pictures. Tell Grandmother I will write her in a few days. In haste. C.

Whoever "the music lessons" were with, they cannot have been part of the Hopkins Grammar School curriculum, else the parental excuse would have been unnecessary. The spring term at HGS had started April 17, and "the room" was at 344 Crown Street, a boarding-house owned by a Miss Porter, sometime acquaintance of Aunt Amelia's, who gave private tuition to some of the HGS boys on the side. The school was a few blocks away, on the corner of Wall and High streets, where Yale Law School stands now.

May 7 1893 was Charles's first Sunday at St Thomas's, and two days later he wrote his father:

Yours just rec'd. I am in no particular hurry for the music etc. as there is quite a lot of good organ music in the church, and with what I brought with me I will have enough for 2 or 3 Sundays more . . . I wrote to Uncle Lyman yesterday telling how the service etc went. I had most trouble with the chants, and found the best way to learn them was to commit the music to memory and then follow the words. They sing their hymns faster than I am accustomed to, and it is rather hard to get used to it . . .

No further correspondence with home for the next eight weeks. Charles and his parents were hopeful that he might enter Yale in September, but he was finding work at Hopkins heavy going—especially as he was on the school baseball team, which took him away from his study. Nor did he get on well at first with Charles Bonney, who was English—Charles's first exposure to an Englishman, and he resented his prosaic ways: "everything had to be just so—a drillmaster . . ."

Aunt Amelia and Uncle Lyman paid him a visit the first week in July. Charles wrote his father again on July 5:

. . . enclosed please find check which I have rec'd from Mr Bonney, and also receipt for the room. I suppose Uncle Lyman told you I was going to the boat race, and I suppose you heard that Yale won again, as usual, though they had hard luck in the Base Ball Game.

The Hopkins B B pictures are done, and I have one for myself and will get one to send home if you wish . . . they cost $1.50. I haven't seen Miss Porter yet as she is out of town till tomorrow. The services at the Ch. went smoother than I thought they would, especially at the Choral Evensong the Sunday before last, when I only left out the "Amen" ( ( ( ! ) ) ). You ought to hear the choir sing Stainer "Alpha & Omega." When does Mother expect to come to Westbrook ?

( (Leaving out the "Amen" was not carelessness on Charles's part. In his *Memos*, he talks about the Presbyterians and Episcopals expecting the Amen as a rite, regardless of whether it was appropriate to the Hymn or not. The Baptists and Methodists, on the other hand, might choose to sing it or leave it out, as the spirit moved them.) )

And on July 9:

. . . I kept putting off writing last week until I heard from Miss Porter, who I was unable to see until Thursday night. She says it would be better for me to wait till Sept to study with her. I haven't heard about all the examinations yet, but I guess most of the fellows passed. I see that Jack Bliss failed . . .

It had been decided, reluctantly, that Charles should not take his entrance examinations to Yale at least until the fall, and his father wrote him on July 11 that Uncle Lyman would be going to a legal convention in Milwaukee and would like Charles to go with him as his "typist"—if Mr Bonney could spare him. The suggestion threw his son into a pother:

. . . Have just seen Mr Bonney who says he doesn't know of anybody now who would play, and as it will be the first Sunday for the choir, it will be particularly hard, besides he would have to have the rehearsals a week before as usual, although he might find somebody later but of course that would be too late. The ass't organist could not do it, as we will hardly be able to get him ready to play the hymns in August. I show him twice a week. He never had anything to do with an organ before so it is easy to show him. Mr Bonney said I hadn't ought to take less than a dollar a time so I get two dollars a wk from it. Even if I could go I don't see how I could get any time for the typewriter, as I will have to study all the time if I get even 6 prelims off next Sept. They are marking very close this year as only 3 of the class passed and half of them flunked who were better prepared than I. I also heard that a pile of Andover fellows got left. It was lucky I didn't take mine. Anyway please let me know the plans as soon as possible . . .

George Ives replied on July 15, gently humoring his son for his grammatical errors—"I don't think 'hadn't ought' is exactly 'proper caper' ":

> . . . your Uncle Lyman has been appointed Commissioner on Equalization of Laws & is to be paid expenses to attend convention in Milwaukee the first week in Sept. He could get a secretary's expense & thought if you could go. He would like to go to Chicago the last week in August ((for the World Fair)) & back to Milwaukee for the first week in Sept. In that case you couldn't get back until one day before the second Sunday in Sept so I think it would be necessary to get a substitute for the two first Sundays in Sept, if you could get one at all, which I doubt. But there is a possible chance & Lyman is anxious to have you go. If you hear of an organist any time this month that would satisfy Mr Bonney, shouldn't think two weeks taken from study would necessarily be any detriment. L D B thinks you might get enough practice on typewriter the first three weeks in August . . .

A substitute organist appears to have been found, as Charles's next letter was from Chicago (Aug 22) where he and his uncle had been to the Fair grounds and "heard Theodor Thomas's orchestra"— the Chicago Symphony, now in its third season. Then from Peru/ Illinois (Aug 28) where they were staying with Uncle Lyman's relations, and Charles had read in the Chicago newspapers that the French organist Alexandre Guilmant was to play at the World Fair at the end of the week.

On September 1, Lyman wrote to his wife in Westbrook:

> My dear Amelia,
>     Your good long letter & Aunt M's came last night and as we have now finished up the business of both the Am. Bar Assoc. & the Convention of Conferences—(except for the Annual Banquet this PM) we can stop to write a little & look round this beautiful city . . . Charley's task as "Secretary of the Con. Commission"

was not very onerous, about four hours in all. He is rejoicing in the prospect of hearing the famous French organist "Guilmant" to-morrow on the Exposition grounds at 1 PM. Charley says he is the best organist in the world & the papers seem of the same opinion . . . Charles will leave for Danbury on the 6th getting there on 7th at 6 PM or earlier . . . You need have no apprehensions as to C's health. He has weighed himself at every stop & has found no deficiency in weight. If there has been any over-action it is in chewing gum—confined strictly to our room . . .

  Charley joins in love to you all
Yours ever
L D B

## An Operatic Venture Discussed

Charles and his uncle traveled to Chicago by the NY Central from Putnam Junction, an overnight train ride of some 20 hours. During the first part of the journey—Monday afternoon and evening, August 21—Lyman Brewster showed his nephew the script of his play, *Major John André*, a rather pallid copy of William Dunlap's melo-drama, concerning the incident near the start of the Independence War where André had been arrested, tried, and shot for giving in-formation to the British. Uncle and nephew discussed the possibility of setting it as an opera. Even in the hands of the most conventionally gifted composer it was not good operatic material, but 18-yr-old Charles seemed flattered and excited at the time. The project came to nothing, and there is no further mention of it in his letters or memo-randa. The idea for an overture became the Overture & March: *"1776,"* completed at Pine Mountain in July 1904.

  In September 1893, Charles returned to New Haven, and after 10 days at Miss Porter's boarding-house, moved to the house of the MacIntyres, whose eldest son Tom was a classmate of his at HGS. On September 30 he wrote to his father:

  . . . Your letter rec'd yesterday noon. I enclose laundry and Mr Bonney's check. I asked Mr Bonney about trying voice last Tuesday after the rehearsal, but he said wait until sometime when we weren't both so tired. I think you asked me in one of your letters, how much time &c I had for studies, music & exercise. The studies take most of the time . . .

On October 4, to his mother:

> . . . I have bought 4 new books, 2 of them 2nd hand. Tell Uncle Lyman I am studying Homer, which is not much more difficult than Xenophon, though it takes more time. I also have German and find that what I studied with Father helps me a good deal. I can do very much more studying here than I could at Crown Street, as it is not quite so handy for the other boys, and Tom has to study a good deal himself. We both play football in the later part of the afternoon, and so I have all the rest of the time for practice and study . . . I wish you would send me that Latin Grammar (Allen & Greenough) . . .

In the postscript of a letter to his father, October 30:

> There was a choral service yesterday and they said it went better than any service went before . . .

And on November 11, to his father:

> . . . Your letter just rec'd. I will meet mother at the room after 1.30. I can't think of anything, she needs to bring. I rec'd your letter, with the check in, the other day. I doubt if I will be able to come home Thanksgiving, as there is to be service at the church that day. I have been playing tennis this week, instead of football, as there are some good courts, on the next block, above us . . . I am trying to finish up the fugue now, which I started last winter . . .

(( . . . This, the first reference to composition since Charles left Danbury in April. One copy of the *Easter Carol*—first performed in Danbury on Easter Sunday 1892—has the note: "St Thomas New Haven  Oct 1893  Mr Bonney"; and an early list of works mentions a "Morning & Vesper Service" at St Thomas's, but no such music has come to light. A letter in May 1894 mentions "a little song I am trying to write . . ." By then, Charles must have been working on Psalm 67—one of his most astonishing works—but his letters make no mention of it . . . ))

The St Thomas's Thanksgiving Service was over early, and Charles was able to get home to Danbury after all, leaving on the 12.10 train and returning to New Haven the following day. His letters home from now until Christmas talk of the possibility of taking organ lessons with a Mr Shelley, and perhaps working up some recitals. Or did his father think it would be better to take lessons from Dudley Buck in New York ? He thought he would be able to pay for the lessons himself. The next week he wrote that he hadn't been in touch with either Buck or Shelley yet—"will talk it over with Mr Bonney first . . ."

Christmas Day 1893 was the last reunion for the entire family at the family house on Main Street. After his return to HGS in the New Year, Charles's letters home are tinged with a faint but growing fractiousness:

> *Sun Jan 21 1894:* . . . I rec'd all the things you sent and asked Uncle Lyman, when he was here, to tell you and the folks so, but I guess he forgot . . . Mr Bonney was sick Friday evening, and was not well enough to be at service today. The music went very well considering . . .

> *Sun Feb 11:* . . . I have not asked Mr Bonney about voice lessons yet, as he has been busy after the Tues rehearsals, the time I thought would be best. I can't do anything more about the recitals until after Lent . . .

> *Sun Feb 20:* . . . I suppose I can come home Wed evening, but there is a card party which I would rather like to go to and then Thurs the as'st organist wanted to have me play at the 4 o'c Lenten service, which they have every day in the week, at which he plays, they have no choir, just hymns &c. I could get out of it I suppose. Then I have a debate Friday which I expected to work on almost all day Thurs . . . And then if I come Easter, which is only about 3 weeks after. Of course if you still think it best I will come. Of course I would like to see you all, but it is such a short time to Easter . . .

> *Thurs Mar 22:* . . . School vacation begins today and lasts until next Thurs 29. I would have come home this week but there is service in church Good Friday, and for that reason it wouldn't give me much time as I could have next week if I cut a day or two at school . . . I wrote a letter Sunday and thought I had mailed it until, having rec'd the telegram, I looked and found it in the pocket of my best coat . . .

> *Sat Mar 24:* . . . Will try to get to D Sunday evening if there is a train—if not the first one I can get Monday morning . . .

I don't like to ask Mr Bonney to let me off Tues and I might as well come back Tues evening as school begins on Thurs. I will bring the clothes and music you want . . .

Charles's position at St Thomas's would be coming to an end in April, and he had auditioned for the post of organist at the New Haven 2nd Baptist Church. He had hoped to hear the result before going home, and his father and Uncle Lyman were even more anxious to know. While he was in Danbury, plans for the future were discussed in detail: how was his school work doing ? did he really think he would be able to pass his examinations for Yale in the fall ? should he have some coaching in harmony & counterpoint from Dr Stoeckel, Battel Professor of Music at Yale ? On March 29 he wrote from New Haven:

. . . Rec'd Uncle Lyman's telegram last evening and your letter this noon. I have finally managed to find Dr Walker, the chairman of the Baptist ch. committee, and he says that the committee have decided on a Mr Hogson, I don't know how the name is spelled nor have I ever heard of him before, except that he was the one who offered to do it for nothing and was the one Mr Wheeler, the former organist, criticized the most . . . I think it would be better for Uncle Lyman to see Prof Stoeckel and the sooner the better, as I heard that he is going away again soon for his health, and that also, Jepson was going to Germany next fall to study, and that will probably leave Centre Church, and the As'st organist at Chapel open . . . The first thing I am going to get the best of is harmony & counterpoint, which I ought to get through without taking too much time to it with Dr Stoeckel. There is also some kind of a music course in college which I will look up. I think it can be taken without extra charge and may be substituted with other things . . . I think if anything the work at St Thomas has had a tendency rather to deaden than give ambition and I think my aim ought now to be to improve in the things I wouldn't have time to with the church work, and also to see and look out for some place in N Y for next year . . . I saw Miss Porter last evening the first chance I got, and she said that I ought to come out all right at Hopkins, that she will speak to Mr Fox. He seemed to be all right today, and asked me how my arm was for baseball. (I think maybe that is one of the reasons he wants me to come back.) I don't quite see what you

mean by the "appearances" it would make. It would be a means
of regular outdoor exercise and don't take much time as I won't
have to practice with the rest. Unless someone else comes I feel
as if I was needed to pitch . . . Of course if you decidedly think
it would hurt me very much, why I won't.

　　While I am writing the letter with the newspaper slip came.
I won't let the N Y trip interfere with work, but am anxious to
see what Wagner Opera is. Please tell Uncle Lyman what I have
said about school and Dr Stoeckel, &c . . .

((The "some kind of music course" was given by Professor Stoeckel
at Yale; when he retired in the summer of 1894—giving his name to
Stoeckel Hall, the home of the Yale School of Music—his place was
taken by Horatio Parker, who had been teaching theory at the National Conservatory in New York under Dvorak. Dvorak also left
his position as principal there during the summer, and went back to
Europe. But no one expected this at the time, and Charles's mention
of "looking out for some place in N Y next year"—in the form
of an organ post—could have been a secret desire to study composition with Dvorak. Certainly there is a deal of Dvorak in CI's composition during the next few years . . . ))

　　The "newspaper slip" was an announcement of the New
York performance of Wagner's *Die Götterdämmerung* at the Metropolitan in two days' time. Charles wrote his father on April 1, the
day following the performance:

　　. . . I bought a libretto with both German & English words. I read
　　the plot over two or three times so I could understand and follow
　　the German words better. I could easily see what Wagner tried to
　　do. You wouldn't notice the music or orchestra, as it all seems to
　　be a part of and go along with the action and story. I don't mean
　　that you wouldn't notice it, because one is interested in the play
　　but, that it feels as if it was only made to help one pay attention
　　to the acting. I don't remember any particular piece or song that
　　you would notice simply for the music itself unless it was the "Song
　　of the Rhine-Daughters" at the beginning of the 3rd Act. There
　　are some things that don't seem exactly natural. For instance, in
　　one place, Siegfried is supposed to be greatly furiated with Brün-
　　hilde and she has a long song in which she is greatly excited and up-
　　braids him, but he, instead of interrupting her, waits until the or-

chestra plays a long intermezzo, and then begins . . . They bring a horse on the stage, and it is supposed to be on the shore of the river but you can hear his hooves on the timbers of the stage, which spoils all the effect. And then too the using of so much horn, reed and kettle drums, grows awfully tiresome towards the end. And about all I can remember of the orchestra now, is that it was all diminished chords, whole-tones, and trombone . . . Everything all together is great, you can see just what his idea was, and it seems funny that nobody ever thought of it before . . . But it seems like a great deal of work over nothing . . .

But in Charles's next letters, the fractiousness returns:

> *Thurs Apr 12* . . . Why don't you think I don't understand your letters ? Maybe I don't write as though I did but I think I understand what you have advised and what I have got to do. You know after first of May which is nearly here I can come over Sundays. Of course if your writing won't do until then, I could come up some afternoon and you might come down . . .

April 29 was Charles's last Sunday at St Thomas's. He wrote his father that evening:

> . . . I expect to take my first lesson, as soon as Mr Bonney gets settled with the new organist. The service ended up in good shape today. I went to Centre Church to see Jepson after service, but he had gone. If I need a tutor at all it will be in Greek, and the best time to have him would be right before the exams. Moss says he is making arrangements by which he expects to go to University of Pennsylvania next fall. I wish I was doing something for my expenses, tho I hope I will be again next year . . .
>
> *Wed May 2* . . . Well I have finally seen Mr Jepson, and he says he will want me to play for him at Centre Church in the mornings, as soon as College opens next fall, if one with whom he made arrangements with a long time ago can't do it, and he says it is very doubtful if he can as since then he has accepted a position at Dwight Pl. and he is very doubtful if they will let him off for the mornings . . . He said he had heard of the organist at St Thomas, but didn't know that I was the one, and was very glad I asked him. He didn't mention any

terms, but suppose he would give me ⅓ or ¼ of his salary
which is $1,000. I would have to be only at the Sunday morning
rehearsal . . . I can have the organ to practice all I want . . .

*Sun May 6* . . . I don't see how Moss could have misunderstood
my postal, as Mr McIntire told me he said he rec'd it before
starting out. I said, as I remember, that we would not play
here anyway, probably would go out of town, and might not
play at all. I waited as long as possible to find out what we
would do. I am awfully sorry that he came, but Tom is going
to write him to come and spend Sunday next, here. I hope
he can come then . . . I took my first singing lesson, Thurs.
He didn't do much except try my voice. He said I had a good
high tenor voice, and also fairly low. Better than he thought
I had. He told me to sing mostly as I speak, naturally you
know . . .

*Tues May 8* . . . I can't think of anything in my last letter that
wouldn't do for the family to hear. Don't they know I'm taking
singing lessons, and if they don't, don't you want them to
know? I don't remember writing anything about extra lessons
in that letter, as I thought that you understood from what I
have written before, that if I considered it necessary to have
any tutors at all, it would be towards the end of term, and
I will look out for that at the proper time . . . I have suc-
ceeded in getting up about 6.30 every morning lately and get
quite a little studying done then. I have been playing tennis
for the last week or so, as I don't need to go to the field to
practice with the nine, except the day before the game. And
I don't see why you insist on blaming everything on ball, or
at least because I didn't write a good letter last Sunday. I
usually study in the evening—until 9.30 or 10—and then go
to bed . . . Mr Fox has not complained to me at all for a
long while, and I am sure he thinks I am doing all I can. I
will try and write Uncle Lyman soon about studies, but as
much as I can say will be what we are studying, etc, and how
I am getting along with them (that is, as to what my opinion
is, but as to what Mr Fox and the teachers think, of course
I can't say . . . Sunday after I had gotten lessons out of the
way, I was working on a little song that I am trying to write
for Garrison . . .

This letter seems at last to have won his father's approval, for his next letters are more relaxed, as though a crisis had passed. For George Ives's part, he had long since been forced to abandon most of his musical activities, and worked as teller at the Danbury Savings Bank, which his father had founded, and as clerk in his brother-in-law's law firm—this to keep his two sons in school. He had never enjoyed spectacular good health, and at the age of 49 had lost the boundless enthusiasm he had brought to his musical enterprises 10 and 20 years earlier. Little wonder if he saw in his son Charles a fulfillment of his own ambition as a musician; that he worried constantly about his having enough exercise; and worried then that time taken out for exercise would interfere with his studies. On Sunday May 13 Charles wrote his father:

> I took my second lesson with Mr Bonney Thurs, he had me sing some of those Concone exercises, but of course paid most attention to the way I get the tone. He believes that singing is only an extension of talking, and makes me say a certain sentence and then sing it with the same kind of voice . . . I will get a tutor if you think best, but I would have a hard time to do the lessons at school and his too. And I am pretty sure that Mr Fox will recommend me now. The baseball season is nearly at an end . . .

> *Sun May 20* . . . I have been very busy this week. We had the mid-term tests, and our final compositions are due Monday (tomorrow) and it took nearly all my spare time getting that ready. I have also been finishing the song for Garry. Rec'd the letter with the $5 check in, for which I am much obliged, also for $1 for the Music Teachers Convention . . . I forgot to say, I was elected permanent capt. of the nine last week, again. I had to accept under the circumstances, it won't take any more time, as season closes next Wed. It might be an item for Moss' paper though, it was in all the New Haven papers . . .

On June 9 Charles began 3 weeks' private tuition with Edward Hume in New Haven. He wrote home on June 27:

> . . . I only went to two of the MTC—the organ and the piano recitals. Mr Clark Lord the old Westbrook organist, and the friend of the Shermans played. Harry Jepson played "Tannhäuser Overture"—the same thing he played 3 yrs ago. Friedheim was the

pianist, and it seemed to me he was a kind of a machine. Tom
went to New York to take his exams for Princeton last Tues. His
father saw him Fri. and said Tom seemed to think he had passed . . .

The tutoring continued in Danbury July 10 through 13, with some
extra coaching from a J B Ryder, who wrote Charles from New
Haven on July 12:

> My dear Ives,
>       Yours of the 6th containing check received, for which accept
> my thanks. Am very glad to hear that you did so well at your
> examination, and it is especially pleasing to me that you passed
> in all your Mathematics . . .

On July 29 Charles wrote his father from Westbrook:

> . . . Fri. I rec'd the letter you forwarded, it was from the organist
> of Dwight Pl. ch. who wants to have me play for him the three last
> Sundays in August. Will give me three dollars—only one service
> (morning)—no rehearsal . . . I think this is the same one that
> Jepson first thought of getting for Centre Ch. so I thought it best
> to write to Mr Jepson first and look into it. I haven't heard from
> him (Jepson) yet but probably will tomorrow or next day . . .

And on August 3:

> Uncle Lyman has just arrived and says you want me to write about
> the studies. As Mr Hume said I am taking more time down here
> with the things Uncle Lyman can hear as English and Latin. Have
> also done quite a deal of German, but have kept to the hours of
> the schedule except for 2 or 3 days . . . I can usually get in about
> 4 or 5 hrs of study, mornings . . .

On September 1 1894, Charles's cousin Howard died suddenly, at the age of 34, in Danbury. Charles was perhaps too taken
up with his impending entrance examinations to be overly affected
by his cousin's death, but it put a sudden presentiment of fear into
him, and he lingered absently by the grave long after the funeral
party had left. His brother Moss had to come back three times to
fetch him.
    The final phase of tutoring from Edward Hume was from
September 17 to 22, and on September 28, Charles telegraphed

his father from New Haven to say that he had passed his exams. His father replied at once:

Dear Charles,

Was glad to rec've Telegram. Want to know particulars but suppose you've been too busy to give details . . . I am to stay in Bank all day which will be the first day I have done so since last week Thursday. I feel awfully weak & shaky, but besides that & a cold & a cough, am about well I hope. Your Mother & Moss each have colds. Mother has another new Nurse, quite a young girl but starts off well. Rest are as usual. Send Draft for $5 as you must need that much at least by this time.

Love from all

Father

# New Haven II

Charles Ives had his first class meeting with Horatio Parker October 10 1894. It was not historic. Parker had asked him to bring along any music he had with him, and Charles showed him *At Parting*—a song written 6 years earlier, when he was just 14; first sung by Mrs Carrie Baker at Danbury Town Hall November 1888/ CI at the piano/and repeated the following February in Brewster/ N Y. The song is 17 measures long, the last 10 measures repeated. But if Charles hoped its pedigree might impress his teacher, he wasn't obviously successful. When Parker's eye reached the final measure he said: "There's no excuse for that—an E-flat way up there, stopping there unresolved, and the nearest D-natural way down two octaves . . ."

Charles recognized the attitude—there had been the same reaction at the early performances, and under the same measure in another copy of the song he wrote: "I played this way at the Brewster concert—and they thought I was a-playing wrong notz—so I cut them out the second time round . . ." But he was dismayed, at this his first meeting with Parker, by the closed mind behind the attitude. He mentioned the incident to his father when he was home next weekend. Ives Sr said: "Tell Parker that every dissonance

doesn't have to resolve if it doesn't happen to feel like it, any more
than every horse should have its tail bobbed just because it's the
prevailing fashion . . . "

But it was all over. 3 weeks later George Ives was dead, and his
son withdrew into his own private musical shell. Tough on George
Ives, of course. Certainly tough on his son. But tough, too, on Horatio
William Parker. Charles Ives could have brought his life a measure
of satisfaction he never dreamed of.

Parker was 31 when he came to Yale—11 yrs older than
Charles Ives, 3 yrs younger than Charles's cousin Howard, who
had died a few weeks earlier. Rather like his cousin Howard, in a
certain rather endearing primness of manner. Charles was very prepared to like him, especially after his own father's death. But the
primness went too deep, to the soul and spirit of the man. Faced
with the boy's personal tragedy, Parker shied like a nervous year-
ling, had nothing to say.

Thoroughbred academics like Parker never stand a chance vis-
à-vis posterity. And posterity's all they're on about, most of them,
most of the time. Around 1904—he was Yale's first Dean of Music by
then—Parker gave a lecture on THE ART OF LISTENING. Its closing
words:

> . . . And it may be, that by fostering a natural aptitude for music
> in your children, the first great American composer will be found
> and trained among us here in New England!

Loud applause and long, from an audience of adoring parent-
folk, many of them with a wistful eye on their own offspring. Some
of them, too, thinking that Parker was being overly modest. He'd
been hailed as "the first great American composer" himself. But then
so had others, before him. And for all the man's breezy sincerity,
his words rang hollow. He'd had his chance 10 years earlier, when
Charles Ives came to him for "training." And he'd muffed it. Worse.
To his dying day he never even realized. Except once, fractionally,
perhaps, around Oct 4 1910.

Who all remembers the names of the great composers' teachers today ?  Remember, that is, without having to go look them up in
a nice music dictionary ?  Mozart, perhaps. He was taught by his
father. But who taught J S Bach ?  Or Beethoven ?  Or Wagner ?  Or

Verdi ?   What about Haydn ?   Or Brahms ?   Or Mahler ?   Who
was Bartok's teacher ?   Schoenberg's ?

At this distance of time, who all really cares ?   They did a respectable job, whoever they were, and died happy in the knowledge
that they'd helped foster a genuine talent, not a bogus one. Their
souls rest easier under a veil of anonymity. Let them be. Why pick
on Parker ?

FOR ONE REASON ONLY. Parker was a fluent, competent, intelligent musician who ought to have been able to recognize a NEW VOICE
when he heard it. No one asked him to acknowledge Ives as America's
musical Messiah—though he'd have enjoyed that privilege. He didn't
have to like what he heard. He even could have hated it. Plenty did.
But he should have recognized the NEW VOICE. And he didn't. He
wasn't even listening.

And I mean REALLY listening—not just letting the ears lie back
in a bubble-bath of agreeable, ready-made sound. Musicians, pre-
cisely the fluent ones, make the poorest listeners, because they get
bemused by the sound of their own voices—singers, players, composers—cannot understand there is anything more to it than fluency
of sound, accuracy of sound, opulence of sound, refinement of sound.
And sound has so little to do with music—nice, agreeable, chromium-
plate sound. Like old Alfred Bell, the Danbury stonemason who sang
at George Ives's Camp Meetings. A lot of people complained about
the sound of his raucous bellowing voice. George Ives used to say
to them: "You'll not get a wild, heroic ride to heaven on pretty little
sounds. But look into old Fred's face—look intently, reverently—
and you'll hear the music of ages. If you listen to the sound, you
may miss the music."

Ives—though he began his formal musical studies 6 years later
than the Viennese composer—was in no better case than Franz Schubert. Schubert's teachers at the Hofkapelle choir school, where he
was one of the Sängerknaben, have been severely blamed for ne-
glecting his education and allowing him to compose without restraint,
and one of them left on record the honest remark that when he tried
to teach Schubert anything, he found the boy knew it already. It is
evidently dangerous to leave such remarks lying around where the
directors of later musical institutions can get at them, but we are not
justified in inferring that his teachers actually taught Schubert noth-

ing. And there is abundant evidence that the 13-yr-old—like 19-yr-old Charles Ives—taught himself with remarkable concentration, if not severity. Schubert and Ives—masters both of extended forms that looked to break all known principles of composition and then miraculously establish their own logic—were very similar composers, and not their least similarity was in their early autodidactic instincts. But whereas Schubert was adored by his teachers, who acknowledged his unruly genius and tried to help him as best they could, Ives, during his 4 years at Yale, suffered only the willful and culpable neglect of Horatio Parker.

Lazy minds say that this was probably just as well, that composition cannot be taught anyway. Lazier minds hold to the prevailing velleity that all education is useless. It is true that the educational system seems to have broken down the world over, but we owe that to educational attitudes, now three and four generations ingrained, implanted by people like Parker around the turn of the century—attitudes that tacitly accepted the teacher as a prima donna of vastly greater importance than his students. It is not the caliber of the teacher, but of the alumni, that brings lasting credit to a school. It may be that Ives's Yale experience would have been no different had he gone to any one of a dozen other famous American schools. But he didn't. He went to Yale. Like it or not, Parker has become key witness in a test case—the case for higher musical education at large. He must take the stand.

> *Parker, Horatio William:* (b Auburndale/nr Boston, Sept 15 1863—d Dec 18 1919), son of a local architect, Charles Edward Parker . . .

((identity of first & middle names—Charles Edward Parker's and Charles Edward Ives's—topic of HWP's first "little joke" to CI at Yale))

> . . . first interest in music at age 14, first music lessons from his mother, a gifted amateur pianist & organist . . .

((at 14, CI is regular organist at Danbury 1st Baptist Church, has written *At Parting* and other songs, *The Circus Parade, Holiday Quickstep, Slow March* ("Adeste fidelis"), &c, &c.))

. . . in 1880, age just 17, Parker is sent to study music theory with George Chadwick, recently returned from 4 years' study in Germany . . .

((at just 17, CI starts writing the *America* Variations, for organ))

. . . in July 1881, financed by a Boston philanthropist, Parker leaves for Germany to study at the Royal Conservatory of Music, Munich, founded 15 yrs earlier by Wagner's patron, Ludwig II of Bavaria, under Hans von Bülow as its first director. Intention is that Parker study with Chadwick's former teacher, Josef Rheinberger. Accepted into Rheinberger's organ class, but fails entrance examination into his class for "foreign composition-students" and has to wait another year . . .

((at the same age CI writes *Psalm 67*, which, for different reasons, would have failed him an entrance examination anywhere in the world. The same had happened to Verdi . . .))

. . . *Parker's diary for New Year's Day 1882, age 19:*

"I have nothing but contempt for such people as come into the world—stay in it for a short time and then leave it without making any impression on humanity (which is the world to me). Every man should contribute to the advancement of the human race, should train himself carefully for work, should do something better than it has ever been done before, and above all, should raise such children, and in such a manner, that their standard of excellence should be higher than that of their progenitors. I wish that I might live to see this policy carried out by all men of the earth and to the utmost extent.

"Everyone would be to my thought ambitious, intensely, yet I think nothing so admirable or so beneficial as an overwhelming ambition if it is supported by sufficient forcefulness of character. I find I have not strength of character sufficient to carry out my great ambition, which is to be pure in mind and body, and to be the first American in my profession . . . "

((*cf:* (1) the previous year, 1881, Nietzsche had published *Also sprach Zarathustra* . . .

(2) also age 19, CI's letter to his father of March 29 1894: " . . . The first thing I am going to get the best

of is harmony & counterpoint . . . There is also some kind of a music course in college which I will look up . . . I think my aim ought now to be to improve in the things I wouldn't have time to with the church work . . . "))

. . . in 1884—his 3rd year in Munich, 2nd in Rheinberger's class for "foreign composition-students"—Parker meets Richard Strauss, 1 yr his junior, at the Hofbräuhaus, "a very tall, thin, consumptive looking chap . . . " (18 yrs later, in 1902, Strauss had become "an absolutely splendid fellow . . . ")

((at same age (as Strauss in 1884), CI enrolls in Parker's class at Yale))

. . . in June 1885, the end of his 4th year in Munich, Parker, age 22, sits his final exam—Reifeprüfung—in composition. For this, Rheinberger has set one 4-hr question, a fugue subject—"a most miserable one," Parker wrote home, enclosing the subject for posterity. The question is unworkable and Parker fails the exam, leaving Munich before the graduation ceremonies . . .

((at 22, CI completes the second movement of his 1st Symphony, later submitted in partial fulfillment of the graduation requirements of his B A))

. . . Parker comes back to America, works for a while with Chadwick, and in June 1886 is appointed music teacher at St Paul & St Mary School, Garden City/Long Island. During the summer he returns to Munich to marry a Bavarian lass he had met there—a piano student—and brings her back home with him . . .

((at the same age, back in 1862, John Knowles Paine is appointed Harvard's first Instructor of Music))

*Sept 1886:* Parker appointed organist of St Andrew's Church, New York, commuting with his Long Island post.

*Sept 1888:* appointed organist & choirmaster of Trinity Church, Boston. Continues commuting.

*Sept 1891:* appointed instructor in music theory at the newly opened National Conservatory of Music, New York: president, Anton Dvorak. Continues commuting with his Boston organ post.

*March 1893:* Parker, age 29, wins Conservatory composition prize with his first major work, a cantata, *The Dream King & His Love.* Dvorak chairman of the jury.

*May 3, 1893:* first performance of Parker's oratorio *Hora novissima* by the Church Choral Society of New York, the composer directing. Dvorak present in the audience.

*Sept 1894:* Parker appointed first "full-time" Instructor of Music at Yale. Continues commuting with his Boston organ post. ((During CI's 4 years at Yale, that is to say, *Parker can never have had the opportunity of hearing him play the organ for services or rehearsals at Centre Church.* He was away in Boston at these times.))

Back to Dvorak for a moment. Mrs Jeanette Thurber, founder of the National Conservatory of Music in New York, had invited Dvorak to become its president in 1890. When, in 1891, he accepted the position, he made his intentions explicit enough: "to establish a school of American composition based on the intelligent cultivation of the resources of indigenous folk music." They provoked a tempest of ridicule from the New York press. *The New York Times* "presumed that 'Dr' Dvorak ((Dvorak had just received a Doctorate of Music *honoris causa* from the University of Cambridge —a distinction later conferred on H W Parker)) has in mind a school which should devote itself to writing variations on *The Old Folks at Home,* and tunes of its class . . ." The atmosphere of official hostility persisted—after the first, New York, performance of the *New World* Symphony in December 1893, it grew acute—and Dvorak decided he had had enough. In June 1894 he resigned his position and returned to Europe, vexed and disappointed by establishment shortsightedness, as he saw it . . .

3 things:

(1) That old gnawbone, NATIONALISM IN MUSIC;

(2) Parker's attitude to this, and to Dvorak as a "national composer."

(3) Ives's relation to all three. He is a "national composer," if you want to call it that. And there is, as I've said, a deal of Dvorak in the pieces he wrote for Parker at Yale.

Nationalism in music is ridiculous when it degenerates into tub-thumping patriotism. Patriotism is not enough. Tub-thumping too much. But music becomes a bore when there is a total absence of national identity. No one's going to tell me you can listen, really LISTEN, to an unfamiliar work by Bach or Mozart or Schubert—let alone Tschaikowsky or Elgar or Debussy—and not know what country they hail from. It's generally easier to identify than the actual composer. Great art is supranational, of course—but, what contributes to its greatness, it breathes the essence of its native soil. An incidental contribution, but still a vital one. On the other hand there's a mass of 18th/19th century music from central Europe (and from America), nowadays sounds downright homeless—if you get to hear it at all. A lot of it written by composers considered celebrities in their day, prized above Bach and Mozart and Schubert.

Not even a Czech would call Dvorak the world's greatest composer. What matters, he was a fine one, and was invited to head the new National Conservatory in New York for good reasons. Jeanette Thurber—it took a woman's intelligence—was concerned that American music had no national identity, that there wouldn't be any great American music until it acquired one. All music sprang from the soil of indigenous folk music one time or another. If, with the music of Bach and Mozart and Schubert, folk music sources had been distilled, over the centuries, into a perfect art form, that didn't give American composers the right to walk in and help themselves. They had to go back to their own native sources and build their own distillery. Take a thief to catch a thief, the old lady brought over a composer with a very definite national identity to show American composers how.

Dvorak had put the cat among the pigeons with his New York press release, and a lot of qualified musicians were perhaps chary about applying for positions. He may have had to make do with what he could get. A young organist from Boston was no great catch— Parker had no reputation as a composer yet. But Theophilus Finck was. He had made a close study of European ethnic music and was just the man Dvorak needed. Finck and Parker had both studied at the Royal Conservatory in Munich. Finck may have recommended Parker.

Was Parker sympathetic to Dvorak's ideas ? He must have been reasonably sympathetic or he'd not have got the job. He was ambitious—"I think nothing so admirable or so beneficial as an overwhelming ambition." And, at age 19, unusually frank—"I find I have not strength of character sufficient to carry out my great ambition." It seems unlikely, nine years later, that he would have feigned sympathy for the sake of getting a job. But how far did Parker understand the ramifications of Dvorak's ideas ? Not far, to judge by his later indifference to Ives at Yale. Not far, to judge by the two works of his that Dvorak heard—*The Dream King* and *Hora novissima*. Whatever their merits, a positive attitude towards "national identity" was not one of them. And then Parker adopted Jadassohn's harmony textbook for his theory class at the Conservatory . . .

AN EXTRAPOLATION. Jadassohn was Rheinberger's teacher. Chadwick's also. Parker thus came by his textbooks from a twofold source. He was impressed and wanted to pass their knowledge on—he must have been gratified to learn that Ives had worked from Jadassohn with his father. The flaw in Jadassohn's reasoning—shared by many music theorists—was not in his harmony textbook as such. It lay in a later textbook that revealed an attitude of mind to an earlier principle: *Canon & Fugue.*

"Fugue" is a texture. It was intrinsic to the fabric of all music-making till the end of the 18th century, had been for 300 years and more—an era when style and form were dictated by CONTENT, something reflected in the way people lived their lives. There are 2 basic kinds of Fugue—"real" Fugue and "tonal" Fugue. Experts do not agree on the ultimate subtleties between the two, and never did. As I hear it, the broad, rule-of-thumb distinction between them is this:

A "real" Fugue tends to sound more fluent, more immediately agreeable to the listener, ∴ stands less chance of being memorable; while a "tonal" Fugue calls for a little more ingenuity, a little more creative imagination from the composer, requires him to LISTEN more attentively to what he is doing, tends to sound more startling, is ∴ less immediately acceptable to the listener, ∴ stands a greater chance of enduring. Both categories—"real" Fugue and "tonal" Fugue—are determined at the outset by the composer's choice of a "real" or a "tonal" SUBJECT, i.e. the fugue's initial phrase. The choice is the composer's utterly. Now:

> (1) 3 of the choral movements in *Hora novissima*—nos 4, 10 & 11—are treated as fugues. All of them "real" fugues . . .
>
> (2) the fugue subject Rheinberger set for Parker's final

examination in Munich was "real"; it also was musically derelict, and if Rheinberger was really LISTEN-
ING to what he wrote when he wrote it, then the man
was a charlatan . . .

(3) Jadassohn, in his *Canon & Fugue,* dismisses the problem of "tonal" fugue-writing within the space of a
few lines, saying "it is far better avoided," that the
"safe" fugue will always be a "real" one . . .

How does all this tie in with indigenous sources, national iden-
tities, &c ?  In this way. The Fugue derives from the Canon, the
Canon, in its prime state, from the ancient rite, the children's Round
—earliest known musical device for combining voices in counterpoint: *Sumer is icumen in, Frère Jacques, Three Blind Mice,* &c. Folk
music's first step towards art music. Fugue-writing went out of fashion
when music started "playing safe."

Counterpoint—like fugue, like canon—is equally a texture,
less rigidly disciplined by its materials, .·. requiring closer self-
discipline. The only works of Ives—apart from exercises—that had
Parker's nominal supervision were the fugue which became the first
movement/1st Spring Quartet ((later, much later, the third move-
ment/4th Symphony)), the 1st Symphony, which contains little
counterpoint but some astonishingly fine bass-writing ((sure evidence of a good contrapuntalist)), and a substantial part of the 2nd
Symphony, which, though a generally unsatisfactory work, shows in
its first movement a command of counterpoint equal to that of
Brahms. ((The last, fifth, movement has the Stephen Foster parody that
is generally identified with the horn figure in Dvorak's *New World*
Symphony; but the opening of the first movement, with its glorious
counterpoint, is strongly evocative of Dvorak's F major Symphony.
How this wonderful opening movement could be allowed to degen-
erate into the tawdry, flaccid writing of the second movement is a
total mystery. The "penny-whistle song" subsidiary theme, by the
way, is not "The Peagreen Freshmen"—a Dartmouth song that only
appeared in the Yale Songbook in 1902—but a parody of the
hymn tune *Hebrew Children.* A college song would have been out
of place in the hymn-tune context of the second movement in any
case . . . ))

Counterpoint, too, is the only aspect of composition that *can*
be taught a creative mind. Certainly harmony—Jadassohn's or any-

one's—cannot: to try, as music conservatories constantly do try, is like trying to inculcate the standard clichés of 18th century literary classics in a course on creative writing. Any composer worth his salt knows them—like Schubert—already. But counterpoint, like embroidery or tapestry-work, can be taught. Yet, though his own reputation rested on a command of counterpoint, there is no evidence that Parker taught any to Ives. He had him working on canon his senior year, but that is normally an introduction to counterpoint. Ives did not abandon counterpoint in his later works—far from it—but he was drawn to other textural possibilities: e.g. ragtime—the long chains of "walking bass" in the Emerson movement/*Concord* Sonata, the last movement/4th Symphony, last movement/2nd String Quartet, &c, &c. These were vehicles of composition quite unknown to Parker—quite unknown to most music conservatories to this day. Ives knew them instinctively; they belonged to the vernacular, the people. Like canon & fugue, originally.

Another aspect of composition that cannot be taught is orchestration—something every original composer *must* learn for himself. Instrumentation, the composer's stock-in-trade—this can be taught, and there is evidence that Ives's training in this area was scandalously inadequate. But orchestration—the manner in which a composer combines the different instruments—this is something that instantly identifies a great composer, frequently with a single chord, a single note. Parker's orchestration, though fluent, was completely anonymous— any able, fluent, unimaginative student today could have done it. Ives's orchestration progresses from the *quasi* Dvorak models at Yale, through a long period of often clumsy experimentation, to the instantly recognizable qualities of his later works.

Beethoven found Haydn a bad teacher, the anonymous Albrechtsberger a good one. There is surely a moral to be learned here. A famous figure, whether or not his fame is ephemeral, seldom makes a good teacher. It is the anonymous teacher who cultivates genius, because he is only concerned with what can be taught, has no concern for furthering his own reputation, is never dismayed when his students outgrow him. That is what he expects, what he hopes for, his vindication. Institutions of higher learning, on the other hand, especially in the creative arts, are disastrous for a student of genius, potential genius, near genius. If he survives—and, embarrassingly, he does survive—it is always in despite of them. Talent, not genius, is what they handle best—for talent can be stereotyped, made to conform.

This, then, the legacy that Ives inherited when he came to Yale. What counts, he had, "the experience, what lies under." What counts equally, he lacked, the self-confidence, what Horatio Parker might have given. And it would have cost the man so little, save a generosity of spirit . . .

# New Haven III

My Business is Circumference—
EMILY DICKINSON : *letter to Col Higginson*

Charles's last letters home chuckle with domestic sunlight . . .

. . . has a room with Mandeville Mullaly in South Middle . . . all he needs for himself is a small bedstead . . . but *together* . . . measurements of whole room not deducting border of stained part of floor   brdth = 12 ft 10 ins   length = 15 ft 1 in . . . that would need a rug 11½ × 13½ ft . . . next a Franklin stove medium size (and andirons if there is any in the store house) . . . and 2 desk chairs, and 2 or 3 easy chairs, and 2 heavy curtains for the doors from the closet and bedroom . . . and something thin for the 3 windows . . . and curtain rods . . . lamps (one to put in middle of room to study by and one portable one) . . . and wash stand . . . Mullaly will pay half expense . . . saw Mr Bonney today, says he's very busy . . .

. . . didn't write Sunday as Uncle Lyman was here . . . hasn't quite settled in yet but hopes to after they put up shades and curtains and they say they will tomorrow . . . about as slow here as they are at Uncle Joe's . . . will write to Uncle Joe soon . . . rec'd last check . . . going over to Mr Hume's tonight, and it's about time now . . .

. . . distance between window frames for pole or rod is
3 ft 4½ ins . . . some colored stuff would be better than white,
something like that in music room at home . . . bought ticket
of Mr Hume for series of chamber concerts, this winter, Kneisel/
Beethoven quartets, $2.50 . . . hopes to hear symphony concert
((conducted by Parker)) Tuesday . . . please send Garrison
some more lessons, if only a little . . . can go over them with him
together . . . also please send MS of *March* . . . Mr Parker
gives an organ recital this evening in Battel . . .

. . . started letter Sunday evening, but left it to go over to
Dwight Hall to hear the Rev Mr Twichell of Hartford . . . both be
glad to have Grandmother send them the "Outlook" and will
read it . . . sees Howard Starr quite often, was over here this
evening . . . expects to write Grandmother and Uncle Joe very
soon . . . *please send March,* also music sheet paper, & that book
of B Cornwallis, that Dr Stoeckel used . . .

And the March, when it came, a winner, anticipating the zest
and precision of the best musical comedy traditions by 40 and 50
years—Charles's music, Charles's words:

> All summer long, we boys
> dreamed 'bout big circus joys!
> Down Main Street, comes the band, Oh!
> "ain't it a grand and glorious noise."
>
> Horses are prancing,
> Knights advancing;
> Helmets gleaming,
> Pennants streaming;
> Cleopatra's on her throne!
> That golden hair is all her own.
>
> Where is the lady all in pink ?
> Last year she waved to me I think.
> Can she have died . . .

. . . His father died, in the early hours
of Sunday morning, November 4 1894, of a sudden heart attack.
Charles, summoned by telegram, left after morning service at Centre

Church by the 12.10 for Danbury. Next day, the *Danbury News* reported:

> . . . his personality was so bright, so genial, as to cast a gloom over the whole community by its removal . . .

As much as the personal anguish, Charles resented that there had been no formal leave-taking between them, almost resented his father himself that he should have died so abruptly, leaving him without guidance and approval. It was a wound that remained with him to the end of his own long life. Whatever he did later, there was a constant subconscious referral to his father for sanction, a sense that, whatever it was and however ill received, at least "father would have understood."

After his initial grief, Charles had to make a quiet assessment. His first meetings with Parker had not been encouraging. He was open enough on the surface as a person, but you couldn't get near the man himself. He would brush away any approach at the personal level with one of his infernal "little jokes." As a musician, Parker was intractable. Charles felt he regarded him as a gauche, wayward, mediocre talent, badly trained by a small-town bandmaster father who had filled his head with a lot of crackbrained musical nonsense, and was set on trying to teach him the textbook rules over from scratch. That meant Jadassohn, and he had studied all the Jadassohn he wanted with his father.

Escape ? Any hopes he may have had of going to New York and studying with Dvorak had been dashed when Dvorak resigned from the National Conservatory last June. His departure for Europe had just been announced in the press, and, even here, Parker could not leave well enough alone: "I see Dvorak's gone off in a fearful huff . . . back to Europe, where he belongs . . . and good riddance, I daresay . . . he was never happy here . . ." (followed by the inevitable "little joke" about "having to make do with the American goods now . . .") Should he, Charles, try and go to Europe too ? No, that would never do. Coming to Yale had meant so much to his parents, maybe working too hard to make it possible had hastened his father's death. He was head of the family now, and any thought of going to Europe would seem ungrateful, irresponsible. More than that, a betrayal of his whole musical ideal, something that

his father never would have condoned. Besides, where would the
money be found ? And what would Aunt Amelia say ?

Best stay at Yale—as Dr Griggs, the new choirmaster at Centre
Church suggested. He had just returned from Germany himself—but
graduated from Yale, class of '89, before going. As he pointed out,
Parker's course was only one of many Charles would have to take,
and the others would make up for what he lost in music. As for
music, he could do what Parker required him to do and no more.
For the rest, go his own way, not bother the man with his own ideas.

Griggs was only 2 years younger than Parker, but hadn't
lost an inquisitive ear for music. He had earned a Ph D from the
University of Leipzig the previous year—1893—with his disserta-
tion, *A Study of Music in America*. His adviser: August Ferdinand
Kretzschmar—the same who later made an analysis of "indigenous
American sources" in Dvorak's *New World* Symphony, and angered
the composer. But however mistaken the old Saxon's notions of what
constituted "American music," at least he endorsed his student's
conviction that such a thing existed—a conviction not everywhere
shared at that time, in Germany or America.

Charles had been playing the organ at Centre Church regularly
since September 30—before classes started at Yale—but his contract there was not confirmed till the following March 4. He had
been taking organ lessons with Dudley Buck in New York, Thursday
afternoons twice a month, since January 24—at $4 a lesson—and
this may have helped towards his appointment. The contract letter
offers him "the position of organist under Dr Grigg's direction, for
one year from May 1st 1895 at a salary of $200.00"—less than he'd
been hoping for—and goes on to ask him "to come into the office
to get some of the money now due to you for services." Official recognition clearly helped his morale, and almost at once he wrote *The
Light That Is Felt*, for mixed chorus—to a plebeian text by John
Whittier—first performed at Centre Church June 4 1895, Griggs directing.

His next choral works for Centre Church are more startling:

*1896:* pencil sketch of first 4 verses of *Psalm 54.*

((The central section—verses 3/4—is a double canon of great complexity and shows astonishing mastery of contrapuntal techniques—

Parker can have been of no help, as this is "dissonant" counterpoint, way out of his depth. There is no record that it was ever performed at Centre Church, and CI, with his contract up for renewal, probably was not anxious there should be a performance. The lost music to verses 5/6 has been constructed by Gregg Smith, inverting the material used in verses 1/2.))

> *Psalm 150*, for double chorus of boys' & mixed voices, with organ. At foot of final page of MS: "Dr Griggs and Choir sing in Praise Service Centre Church New Haven Sunday June 14 1896."

((The boys' choir is the more stable, the mixed choirs weaving flights of fancy around them that still sound electrifying. The central section is an energetic fugue.))

> *1897:* 8 measures of an unfinished—or lost—*Kyrie*, for mixed voices a capella. Contains soprano & alto entries as for a fugue.
> *Psalm 25*, for mixed voices and organ. Verses 8/22 reconstructed by CI *c* 1909, after originals had been lost. The second page of MS contains CI's famous diagram towards a 12-tone row, which anticipates the Vienna serialists by nearly 30 years. The row is maintained by the choir through 4 verses.

((CI took *Psalm 25* and *Psalm 90* (written the following year) with him to the Central Presbyterian Church, N Y after he left Yale. At the foot of the final pages in the ink copies of both, the note: "Score & parts were in Choir Library, Cent P Ch W 57 st—see mean letter from Prof Hall—Feb 18 1903 (in office file)." CI left Central Presbyterian June 1 1902. "Professor" Hall was the Librarian—CI had a habit of labeling people "Professor" he didn't like, or didn't like his music—and the lost letter probably said his music had been thrown out as no one had any use for it.))

> *Psalm 24*, for double mixed chorus a capella. As with *Psalm 25*, no record of a performance at Centre Church.

((This furthers CI's use, in the tentative Organ *Burlesque* of 1889, of "interval series"—the first 7 verses all starting on a unison C, verse 1 spreading apart by semitones, verse 2 by whole tones, verse 3 by minor 3rds, verse 4 by major 3rds, verse 5 by 4ths, verse 6 by augmented 4ths, verse 7 by 5ths. Much of it sounds like the male chorus in the fairground scene of Berg's *Wozzeck*—though predating it by 28 years.))

Also in 1897, two organ pieces:
(1) a *Prelude*, on "Adeste fidelis."

((This was played at Bloomfield 1st Presbyterian Church, Christmas Day 1898. CI's footnote: "Rev J B Lee, others & Mrs Uhler said it was awful . . ."))

(2) A *Prelude & Postlude*, for Thanksgiving service, Centre Church, November 27, 1897. Later used as basis for final movement of *4 New England Holidays— Thanksgiving, or Forefathers Day·*

((CI's *Memo* reads: ". . . the first piece that seems to me to be much or any good now. Parker made some fairly funny cracks about it, but Dr Griggs said it had something of the Puritan character, a stern but outdoors strength, and something of the outdoor feeling. He liked it as such, and told Parker so. Parker just smiled and took him over to Heublein's for a beer."))

If Parker had grown more indulgent of Charles Ives, his attitude towards him in the classroom had not become any more lenient. There he was still having to do counterpoint exercises and write canons at the 4th/5th/7th/8ve/& 10th—above and below. Parker's demands on the boy may have been more exigent than his father's had been, but to what end ? They only alienated him still further, so that he came to regard Fugue as "an exercise on paper, rather than on the mountains." Who knows that, but for Parker's influence, the *Kyrie* might have been finished ? Or, had it been greater, the fugue from *Psalm 150* might never have been written at all ?

The previous spring, Parker had discussed with him a project for his thesis. Charles showed him the first movement of a Symphony in D minor written two years earlier—"finished 76 So Middle YALE May 29 1895." The first subject went through eight different keys; Parker had a fit, and made him write another first movement. Charles started work during the summer and finished at the beginning of May 1898. In the meantime he had written the fourth movement, completing the sketches over the Christmas vacation home in Danbury. The second and third movements were already written—the second during the summer of 1896. But he was still dissatisfied with the new first movement, and told Parker he would much prefer to use the original one. "Parker smiled and let me do it, adding 'But you must promise to end in D minor!'" In the end, only two (or three) movements were submitted. On the title page of the full-score:

> Symphony No 1   1897   2nd & 4th movement (& 3rd ?) accepted as part of thesis, Parker course June 1898—*not* the first 1st movement composed over for Prof Parker (and not kept).

A year earlier Charles had written an Organ Sonata—now lost —"played in part" at Centre Church. The Largo from the Sonata later became the slow movement/2nd Symphony. At the top of the first page of MS:

> This was the one played in Centre Church. When scored later, it was made "better" and spoiled (by advice HWP). This was scored as below on long score paper but lost (middle sections remained the same). P said—a movement in Key of F should start in key of F: so change and weaken it !!!!!!!!!

((The slow movement starts on the chord of G-flat—the Neapolitan of F. John Kirkpatrick thinks that this movement was the original second movement to the 1st Symphony, taking CI's *Memo* as his evidence. On the evidence of the MSS it seems more likely that CI, recalling events 35 years earlier, simply confused the movements in question. The slow movement of the 2nd Symphony undoubtedly was revised—"*à la* Brahms, at Parker's suggestion"—but the "middle sections remained the same." The middle sections of the two slow movements, as they now stand, are entirely unalike.))

Parker was not all bad. He liked Charles's 1895 orchestration of an 1890 Organ *Postlude* in F ((F, you may be sure, was his favorite key)) well enough to try it over with the New Haven Orchestra. More than most University conductors would do for a student today.

During the afternoon of March 30 1898, George Whitefield Chadwick, 43, paid a surprise visit on Parker's composition class. He was down from Boston to receive a Yale M A, *honoris causa*, in recog-

nition of his work at the New England Conservatory, and next evening, in honor of the occasion, Parker was doing his *Melpomene*
Overture with the New Haven Orchestra. ((Parker, 34, had received
the same degree, *honoris causa,* when he became Instructor of Music
at Yale 3 years back.)) Chadwick wanted to hear the final rehearsal
of his Overture that evening in any case, and dropped by the class
on the spur of the moment to see how his old student was getting
along. CI's account, jotted in the margin of two of his songs—*Ich
grolle nicht* and *Feldeinsamkeit:*

> Geo W Chadwick came into class this afternoon (on way back from
> Heublein's) and sat down behind me . . . Lord! beer breath!
> When Chadwick came in, Parker objecting to the too many changes
> of key in the middle of *Summer Fields* ((CI's translation of *Feldein-
> samkeit*))—Geo W C grinned at it and H W P. Of the other song
> Prof Horat P said it was nearer to the *Grolle* of Schumann than
> the *Summer Fields* was near to Brahms—but Chadwick said that
> *Summer Fields* was the best . . . "The melodic line has a natural
> continuity—it flows—and stops when it's finished—as only good
> songs do. And, different from Brahms, as in the piano and the
> harmony it takes, a more difficult, almost opposite aspect to Brahms,
> for the active tranquillity of the outdoor beauty of nature is harder
> to express than just quietude. In its way, almost as good as Brahms
> . . . " He winked at H W P and said "That's as good a song as you
> could write."

Such frankness between colleagues, in front of their students, might
be thought indiscreet to the mealy-mouthed. It wasn't 80 years ago
—or else Parker put the comment down to jealousy on Chadwick's
part. He should have taken note. Chadwick's assessment of Charles's
song was shrewd—meant he was really LISTENING—and if his final
comment piqued Parker, it gave Charles much needed encourage-
ment. That was probably Chadwick's intention. He knew, from
teaching him, what a martinet Parker could be.

*In Summer Fields* and *Ich grolle nicht* were later included in
Ives's collection of *114 Songs* (as nos 82 & 83). CI's footnote to the
1st (1922) edition:

> The writer has been severely criticized for attempting to put music
> to texts of songs, which are masterpieces of great composers. The

song above and some of the others, were written primarily as studies. It should be unnecessary to say that they were not composed in the spirit of competition; neither Schumann, Brahms or Franz will be the one to suffer by a comparison,—another unnecessary statement. Moreover, they would probably be the last to claim a monopoly of anything—especially the right of man to the pleasure of trying to express in music whatever he wants to. These songs are inserted not so much in spite of this criticism as because of it.

These songs were among the last of over 40 written during Charles's four years at Yale—his music course, remember, only one of several he was engaged in. Some of the songs—like these two— "were written primarily as studies"—certainly for Parker—and have an academic interest in the comparison that could be made with their prototype texts:

*1894: The Old Mother (Du alte Mutter)*
    (Vinje, German tr Lobendanz, English tr Corder)
    no 81 of *114 Songs*        cf Grieg, Op 33/no 7

*1895: Rosamunde* (Wilhelmina von Chézy, Fr tr Bélanger)
    no 79 of *114 Songs*        cf Schubert

    *Ein Ton* (Cornelius, English tr Laubach)
                        cf Cornelius, Op 3/no 3
((basis for *Night Of Frost In May*, 1899, no 84 of *114 Songs*))

    *Songs My Mother Taught Me*
    (Heyduck, English tr Natalia Macfarren)
    no 108 of *114 Songs*        cf Dvorak, Op 55/no 4

    *Grüss* (Heine)             cf Mendelssohn, Op 19a/no 5
                             Franz, Op 41/no 1
((basis for *The World's Wanderers*, 1895, no 110 of *114 Songs*))

    *Die Lotosblume* (Heine, tr CI)
                        cf Schumann, Op 25/no 7
((basis for *The South Wind*, 1899, no 97 of *114 Songs*))

    *1896: Frühlingslied* (Heine)     cf Franz, Op 20/no 1
((basis for *I Travelled Among Unknown Men*, 1901, no 75 of *114 Songs*))

*1897: Du bist wie eine Blume* (Heine)

cf Schumann, Op 25/no 24

((drawn from *When Stars Are In The Summer Skies,* c 1893, no 113
of *114 Songs*))

*In Summer Fields (Feldeinsamkeit)*    (Almers, tr Chap-
man)
no 82 of *114 Songs*                            cf Brahms, Op 86/no 2

*1898: Ich grolle nicht* (Heine)
no 83 of *114 Songs*                            cf Schumann, Op 48/no 7

*Wie melodien zieht es mir* (Klaus Groth)

cf Brahms, Op 105/no 1

((basis for *Evidence,* 1910, no 58 of *114 Songs*))

And others, then and later. What matters, they are evidence that
Charles had access to *Dichterliebe* and other song collections by
Schumann, Brahms, Franz, Cornelius, &c, giving him a varied insight into the vocal styles of these composers. The experience, too,
of adapting fresh texts to existing music. This brought flexibility.

Other songs written at Yale—though not for Parker—have another category of interest, their marginalia (and their texts, all by
CI) more revealing of an attitude of mind towards music-making
than the music itself: e.g. *In The Alley,* written 1896, later no 53
of *114 Songs.* Below the title:

AFTER A SESSION AT POLI'S (Not sung by Caruso, Jenny Lind, John
McCormack, Harry Lauder, George Chappell or the Village Night-
ingale . . . )

Poli's Bijou Theatre, on Church Street, was the home of minstrel
shows right up until the end of the 19th century. George Felsburg
was the pianist there, the kind of rough-diamond musician Charles
took to his heart:

. . . George could read the newspaper and play the piano better
than some pianists could play the piano without any newspaper at
all. When I was in college, I used to go down to Poli's and spell him
a little if he wanted to go out for five minutes and get a glass of beer,
or a dozen glasses. There were black-faced musicians then, ragging
their songs . . .

George Felsburg is immortalized in measure 5 of *In The Alley*, where, just after the voice entry, the left hand accompaniment takes over for 1 measure, leaving the right hand free to "turn newspaper . . ." And at the climax of this short gem, an optional dominant 7th chord carries the injunction: "use Sat night."

A third species of song was one that earned Charles Ives some local, even general acclamation—if no money. A Republican campaign song for William McKinley, *William Will*, written in August 1896 at Keene Valley, published with expedition by Willis Woodward & Co, 842/844 Broadway NYC, now expediently forgotten. A partsong, *For You & Me*, performed by the Yale Glee Club early October 1896, published in November by Geo Molineux, 10 East 14th Street NYC, no 966 in "Molineux's Collection of Part Songs and Choruses for Male Voices." Another song, *A Scotch Lullaby*, to words by CI's classmate, Charles Edmund Merrill Jr, published in the Yale *Courant* for December 1896; and another partsong for the Yale Glee Club, *A Song of Mory's*, to Merrill's words again, published in the *Courant* for February 1897.

Also in 1897, *The Bells Of Yale*, words by Huntingdon Mason (class of '99), for baritone solo, TTBB, 'cello, bells, and piano, sung by the Glee Club on their transcontinental Christmas tours by pullman coach, published in 1903 by Thomas G Shepard & Co, NYC. Until recently, this undoubtedly was Ives's most widely performed piece, and certainly earned him election in June 1897, to the Wolf's Head.

((The sketch of *The Bells Of Yale* was made on the back of one of the parts his father had copied for CI's *Communion Service*, in 1890. Years later, CI added the marginal note: "This shows that in those days music was a heavy expense. This song for Yale Glee Club was written (on back of father's copy) some 6 or 7 years later —to save buying new paper . . ." Had this been the only instance!))

Between 1894 and 1898, seven more partsongs, five lost, the other two unpublished . . .

Charles's associations with the Yale Glee Club were not always so cordial. Earlier in 1896 he had written them a piece for chorus & orchestra, *The All-Enduring*—"but they couldn't sing it T(he)

G(reat) S(issies) NG." So he arranged it for baritone solo and it was sung by John Griggs at Centre Church, Sunday June 14 1896.

4 weeks earlier he had been elected into the Junior Fraternity, Δ K E. Their spring show took place next evening, and Charles produced a diverting trifle, for clarinet & piano. This was in a lurching Russian/Irish waltz rhythm that took off the 5/4 "waltz" movement from Tschaikowsky's 6th Symphony—first performed in New Haven the previous week by the visiting Boston Symphony Orchestra under Emil Paur, the 5/4 movement causing widespread alarm.

((This, so far as I find, is CI's first use of parody of any kind during his Yale period—the lost Organ Sonata, with prototypes for the third and possibly the first movements of the 2nd Symphony, was not begun till July 1896. The Δ K E piece, to words added by CI (after Pat Rooney) in 1921, became *The Side Show*—no 32 of *114 Songs*))

The following November, the sketch of a program for the Hall of Φ, Δ K E show, November 21 1896. The program, and MSS of any music, lost.

On May 28 1897, "Hell's Bells"—an initiation play given by Δ K E. Copied from the program:

> Mr C E Ives has furnished much original music for this play; his latest masterpiece will be sung at the close of the 3rd Act. The words were written by F G Hinsdale. You are all requested to join in the chorus, but kindly wait until it sounds familiar . . .

The program, and MSS of the music, lost.

Aside from Charles's thesis work, the 1st Symphony, there was not very much in the way of orchestral music. An unfinished—or mostly lost—Overture in G minor, c 1895. The MS of a Band Overture, *Town, Gown & State*, played by the Hyperion Orchestra under Franz Fichtl at Savvin Rock, New Haven, 1896—lost. A *Down East* Overture, c 1896, one of a projected series, "In These United States"—lost, though the prototype of *Old Home Day*, written 1913/14, later included as no 52 of *114 Songs*, starting with a short passage of Virgil that Charles had learned at Hopkins Grammar School: "Go, my songs! Draw Daphnis from the city!"

Chamber music: the 1st String Quartet, its second and fourth movements—*Prelude* and *Postlude*—originally written for organ, "played at Centre Church at a (mild) Revival Service, October 2

1896 . . . " ((the second movement also "arranged for piano &
copied by Tams & Co!"—CI's first use of the professional copying
service in New York . . . )). The 1st Quartet's first movement,
*Chorale,* originally written as a fugue for Parker, 1897/98, ultimately transfigured into the third movement/4th Symphony, 1909/
11 . . .

Also written at this time, the "Greek" Fugue, for string quartet
—this, the astonishing prototype for *Aeschylus & Sophocles,* for
solo voice, piano, and string quartet, to the words by Walter Savage
Landor: "We also have our pest of them which buzz around our
honey, darken it, and sting . . . "

And, certainly before he left Centre Church, in June 1898—
the start of the Cantata, *The Celestial Country,* for tenor & baritone,
two solo quartets of voices, mixed chorus, string quartet, trumpet,
euphonium, and organ; and the first of the *3 Harvest Home Chorales,*
for mixed chorus, 4 trumpets, 3 trombones, tuba, and organ.

Charles Ives was 23 when he graduated from Yale. After 15
months' almost entire silence at Hopkins Grammar School, he wrote,
in the space of 4 years at Yale, more than 80 works, many slight,
some substantial, several remarkable, all speaking an attitude of
mind, a NEW VOICE. This from a young man who was not a Music
Major—there was not such a thing at the time—who never earned
an A from Parker, whose average grade in music was B-minus. So
far as his other professors were concerned, his main academic inter-
ests were classics and mechanics. And there were courses available
in Life Insurance at both Yale and Harvard by that time . . .

# Ricercar I: 1894/98

*1894:*

Charles had first read Thoreau with his father—what, 12, 14 years ago ? And then, at Danbury Academy, heard some school-teacher dismiss him as "a crank who styled himself a hermit-naturalist and idled about the woods because he didn't want to work." Again, James Russell Lowell—"Poor Thoreau; he communed with nature for forty odd years, and then died." Much later, in *Essays Before A Sonata*, Charles Ives wrote:

> . . . The "forty odd years"—we'll still grant that part, but he is over a hundred now, and maybe, Mr Lowell, he is more lovable, kindlier, and more radiant with human sympathy today than, per-chance, you were fifty years ago. It may be that he is a far stronger, a far greater, an incalculably greater force in the moral and spiritual fibre of his fellow-countrymen throughout the world today than you dreamed of fifty years ago. You, James Russell Lowells! You, Robert Louis Stevensons! You, Mark Van Dorens! with your literary perception, your power of illumination, your brilliancy of expres-sion—yea, with your love of sincerity, you know your Thoreau—but not my Thoreau, that reassuring and true friend, who stood

beside me one 'low' day, when the sun had gone down long, long before sunset . . .

That was when his father died, at the beginning of his freshman year at Yale, and he turned back to Thoreau for solace and inspiration. That was the real beginning, the insight.

*1895:*

In the fall of 1895 Stephen Crane, aged 24, published *The Red Badge Of Courage.* Charles Ives bought a copy, in its straw-yellow buckram binding, imprinted in red, black and gold. On the flyleaf, his youthful monogram, and the date—"November 4 1895"—anniversary of his father's death. The ambience of the battle scenes: Chancellorsville. His father's regimental band had played there— Crane even mentioned the sound of band music. Crane's technique: to evoke fantasy with objective, minimal resources—"reviewing every facet of the battle with a simplicity of words that cast back, like the reflection in a clear mirror, every leaf and every hurt that passed through his imagination." Crane's ability: to create a constantly shifting background from the smoke-shrouded woods and valleys of the battleground, through which larger-than-life figures spring, suddenly, in overpowering perspective. Crane's example: a reminder of youthful genius that had been unfettered by academia, and served as an anchor for Charles's far-ranging musical intelligence. This brought strength, craft, design . . .

*During the summer of 1896, a coincidence of 4 events:*

(1) Susan Benedict Hill wrote a poem—a campaign poem for the Republican Party, replying to the Democrat's free-silver campaign:

> What we want is Honest Money,
> Good as gold, and pure as honey,
> Ev'ry dollar sound and true . . .

Mrs Hill had put together James Montgomery Bailey's *History of Danbury* after he died two years earlier, and Judge Brewster, who oftentimes collaborated with Bailey, helped her. Now the poem was writ, Lyman Brewster showed it to his nephew. He'd be able to write a rollicking good tune that would set the Democrats by their heels—

if he'd only keep off all this modern stuff. Charles did as he was bid. But not in Danbury. He had his mother and his grandmother to think of. He waited, meantime working on the Organ Sonata over at the Baptist Church.

(2) On August 4, David Twichell wrote inviting him up to stay with his family at Keene Valley. He'd met David when his father gave an address in Dwight Hall two years ago, just before his own father died, had since become close friends. The Twichells seemed traditional Republicans—best write this song for Uncle Lyman up there. Even if they weren't, it would still be good for a laugh—and *"wer spielt Klavier, hat Gluck bei Frauen,"* as they said in German . . .

(3) Joseph Twichell's diary for August 1896:

"At Keene Valley as guests again of Judy's father-in-law Mr C O Wood, in his cottage 'Waldruhe.' All the family, except Judy, were there, part of the time also, Fred Ware and Bartlett Yung, whom we count of our number, and in the course of the season several young men and women friends of Harmony and Dave. We had plenty of delightful company, and never enjoyed a season more . . . "

(4) On August 27, a telegram:

"Grandmother wants you home. Start Saturday if possible. Nothing serious. J Moss Ives."

Grandmother was 88. Probably had taken a turn for the worse. *But what if she'd found out about "the song"* ? Lord! There'd be hell to pay . . .

*1897:*

At Thanksgiving service, Centre Church, Charles met David's brother, Edward Carrington Twichell, and later dedicated the last of the *4 New England Holidays—Thanksgiving, or Forefathers Day* —to him. Edward—"Uncle Deac" as he came to be called—was a Thoreauesque character who later still lived in a cabin on Charles's property at Umpawaug Road, West Redding—"Mr Carrington

Twichell, alias "the Albuquerque Terror"/Alkali Kid, Poultry Crest, Scratchfeed Terrace, P O Box 23, on your way . . ."

*1898:*

The class of '98 graduated on June 29—David Twichell *in absentia*. Like many other young men, he was already in uniform, fighting in the Spanish/American War. From Hartford, Mark Twain fulminated against the war. From Cuba, Stephen Crane was sending home dispatches for the New York *World*. David Twichell's father was Mark Twain's closest friend. Stephen Crane had taken the job of war correspondent with the *World* only after being turned down for the Navy. Who was right ?

This was a "politicians' war" if ever there was one—or that's what Mark Twain said, at any rate. And then the Civil War too. Mark Twain had been involved in that, for a few weeks, fighting for the Confederates. Or so he said—and was very satirical about it. Yet Crane seemed the greater artist—Charles didn't know what posterity would say, but that's what people were saying now. And Crane had had no first-hand experience of war at all when he wrote *The Red Badge Of Courage*. The Civil War. Chancellorsville. Father. Thoreau. Stephen Crane. There was a thread running through it all somewhere. And Mark Twain standing outside, poking fun. Was there an aspect to the Civil War that had made it "above politics" ? Made it different from this war ? Yet Stephen Crane had wanted to enlist in this war. There was something Byronic about him, a self-destroyer. Was there something like that about every significant artist ?

And "posterity." Parker had always been on about "posterity." He was certainly going places—being invited to England next year to conduct *Hora novissima* at the 3 Choirs Festival. Did Parker ever think about the issues involved in this war ? *Any* war ? Did Chadwick, at the New England Conservatory ? Did John Knowles Paine, up at Harvard ? Or MacDowell, down at Columbia ? If they did, it certainly didn't show in their music. Not even a trace of Mark Twain's satire showed.

Charles thought about the present. Parker had asked him what he was going to do—just out of formality. He wasn't really interested in knowing. His interest now was entirely focused on "that astonishingly gifted young man," David Stanley Smith, who had arrived at Yale in Charles's junior year. Charles might have said he was going to the moon and Parker wouldn't have turned a hair. Probably made some "little joke" about hoping he'd find a decent organ position there. Dear man, he would have his little joke.

Well, what *was* he going to do ? He had this job he'd just started, as organist at Bloomfield 1st Presbyterian Church, across the Hudson river in New Jersey, but that wouldn't last forever. And he had moved down to New York City and was staying at the Yale Club on Madison Square North, where the old Delmonico used to be. He'd made a lot of friends at Yale. One of them, in the class ahead of his, had been baseball captain—Harry Keator. He was living in a fourth-floor cold-water apartment on the Upper West Side, said there would be room for Charles in September when three of the present inmates moved out. They were all studying medicine at Columbia Medical School, but that didn't matter. Actually there were two apartments, either side a central stairwell. Charles could move into the non-medical side. They'd called the two apartments "Poverty Flat."

One thing was for sure. Whatever he did, Charles was going to go on writing music. His organ position would barely pay the rent and he would have to find another job to supplement it. But whatever it was, he would regard it simply as a job, do it to the best of his ability, and save his real energy for his real work. Then a distant relative of his mother's, Robert Grannis, Vice President of Mutual Life Insurance, offered to find him a job in the insurance business. There was a faint stirring in Charles's distant subconscious. He couldn't remember what. But, anyway—yes. He'd take the job.

# SECOND FUGUE

# New York I

The view taken of Transcendentalism on State Street
is that it threatens to invalidate contracts . . .
EMERSON: *Journal for Oct 8 1841*

The first address of Poverty Flat was 317 West 58th Street, one block south of Columbus Circle, just west of Broadway. Above the Circle, Broadway still was known as The Boulevard in 1898, and way to the north, between Morningside and Amsterdam avenues at 114th Street, Columbia University's College of Physicians & Surgeons at St Luke's Hospital lay in the space and quietude of open countryside. To the west, filling one whole block on Riverside Drive between 73rd and 74th Streets—Charles Schwab's projected château, that was to excel even the splendor of the Vanderbilt residence on Millionaire's Row, at the 5th Avenue end of 58th Street. One block south, on West 57th Street: Carnegie Hall, 9 years old, and the Sherwood, center of New York's Bohemian community.

When Charles Ives started work with Mutual Life in October 1898, he used to take the Broadway cablecar—one of Stephen Crane's "long yellow monsters"—downtown through Long Acre (now Times Square), past the Metropolitan Opera and the Globe Theatre at 39th Street, through Greeley Square, Madison Square and Union Square, past Grace Church and Fleischmann's Vienna Model Bakery ((meeting-place for Anton Seidl and the stars of the Metropolitan (3rd floor: "Geo W Pettit's School of Music"))), past Fulton Street, City

Hall and Liberty Street, to Wall Street. From there, Nassau Street
was one short block to the east. A few doors back up to the north: nos
32/36, head offices of The Mutual Life Insurance Company of New
York.

Charles soon blotted his copybook. During the great blizzard
of 1899, he was able to get to Bloomfield for the Sunday services
on February 12, but not to the office next morning. On St Valentine's
Day, the New York *Tribune* reported that "snow, flying horizontally
across the city on the wings of a fully-fledged gale, is sticking to
everything like a coat of lead." The storm threatened to outdo the
1888 classic, and Charles remained contentedly at home, working
on the 2nd Symphony and his cantata, *The Celestial Country*. But
when he finally returned to the office, he learned he had been the
sole absentee. All through the blizzard, the Broadway cablecars had
kept running—"covering themselves with glory," said John Tatlock,
the department head, quoting the morning newspaper at him. Up
on the carpet, Robert Grannis interceded for him, and Charles was
transferred to one of Mutual's general agencies, Charles Raymond
& Co, round the corner at 32 Liberty Street. Here he was to replace
the applications clerk, Julian Myrick, 6 years his junior, who was
being sent on sick leave.

It still seems incredible that Charles Ives didn't know what he
was getting into. Life Insurance by the turn of the century was so
corrupt it seems incredible that everybody didn't know it. But that's
how corruption gets away with it. Nobody does know, except those
who are involved. And they aren't about to tell.

The first major New York life insurance company started out
in 1830—New York Life & Trust Company, capitalized at $1 million.
Mutual Life followed in 1842, founded by Morris Robinson, began
issuing policies in February 1843, all policyholders members of the
company. So far so good. Then, during the depression of 1857, they
engaged a young cashier named Henry Baldwin Hyde. Two years
later, Hyde left Mutual and set up on his own—the Equitable Life
Assurance Society of the U S—sold $1 million in policies by the
end of 1859, $3,267,000 by the end of 1860, by the end of the
Civil War, with his aggressive sales methods, had built up Equitable
to the point where it was becoming a serious threat to Mutual. In
1865, the end of the first 5-yr dividend period, Hyde distributed
$10,787 to policyholders and $16,200 to himself, out of an actual

surplus of less than $5,000—which meant around $22,000 water.

By 1898, Mutual, under Richard A McCurdy, was entirely dominated by Standard Oil and spending 98% of first-year premiums to get new business. The Raymond General Agency, as late as 1903, was receiving up to 80% commission on first-year premiums and paying their local agents up to 65%. 96%, 80%, 65% of policy-holders' money that they held in trust. Small wonder they were slow in paying out on claims. Richard McCurdy's son, Robert, was general manager of the Raymond Agency, received a salary of $30,000 and $100,000 in foreign commissions, while his father, as President, drew a salary of $300,000. His brother-in-law, Dr E J Marsh, was Mutual's medical director, his son-in-law, Louis A Thebaud, held a 75% interest in the Raymond Agency, Thebaud's cousin was In-spector of Risks for Mutual Life. Charles Ives himself was a distant cousin of Mutual's vice president, Robert Grannis, whose salary was around $200,000.

That can be the only reason how Charles survived. He made a reputation for himself later, but in the early years, in a clerical capacity, he must have been almost useless. The typewriter was still a cumbersome affair, far from being standard office equipment, and Charles's longhand was atrocious, constant target for snide re-marks about his "college education." When Julian Myrick came back off leave, Charles was sent out to work with the agents. But here again it was no good. His nature was too impulsive, too gen-erous. A good insurance salesman had to be the mean, aggressive, foot-in-the-door type. Charles would never make it. He was called into Colonel Raymond's office, assured by everyone that he was going to be fired.

Charles Ives never related how he survived that interview. Being a Yale man, a member of Δ K E and Wolf's Head must have helped. Being a distant relative of Mutual's vice president may have helped. And perhaps Colonel Raymond spotted other qualities in this big, shy young man with the soft New England drawl and ideas of his own about how the business should and could be run. At all events, he was kept on, and seems to have been left very much to his own devices.

In September 1899, David Twichell joined the Yale com-munity at Poverty Flat. He had stayed in the Army for a year after the Spanish/American War ended, quartered at Summerville/S

Carolina. Now he wanted to be a doctor, and had enrolled at the College of Physicians & Surgeons. Meanwhile Charles's brother Moss, after 3 years' intensive apprenticeship to Uncle Lyman and 1 year at Yale Law School, had graduated LL B and been admitted to the Connecticut Bar, joining his uncle's law firm in Danbury. "Brewster, Davis & Ives." Looked great. At least someone in the family was making good.

Charles had been up to Yale for his brother's graduation, now went back again in November with David Twichell, for the Yale/Princeton ball game. The event became instant music:

> Sketch of Y-P Football Game in Tones    completed & copied &
> sent to Hunt Mason in Chicago in 1899 . . . a "take off" of 2
> Halves in 2 minutes . . . OK by Dick Schweppe    318 W 59    Nov
> 1900 . . .

((CI—and his piano—occupied the rear room of the 4th floor at 317 West 58th Street, and the sound of his music-making carried across the back yard to the rear 4th floor window of Dick Schweppe's room. November 1900 was warm, and the windows were open. When CI played over the Yale/Princeton "take off" from the sketch—anniversaries were a ritual—Dick Schweppe called out his approval. CI learned his name—across the intervening yard—but never his occupation; for this reason, always accounted him one of his astutest critics . . . ))

> *Right-hand margin:* Playing this for Hunt Mason & unknowns at
> The Spot ((meeting-place of the sophomore society, Hé Boulé)),
> he said "that may not be good music but those sounds make sense
> to me—why shouldn't a symphony give out in new sounds our
> experiences today, and not always those of Ariel or a Classic ?"

> *Page 3 of MS sketch, over bassoons:* fat guards pushing and
> grunting . . . *under oboe:* dodging Half Back . . . *over piccolo
> trill:* 1st Down . . .

> *Page 4 of MS sketch, above:* Run around left . . . *above "wedge"
> figure:* Close formation (Wedge) . . . *below:* when Trumpet =
> running Half Back (Charley Desaulles) reaches this measure, every
> other instrument must make a hell of a noise & stop . . . *over*

*final measure:* Touchdown   Game over & won   Everybody tired
Players & Spectators   Repeat first 11 measures ending with Greek
cheer . . .

((The full-score, "completed & copied & sent" to Huntingdon Mason
in Chicago, November 1899, is lost. According to a letter from his
brother in 1933, it was thrown out by his family after Hunt Mason
died, prematurely, in 1914. Only the first 4 pages of sketch are
extant . . . ))

With the end of the year—and the century—Charles resigned
his post at Bloomfield Presbyterian Church, and in April 1900 became organist and choirmaster of Central Presbyterian Church,
round the corner from Poverty Flat at Broadway and 57th Street.
This was not quite the same order as the Presbyterian Church over
on 5th Avenue and 55th Street, where, of a Sunday, its pastor "might
count on preaching to $250 millions"—where the service was speci-
fically designed to attract the cream of wealth and society, and
the departure of J Pierpont Morgan, won over to the Episcopalians,
had given Dr John Hall a nervous breakdown. Dr Wilton Merle-
Smith, pastor of Central Presbyterian Church, was less highly
strung. But he still numbered among his congregation figures like
Senator Chauncey Depew, from West 54th Street, and Julia Baird,
from the Sherwood—model, 5 years ago, for Augustus St Gaudens'
controversial statue of Diana in Madison Square Garden. And he
was anxious to keep them. He knew, too, that these people came as
much to hear the music as listen to his sermon—if in fact they came
for either, and not just to be seen. Like his sister church over on
5th Avenue, he had a paid nucleus of singers, and, like Dr Hall,
held intelligent though narrow views on church music in general.
Realizing, as with Horatio Parker, that discretion must again be the
better part of valor, Charles resolved to be a "good boy" and play
"nice" music. It was more than a year before he slipped a piece of
his own into a Sunday service, a further eight months before he began in earnest releasing a series of musical explosions that was
heard the length of Broadway and across to Fifth Avenue.

Obviously Charles auditioned for the post—a plum—and was
appointed in the face of fierce competition from ranks of redoubt-
able organists of experience and influence. That he was awarded

the position on his own merits—at 25 a virtuoso player, but without influential support of any consideration—spoke well for church music politics of the time. But the first contact must have been one John Catchpole, a tenor in the Central Presbyterian choir. Back in the summer of 1898, at the Yale Club, Charles had adapted some "nice" music, written when he was 15, to the Pike County ballad *Because Of You*. This, according to a note on the MS, "at the request of Mr Catchpole, who wished a pretty encore to sing . . . "

((The Pike County Ballad originated in 1871 with a collection of poems by John Hay, that made use of regional dialects from Missouri, Arkansas, northern Texas and southern Illinois. The style and sentiment of text and subsequent musical settings were the progenitor of Blue Grass and Country & Western . . . ))

The last week of January 1901, Charles gave an organ recital at Central Presbyterian, which included his Sonata for Trumpet & Organ ((lost, though it was used in the first movement/4th Violin Sonata)). On May 8 1901, at another recital, a Toccata for organ ((also lost, though it became the second movement/3rd Violin Sonata)). At Sunday service four days later, his first organ *Postlude* for Central Presbyterian. This also is lost, but became the second movement/3rd Symphony. On a page of the full-score sketch:

from Organ Postlude May 12 1901 C P Ch    Geo Fleming smiled

((George Fleming was the baritone soloist—perhaps, the smile conspiratorial, reminiscent of John Griggs at Centre Church, New Haven . . . ))

Three days later Ellis Ellsworth Giles, tenor soloist of Central Presbyterian, sang two of Charles's songs at a meeting of the Apollo Club in the ballroom of the Waldorf-Astoria: *An Old Flame* ((later no 37 of *114 Songs*)), and, as an encore, *My Native Land*. Marginalia on the MS:

> This song is no good—written as encore for Ellis Giles, who sang it in a concert at the Waldorf. An organist, in NY then, came up after the concert, shook hands & said I had the gift of good melody, harmony & workmanship. This man later was a Prof of Music (I think at Columbia). His remark showed what a soft headed, restricted condition music was in, in N Y at this time . . .

Summer vacation—August 1901—was spent in Ridgebury, near Pine Mountain. Here the preliminary sketches of the 1st Piano Sonata, and the completed sketch of *From The Steeples & The Mountains*, for trumpet, trombone, and 4 sets of bells.

((According to the Cowell biography, *From The Steeples* is based on CI's recollection of his father standing outside their house during a rainstorm, listening to the bells of the nearby Congregational Church, and running indoors at intervals to try and reproduce their sound on the piano. CI's mother had another, more sinister, more authentic recollection:

> Late one night, soon after we moved to Stevens Street, a violent thunderstorm blew up over Pine Mountain, and a thunderbolt fell in the village, setting light to some houses. There were no fire alarms in those days—the only alarm was the church bells, and the telephone bells that used to be fixed to the telephone poles outside people's houses then. First the bells of the Baptist Church started ringing, then the bells of the Congregational Church next door, next the bells of the Episcopal Church down on Main Street. Then the telephone bells started to ring outside the firemen's houses, and the gong on the fire-cart as it started towards the fire. Pretty soon the air was alive with the sound of ringing bells—you could hear them even over to St Thomas's in Bethel, and up to Brookfield— and the thunder and the pouring rain from Pine Mountain. The glare of the fire in the dark and the continual lightning flashes was very frightening. But my husband stood outside on the back porch in his night clothes like a man entranced, till the bells finally died out and the fire was stopped. I went back upstairs several times to look at the children. Bless them, they were sleeping soundly as angels, both of them. But Charlie was awfully cross, next morning, when he heard what he'd missed . . .

On the MS sketch of the score, the title:

> From the Steeples—a new sexton    Telephone Smith's

and at the end:

> From the Steeples—the Bells!—
> then the Rocks on the Mountains begin to shout!

The opening trumpet-figure is "Taps"—which CI always associated with his father. And the trumpet itself . . . ))

In September 1901, Poverty Flat moved to 65 Central Park West, on the north-west corner of 66th Street. By this time they had been joined by David Allen, George Lewis, William Maloney, Keyes Winter and Edwards Park. Earlier in the year—before the move—David Stanley Smith, Park's roommate at Yale, called on him and overheard Charles working on the hymn-anthem setting of "Abide With Me":

> While I was living at 317 West 58th Street with classmates who were studying medicine at the College of Physicians & Surgeons, Dave Smith came in one afternoon to call on Ned Park. I was then working on the *Abide With Me* organ and chorus pieces, built around the tune in off-beats, and with the three keys used as the three triads of the main key . . .

((tonic: Db major; E major used as "dominant," Bb major as "subdominant"))

> . . . Dave said, "Why do you have to take a good tune like that and spoil it with a lot of burlesque ?" At the time, I didn't know but what he might be right. But the last time I heard this piece played, not many years ago, I came to the conclusion he was decidedly wrong. There was no sense of burlesque about it. In fact, the namby-pamby, nice up-and-down, jumpy, precise little way I've heard some church organists play this hymn (some of them "celebrated," so-called) approaches the burlesque much more . . .

By the autumn of 1901 the 2nd Symphony was finished, *The Celestial Country* and the *3 Harvest Home Chorales* nearing completion. Charles decided to launch a musical campaign at the church. It began with an organ *Prelude* ((lost, though it became the basis for the third movement/3rd Violin Sonata)). On November 21, Annie Wilson, soprano soloist at Central Presbyterian, sang a prototype of *Watchman* ((later no 44 of *114 Songs*, partial basis for the Prelude of the 4th Symphony)) at a YMCA service in the church. In early December, a piece for Communion Service—lost, though later the third ("Communion") movement/3rd Symphony. On December 12, another *Prelude*—also lost, later the second movement

of the 3rd Symphony. And on December 15, an Adagio for Violin
& Organ, played with William Haesche, a classmate of his from
Yale, who had played in a Danbury concert with him 12 years
earlier, in February 1889.

An innocent beginning, it must seem now. But not at the time.
To Max Smith—another of Charles's classmates, then music critic
to the New York *Press*—the two organ pieces that were later used in
the 3rd Symphony were "hideously modern . . ."

But even for Ives, the screw now began to turn. The same month,
December 1901:

(1) the *Memorial Slow March*, for President McKinley, who was
shot at the Buffalo Exposition on September 6 and died at Milburn
House, Buffalo, September 14. ((This again is lost, but became the
monumental cornerstone to the last movement of the 4th Symphony.))
Throughout the final day, while the nation prayed for his recovery,
the dying President had had on his lips the hymn *Nearer, My God,
To Thee*. The impulse for the *Memorial Slow March* came from a
scene at the Café Boulevard, shortly after news of the President's
death reached the city, when everyone stood up and sang the hymn:

> It brought back an incident in my father's life showing one of the
> finest sides of his character. It was a fine and deep personal experi-
> ence which is better to remember than put into words . . .

(2) the *Processional*, "Let There Be Light," for 4-part male chorus,
two organists, optional 4-part female chorus, string orchestra, and 4
trombones:

> To the Choir of the Central Presbyterian    Dec 1901

At the top of the MS score—for the benefit of the copyist, George
Price:

> All the consecutive 5ths, 8ves, etc
>   *"*  *"*  covered  *"*  *"*  *"*  are
> NOT to be changed
> NOT to be corrected and made pretty . . .

(3) in January 1902, the *Hymn-Anthem* "Abide With Me," for organ, offstage piano ((("in the Sunday School room"))), harp, and
male chorus, done Sunday January 12, at Evensong:

N G Dr Merle-Smith turned around and glowered at the choir . . .

Notwithstanding, a month later, the *Anthem* "There Is No Unbelief":

> Rev Wilton Merle-Smith gave me these words & asked me to compose
> music for them—but didn't like the music. Miss Wilson sang it in
> church Feb 16 1902 . . .

((In 1911, "made over into a nice song"—*Religion* (later no 16
of *114 Songs*)))

On March 9 the *Hymn-Anthem* was repeated, and better received. Charles was mollified, and for Easter Sunday, March 30,
produced his *Easter Carol,* for solo quartet, mixed chorus and organ,
written 10 years earlier for the Easter service at Danbury Baptist
Church.

Finally, on April 18 1902, the first performance of *The Celestial
Country,* to a text by Henry Alford written in 1871, and thought then
to derive from Bernard de Cluny, *De contemptu mundi.* The cantata's
seven movements:

(1) *Introduction* (String Quartet & Organ) and *Prelude*
(Chorus, String Quartet, Euphonium & Organ) "Far o'er
yon horizon . . ."

(2) *Prelude* ('Cello & Organ) and *Aria* (Baritone Solo &
String Quartet) ((sung at this first performance by Emma
Williams, contralto, George Fleming being indisposed))
"Naught that country needeth . . ."

(3) *Solo Quartet,* with String Quartet & Organ "Seek the things
before us . . ."

(4) *1st Interlude* ('Cello & Organ)
*Intermezzo* (String Quartet)
*2nd Interlude* ('Cello & Organ)

(5) *Double Solo Quartet* (a cappella)
"Glories on glories . . ."

(6) *Aria* (Tenor Solo, String Quartet & Organ)
"Forward, flock to Jesus . . ."

(7) *Introduction* (Organ), *Chorale & Finale*
(Chorus, String Quartet, Trumpet, Euphonium & Organ)
"To the Eternal Father . . ."

And the performers:

|  |  |
|---|---|
| Miss Annie Wilson . . . . . . | Soprano |
| Miss Emma Williams . . . . . | Contralto |
| Mr E Ellsworth Giles . . . . . | Tenor |
| Mr George A Fleming . . . . | Baritone |

The Kaltenborn String Quartet

|  |  |
|---|---|
| Mr Franz Kaltenborn . . . . | Violin |
| Mr William Rowell . . . . . . | Violin |
| Mr Gustave Bach . . . . . . . | Viola |
| Mr Louis Heine . . . . . . . | 'Cello |

Mr Charles E Ives . . . . . . Organ

assisted by:

Mrs Springer
Mrs Delaney
Mrs Caroline Andresen

Miss Mary Grout
Miss Mansfield
 (*Mezzo Soprano*)

Miss Martha Snead
Miss Charlotte Snell
 (*Soprano*)

Miss Sarah Edwards
Miss Mina Andresen
Miss Dolores Reedy
 (*Contralto*)

Mr John W Catchpole

Mr A C Eadie

Mr Harry B Mook
 (*Tenor*)

Mr Edwin F Fulton
Mr Frederick Ballantyne
 (*Basso*)

Mr Herman Trost
Mr Thomas

Horns: in B flat (*Euphonium*) Mr W S Phasey
in A (*Trumpet*) (player to be announced)

The performance, which included some organ solos and a Beethoven quartet movement by the Kaltenborn Quartet, rated a paragraph in *The New York Times*, a lengthier review, quoting *The Times*, in *The Musical Courier*. ((Over these reviews, CI scrawled later: "Damn' rot and worse . . . ")) Charles decided to quit while he was ahead, so far as the Presbyterian Church was concerned, and handed in his resignation. Dr Merle-Smith persuaded

him to stay until a replacement could be found—although his contract was up, his resignation was completely unexpected—so Charles
agreed to stay till June 1. That was his last Sunday as a regular organist anywhere. He was getting on for 28—the age his father had
married his mother—and resolved, for better or for worse, from
now on the insurance business must be his sole subsidy, for music
*and* for marriage. His brother Moss had been married for over a
year, now had a son, Richard Goodman Ives, born two months ago.

With his departure from Central Presbyterian, Charles began
work on the *Orchard House* Overture, a musical portrait of Bronson
Alcott and his family. Since (unlike Emerson and Thoreau) there
was no body of writing by Alcott himself, Charles had to discover
his personality by easy stages, working on the score at intervals over
the next two years. Yet it contains his first reference to the terse
opening figure of Beethoven's 5th Symphony. That implied a far-
ranging stream of consciousness that went to the root of Ives's philosophy, finally crystallized round one thing, one issue, one ideal:
Abolition . . . "a sense of PAST, his marriage of spirit to source."

Labor Day weekend 1902 was spent in Danbury with his
mother, now 53. A fragment of sketch for piano duet has:

> Drum Corps or Scuffle   "Barn Door and Backwoods"—Practiced
> in Benedicts Hall for hour Labor Day Sept 1902   Danbury Ct

That must have been during the morning. Later in the day he was
back at 65 Central Park West, sketching another idea he had conceived over the weekend:

> Skit for Danbury Fair   Tent Band (between races) Labor Day
> Sept 1902 ((this contains the parodies: "How Dry I am . . . Bring-
> ing in the Sheaves . . ."))

He played the sketch over for some of his friends at the Flat, and seems
to have caused a little trouble. The footnote on one of the extant leaves
of MS:

> Davey Allen beats up Keyes—smiles, scolds, smirks—then over to
> Healey's . . .

Healey's was the restaurant and bar, at the corner of Columbus Avenue and 66th Street, where they all used to go at weekends and holidays—on weekdays, they had someone come in and cook dinner for

them. Keyes Winter was an ardent champion of his music. At the time, Charles was also working on the *Country Band March,* for chamber orchestra—now mostly lost. Page 4 of the score sketch has:

> Keyes says these notes are OK   He is the best judge as he doesn't know one note from another . . .

((Shades of Ulysses S Grant, at Richmond ?   The parodies used in the existing fragments bear out such an association of ideas: "Marching through Georgia," "Massa's in de cold, cold ground . . ."))

Later in September they were joined by Bartlett Yung, just graduated from Yale, where, among other things, he had been leader of the Banjo Club. He was a close friend of the Twichell family, his father one of their next-door neighbors on Woodland Street, Hartford. Charles had first met him at Keene Valley in 1896, when Bartlett was 17, and they had worked out an arrangement of *William Will* for banjo and piano. *"Wer spielt Banjo . . . "* Bart had an Oriental charm that was very engaging.

The bulk of Charles's writing now was directed towards pieces for chamber or theater orchestra, that he stood some chance of getting performed. Nearly all have been lost, but they reveal two things: (1) many of them are referred to, as sources, in pieces that are *not* lost; and (2) he had now, for some time, been earning enough money in business to engage the services of a full-time copyist whenever he needed one. One example is a ragtime piece, written for theater orchestra between 1902/03, though not performed till 1905. This is identified (1) on page 1 of CI's ink copy of the *first* movement/3rd Violin Sonata:

> Adagio—1st verse & 2nd & 3rd verses & Refrains, from Organ
> Preludes, played C P Church   Nov 1901

and above:

> II Movement from Theater Orches Score played 14th Nov 1905

(2) on the title page of CI's ink copy of the *second* movement/3rd Violin Sonata:

> Sonata No 3   2nd movement

and below:

> some of this movement was in a Ragtime Piece—Theater Orchestra
> —a short piece & played in Globe Theater 14th Nov 1905—put in
> this movement later

and on the first page of sketch for this same movement:

> started as Organ Toccata for Central Pres Ch concert May 8 1901—
> later used in a Violin Sonata

(3) on page 22 of the fair copy, second movement/3rd Violin
Sonata, directions for the pianist, Stuart Ross, for a performance
with David Talmadge, violin, in 1917:

> Mr Ross—This movement was written first for small Theater
> Orchestra in 1902/03 & played in Globe Th N Y Dec 1905 &
> throwing the Fl & Clar, Strs & Cornet into the piano causes the
> awkward passages (it's easier for 4 hands)

This identifies, with fair certainty, TWO RAGTIME PIECES as the
sources of two later violin sonata movements. But CI, in a list of
pieces, has:

> Ragtime pieces (about a dozen)—mostly for small theater orchestra.
> Some of these were arranged for various combinations of
> instruments, some for piano and used as scherzos in some of the piano,
> and violin & piano, sonatas, and orchestral sets later . . .

Again, above the title in the full-score, second movement/2nd
Orchestral Set:

> first written as short series of ragtime pieces for small orchestra,
> shown to Kaltenborn for St Nicholas Rink Concerts NY 1902—said
> too hard to play! then . . .

At the top of a page of sketch for the same movement:

> piano arrangements from 1st & 2nd Ragtime Pieces (Fiddles Clar
> Piano Trombone played by Fichtl Hyperion Orchestra New Haven
> May 21 1904)

At the top of another leaf of MS, that contains sketches both of this
same movement, and the second movement/1st Piano Sonata:

Tams 124 W 28    no telephone    return 317 W 58 NY

& at the foot:

C E Ives    65 C P W    NY

So another segment of the puzzle falls into place. William Tams Copying Bureau, at 124 West 28th Street, employed a fleet of copyists, the best of whom—certainly in his own estimation—was currently (1901) George Price. A later recollection:

> Mr Price was an ultimate type of the "perfect man" (in Mr Price's opinion). He came from Wales, and if Wales and the United States should both wipe each other out, that wouldn't bother Price—but tell him he wasn't perfect and had made a mistake, and he would be mortally insulted. A man completely conceited has the best and easiest time in the world. Price never made a mistake! What mistakes he made were yours. If he thought you had put down a wrong note he would put it *right* (right or wrong), and blame you when you had the audacity to say that, every time there's a C natural, all C sharps that happen on the same beat should be scrapped. Then he would get mad, and want to charge you for correcting your right notes into mistakes. In business and in politics, and in almost every department of life, I know many Prices. But his penmanship was as beautiful as a Michelangelo—to look at a page of those "statuettes" made it hard for you to jump on him . . .

George Price was only one of several copyists—most of them unidentified—that Ives employed, even from the start. Copyists—an unusual (and unfortunate) luxury for a young composer—were necessary for Ives because, even at its best, his handwriting was nearly as bad as Beethoven's at its worst; nor did he possess Beethoven's self-confidence, that, in the last analysis, makes his MSS legible. Unfortunate, because Ives could afford not to have to make his intentions patently clear—a common pitfall among inexperienced composers, but rare among those of genius. And then many of his copyists produced work that, aside from its flagrant inaccuracies, was worse than his own—especially in the later years. But that is another, later story, of genius betrayed.

Then, again, Ives wrote at immense speed, ideas spilling out on the page with such speed that he had no time to turn the leaf, and would grab the nearest blank sheet that lay to hand. That sheet, often as not, had other music already written on its reverse side. And the worst yet to come, 10 and 15 years distant. There is scarcely a page of sketch for the final masterpieces that does not have other, utterly different music on its reverse side, or is not patched with scraps of paper cut or torn from other pages that, in turn, have other music on their reverse sides. Nor were the copyists' copies immune. Any open space—empty staves, a leaf left blank on one side—was fair game.

The marvel was, that Ives could keep so much material, such a profusion of disparate ideas, all in the air at the same time, always at his mental fingertips—had instant recall, before the disaster, without recourse to diaries and calendars, of the whereabouts and when of each single page, what was written on its reverse and when, where it had been played or not played and when and why or why not. And it makes his very occasional lapses of memory all the more significant. As for the copyists, the skilled ones learned in time, the incompetent are still being found out.

By the end of March 1903, David Twichell was completely exhausted preparing for finals, and went for a month's rest back to Summerville/S Carolina, where his sister Harmony came and nursed him. In June, he graduated MD from the College of Physicians & Surgeons, and joined Dr Trudeau's TB sanatorium near Saranac Lake. Charles wrote him that September:

> . . . finally succeeded in placing the shanty on the mountain near Ridgebury, but did it unbeknowed to Aunt Amelia, fearing adverse suggestions . . . George Lewis went up with me last month, taking "Saturday afternoon off—what!" We spent the night on the mountain. Having no curtains on the windows, it took two hours of kind talk to get the old scrunch to disrobe, he being afraid that some of the farmers' wives in the next house (about three miles down in the valley) would peek at him . . . The flat is filled with two new dogs, Harry Farrar of Bart's class, and Walter McCormick, a cousin of Vance . . . Willis Wood spent a day with us recently, tells us you're in good form . . . Del Wood took me to his father's place at Keene Valley over Labor Day . . .

ADDENDA
*Sept 1902:*

(1) Danbury Hatters Case. Loewe's Hat Shop declares for open shop, Hatters Union call strike, impose effective boycott, are cited in violation of the Sherman Anti-Trust Laws. Judgment of $80,000 against defendants is appealed. 13 years later, Supreme Court upholds original verdict, Hatters Union forced into bankruptcy, 125-yr-old Danbury hat-trade goes virtually out of existence.

(2) The offices of the Raymond General Agency move, three doors east, to more spacious accommodations on the 2nd floor at 26 Liberty Street . . .

(3) The Flatiron Building appears, like a surrealist nightmare, at Broadway and 23rd Street, monstrously tall and thin and frail . . .

(4) Julian Myrick takes up tennis. He has met the Washburn family, fiends for tennis, feels drawn by the net of the tennis set. His one ambition, to give 16-yr-old Marion Washburn a game. Charles Ives, a strong tennis-player since boyhood, coaches him two or three times a week on the courts over at 67th Street and Amsterdam. So Julian comes to know Poverty Flat as well . . .

(5) Horatio Parker leaves on a year's sabbatical to Europe, his place as Battel Professor of Music at Yale taken by 33-yr-old William Haesche, a classmate of Ives. On his return in September 1903, with an Honorary Doctorate from Cambridge University, Parker becomes Yale's first Dean of Music. David Stanley Smith joins the Music Department . . .

# New York II

There is no truth in the proverb, that if you get
up your name, you may safely play the rogue.
Look into the stage-coach and see the faces! Stand
in State Street and see the heads and gait and
gesture of the men; they are doomed ghosts going
under Judgement all day long . . .

EMERSON: *Journal for Sept 24 1838*

Christmas at the Main Street house in Danbury was a family ritual.
But Charles arrived home in 1903 to find Uncle Lyman, now 71,
ailing fast, Aunt Amelia watching over him like a tired, pathetic,
broken old rooster-hen. By tacit consent, Charles and his mother,
his brother Moss and his wife Minnie and little Richard, Uncle Joe
and his wife Sally and his daughter-in-law Anna and her three children, and Uncle Isaac and Aunt Emily and cousin George, all spent
Christmas up at Chapel Place.

Charles went over to see his uncle the next day, and found
the old man's mind wandering. How was the opera going ? The
one they'd planned together on that train ride to Chicago . . . 10
years ago ? They'd been to the Exposition and that Frenchman
had played the organ. But how was the opera going ?

Seven weeks later, on St Valentine's Day, Lyman Brewster died.
Moss went into partnership with Samuel Tweedy, Charles started
work on the Overture & March, *"1776"*, based on some ideas from
Uncle Lyman's play, and finished it, appropriately, July 4 on Pine
Mountain. ((Some of its material was later used in *The Fourth Of
July*, third of the *4 New England Holidays*.)) Also finished over
the holiday weekend, the horrifying preliminary sketch for a piece

on *The General Slocum,* the excursion steamer that had exploded in the East river three weeks before, killing 1,200 people:

> . . . I don't believe I had the serious intention of finishing it. This awful catastrophe got on everybody's nerves. I can give no other reason for attempting to put it to music, and I'm glad to look back and see that the sketch is hardly more than a page. It starts with several bands playing popular tunes, on the different decks, and people singing—and then the explosion . . .

> To get a composite sounding noise in some reasonable order was not hard to do. In this (see sketch, *Thanksgiving,* old score sketch, on empty pp 5/6) the rhythms are used in a kind of chemical order:

| | | |
|---|---|---|
| *Deep bells give (constant pitch)* | *: whole notes* | *(1)* |
| *Basses, starting on C, up by ½-tones* | *: half notes* | *(2)* |
| *Basses, starting on C♯, " " " "* | *: triplets* | *(3)* |
| *Cellos, starting on D, " " " "* | *: quarter notes* | *(4)* |
| *Cellos, starting on D♯, " " " "* | *: quintuplets* | *(5)* |

> and so on, all the way up through the orchestra (first piccolo playing 15) . . .

(((cf Alban Berg's *Wozzeck,* the pages immediately preceding the symphonic epilogue . . . 20 years later . . . )))

> I made *The Fourth Of July* from this plan, but much better musically, as each group has a phrase of musical sense, not just a chromatic scale as in *The General Slocum* . . .

Charles was used to working late into the night—often the whole night through. Eight hours at the office was so much *hors-d'oeuvre* to him, a stimulating appetizer for his real *oeuvre,* six or eight or ten hours' writing music. He didn't always work at the piano, but when he did, it caused moments of friction at the Flat. He was their senior member, in length of tenancy, and this gave him a fair hold over the recent arrivals, Bartlett Yung, Harry Farrar, Walter McCormick. But Keyes Winter, George Lewis and William Maloney had been at the Flat since 58th Street days, all now practicing lawyers with heavy briefs, who needed their sleep. Things came to a head one Thursday night the previous March, when Charles was working on an extraordinary piece that later became *On The Anti-*

*podes,* and clear prototype for the gigantic unfinished "Universe" Symphony. A page of sketch has:

> Bill Maloney mad at this    CPW    St Patrick's Day '04
> says just hammers—can't sleep . . .

Thereafter Charles used to call him "Tony Maloney" or "Maloney Bill"—in moments of extreme derogation, a combination of both. But the passages in question warrant some sympathy for the wretched plaintiff—successions of 12-note/12-tone chords, piled up in alternating 4ths and tritones, *ff crescendo.* Charles Ives had a phenomenal stretch—as wide and wider than his Russian contemporary, Rachmaninoff (and approaching that class, as a pianist). But no pianist with only 10 fingers can strike 12 widely spaced notes simultaneously, and Charles early became adept at breaking the chords into four groups of three notes each, carrying the left and right hands over and under at lightning speed. He had the intellectual control to strike the right notes with unfailing accuracy, and the muscular control to do it *ppp* if need be. But the context here demanded *fff,* and his right notes sounded decidedly wrong to Bill Maloney in the next-door room. For Charles would never accept a constellation of sounds simply because they "looked right" on paper. Like Stravinsky, he would go on playing them over and over till they had received the absolute sanction of his inner ear. The ultimate Art of Listening . . .

Another extraordinary piece, certainly written on Pine Mountain that August: the one-page song *Soliloquy,* "a study in 7ths and other things." Though it didn't go to his copyist till 1907, the vertical structure is so nearly identical with the tonal resources he was exploring on St Patrick's Day—and wasn't exploring again till 1911 —that it must have been written about the same time. A marginal note for the 1907 copyist:

> see better copy . . . back of coda page Thanksgiving

And the full-score of *Thanksgiving:*

> finished & all scored on Pine Mountain August 14 1904

((NB The diagram of pitch-rhythms for *The General Slocum*— also used in sketching *The Fourth Of July*—was on the back of pp 5/6 of the "old score sketch" of *Thanksgiving.*))

Pine Mountain was the catalyst for many new ideas. On the same page of *Thanksgiving* sketch that has the first sketch of *Soliloquy*, the cryptograph:

| I   | Mulberry Tree            | Mountain Trees |
|-----|--------------------------|----------------|
| II  | Hanover Square           | Walking Song   |
| III | City Hall Park/Madison Square |           |
| IV  | Thoreau . . .            |                |

In a note on the *Concord* Sonata:

> There was an Alcott Overture composed on Pine Mountain between 1902/04 with a theme & some passages used in sonata . . .

In one of CI's lists, a reference to a 1904 piece that has vanished:

> An Autumn Landscape from Pine Mountain—strings, woodwind, cornet (muted)—is heard from Ridgebury . . .

Also—logically—on Pine Mountain, some early sketches of the Piano Trio, inspired by a visit to the Yale sexennial reunion on June 28. Two pages of sketch are on the back of sketches for the *Alcott* Overture. Sketch for title:

> Trio—Yalensia & Americana    Fancy Names
> Real name: Yankee Jaws—at Mr (or Eli) Yale's school for
> nice bad boys . . .

Also—logically, for it breathes the clear air of Pine Mountain— the fully scored first version of the 3rd Symphony, lovely and gentlest of Ives's works . . . ((This is the version used in the published edition, after the revised 1909 edition, copied by Tams in 1910, disappeared to Europe with Gustav Mahler—another, later, longer story . . . ))

Finally, *Largo*, for solo 'cello, 2 violins, viola, and double-bass, finished on Pine Mountain in August and sent to Franz Kaltenborn in Morristown/New Jersey. A note on the MS sketch:

> Kaltenborn tried it for me in Dec 1904 at his house   NG!

Since the first performance of *The Celestial Country*, nearly three years before, the Kaltenborn Quartet had become Charles's very good friends, always ready to try over new pieces for him—

so long as he didn't expect them played in public. In that first performance, the violist, Gustav Bach, had especially endeared himself to Charles. The Intermezzo, for string quartet alone, is basically in the key of B♭ major, the final note in the viola part, G♭—a case analogous with *At Parting*, the song CI had shown to Parker at their first meeting: a final "unresolved" E♭ in the basic key of G major. In rehearsal, Gustav Bach had wanted to resolve the G♭ to F—"insisted he couldn't stand it not to resolve . . . " At the performance, "he looked at me and winked—but didn't resolve. He is a nice man!"

To commemorate that incident, Charles wrote a short piece (on the back of some pages of string parts from *The Celestial Country*) which he called the "Hootchi-Kootchi Dance." On the verso of a *Celestial Country* 2nd Violin part:

> Practice for String Quartet in "Holding Your Own!" Study dedicated to Gustav Bach (from the line of John Seb Bach)—after a rehearsal Feb 12 1903——65 CPW NY

Gustav Bach thanked him by letter on April 22, recalling the first performance of *The Celestial Country* a year earlier, and the occasion for "the wink." Now, two years later, the Kaltenborn Quartet's reading of his *Largo* had fallen flat, and Charles at once sent the "Hootchi-Kootchi Dance" off to be copied:

> Dec 24 1904   Copy out all repeats & separate parts & return to C E Ives   65 Central Park West . . .

Then he took the afternoon train to Danbury, to spend Christmas with his family.

Since Uncle Lyman's death, his mother's sister, Aunt Nell (Lucy Cornelia), had gone to live with Aunt Amelia. And Moss had broken with Samuel Tweedy and gone into partnership with Thomas Keating. How was business in New York these days, since Roosevelt's re-election?

When Theodore Roosevelt took over the Presidency, after McKinley's assassination in September 1901, there had been grave misgivings among the elder statesmen of the Republican Party. "Now look," Senator Hanna said, "that damned cowboy is President of the United States." By February 1902—the filing of the Federal anti-trust suit against Northern Securities that involved, one way or another, all the big names on the Street—Roosevelt had made it clear that he was out to bust the giant trusts. "The dull, purblind folly of the very rich men," he wrote later, ". . . the responsibility lies upon the railway and corporation people—that is, the manipulators of railroad and corporation stocks—who have been guilty of such scandalous irregularities during the last few years . . . These financiers have no moral scruple whatever . . ." The Northern Securities case had grown out of the 1901 railroad battle between J J Hill/J P Morgan and E H Harriman/Kuhn & Loeb, when the stock market had crashed and the adversaries been likened to "irresponsible cowboys shooting it out in public, with utter indifference to those of the general public who got hurt . . ." By 1904 there were 318 industrial trusts representing mergers of 5,294 separate companies, and a capitalization of more than $7 billion. In the summer of 1904, the Supreme Court ruled Northern Securities in violation of the Sherman Trust Laws and ordered the company dissolved—it was mostly "water" in any case—but it came as no help to the thousands of small shareholders who had been ruined along the way. The case was the first of many, and Roosevelt's re-election in November 1904 came as a predictable landslide. Wall Street was tight-lipped—angry, fearful, resigned—the sanguine preparing to bite on the bullet, the phlegmatic looking for ways of escape. For now it was rumored that the mammoth life insurance companies—Equitable Life, Mutual Life, New York Life—were next in line for "investigation."

By January 30 1905 Equitable had been profoundly compromised. Its 28-yr-old vice president, James Hazen Hyde, who had inherited his father's millions in 1899, threw a lavish "Louis XIV" ball at Sherry's, scandalizing even *The New York Times*. Andrew Hamilton, Equitable's president, threatened to take the matter up with the State Legislature, and James Hyde was compelled to divulge that he had speculated with the Society's—policyholders'—money. New York Life & Trust Company, oldest of New York's "Big 3," saw the writing on the wall and issued an "explanatory" pamphlet to all their policyholders in April. On August 1, Senator Armstrong formed his committee of investigation. On August 11, Charles Evans Hughes was appointed counsel for the investigation. And on September 6, the committee convened at New York City Hall.

In August, Charles went up to Saranac Lake to stay with David Twichell, tired, depressed, disenchanted with it all. Devising new methods for selling insurance, exploring new areas to sell in, had taken up all his time and all his creative energy since January 1905. The only piece he had started was a sketch for a piece for organ & chamber orchestra "as a kind of brass band outdoors, organ indoors, and shown to Franz Kaltenborn . . . But F K wouldn't play it . . . " Now, at Saranac Lake, quietly, two pieces:

> (1) mentioned on the first page of MS sketch, 1st movt/4th Symphony, "started as Horns & Strings piece at suggestion of D C T   Saranac Lake   1905 . . ."
>
> (2) mentioned on a page of fragmentary sketch for 3rd movt/ 4th Violin Sonata, "started as Cornet & Strings piece (with Dave C T at Saranac   Aug 1905) . . ."

(((The 1st was from "the song that Annie Wilson sang at the YMCA concert, Nov 21 1901"—the prototype of *Watchman;* the 2nd "after a visit to a Camp Meeting at Saranac"—based on the hymn, *Beautiful River,* "a favorite of Dave's . . .")))

Then, in a renewed blaze of creative activity—conceived, sketched and finished in three days—the Three-Page Sonata, for piano. At the foot of page 3 of the MS:

> Fine at Saranac L   N Y   with Dave   Aug '05

On page 1:

> Back to 1st Theme—all nice Sonatas must have 1st Theme

and the appended slip:

> made mostly as a joke to knock the mollycoddles out of their boxes and to kick out the softy ears!

The facetious marginalia belie the structural intensity of the piece—a model and marvel of unity-cum-brevity. Style: predominantly ragtime—"old-time" ragtime, Old Style—not the smart, genteel, punch-pulling ragtime of the 20s and 30s, Cole Porter and George Gershwin, but raw, authentic, displaying Ives's marvelous gift for investing a style with a universal, almost mythological perspective. This is the ragtime of Olympus, a crystallization of the Ragtime Pieces for Theater Orchestra, 1902/04, and a miniature portent of the 1st Piano Sonata still to come (((1st full length, that is))) —first sketch "Pine Mt Aug 4 '01"—completed in 1909 as the prelude to the final eight years' stupendous creativity.

But now August was nearly over and Charles had to get back to New York. David Twichell urged him to stay a few days longer. His sister Harmony would be coming up to stay for a week on September 1, would love to see him again, he felt sure. So Charles stayed . . .

Charles was back in Danbury for the October Fair, and sketched at least 8 pages ((the first 6 lost)) of a band piece—his first since his father's death. It later became a song, title:

Runaway Horse on Main Street (during Fair Week) (from Brass Band piece, score not finished . . . )

set to his own words:

"So long Harry, see y' later . . ."

Later still—1914 or 15—*Charlie Rutlage* ((no 10 of *114 Songs*)).

Back in New York, on November 14, Charles went over one of his Ragtime Pieces with the orchestra at the Globe Theatre—until the manager came out and stopped them, saying they were causing too much disturbance . . . Thanksgiving was spent at Poverty Flat, where he finished the second movement/1st Piano Sonata ((based on material from the ragtime piece)), and found a captive audience for a performance, on the piano, of the 1902 *Country Band March:*

George, Bart, Tony Maloney Bill—3 quite right critics!!—say I haven't got the tune right & the chords are wrong——Thanksgiving 1905 . . .

((The "tune" here was probably the one that appears in the *Putnam's Camp* movement of the 1st Orchestral Set, in the Hawthorne movement of the *Concord* Sonata, and in the second movement/4th Symphony. It has caused Ives parody-spotters a headache, because it is a "popular" tune, a good one, and has the durability and familiarity of a good one. But CI was not above inventing a good popular tune for himself—vide *The Circus Band*. What is delightful, the tune sounded so familiar to his three friends, they thought he hadn't got it right . . . ) )

The next recorded event at Poverty Flat was early 1906—an unfinished piece, for clarinet, bassoon, trumpet, and piano: *"Rube Trying To Walk 2 Against 3."* ( (1905/06 was a severe winter, and likely that some of the members of the Flat caught colds. "Rube" could be a contraction of Bill Maloney's middle name—Raymond —spoken by a New Yorker through a heavy cold. Not that it matters . . . ) ) On page 1 of the sketch:

Some of this worked into a song later—"1 2 3"
( (no 41 of *114 Songs*) )

& on page 2:

. . . written as a joke and sounds like one! Watty McCormick only one to see it! and Harry Farrar! at 2.45 AM . . .

This led to a major musical event: *Over The Pavements*, for piccolo, clarinet, baritone saxophone, trumpet, 3 trombones, percussion, and piano, started May 30 1906—Decoration Day. At the top of a page of sketch for the Piano Cadenza:

Storm & distress to "Tony Bill" . . . not so to Delano! ( (Del Wood) ) . . . or to "Disturber" ( (CI himself) ) . . .

At the bottom:

. . . as a Cadenza, to play or not to play! if played, as not a nice one . . .

July 1906 was a trebly rich month: *In The Cage, The Unanswered Question, Central Park In The Dark*. And in August, *The Pond*, for voice or basset-horn, flute, 2 harps, celesta, piano, and strings—consummate mastery distilled into 3 lines of text, 12 measures of music, "that cast back, like the reflection in a clear mirror, every leaf and every hurt that passed through his imagination . . ." CI's text:

> The sound of a distant horn
> O'er shadowed lake is born,
> My father's song . . .

The brief melodic line is echoed at one measure's distance by the flute, the incredibly complex string texture has the sound of gently rippling water, and there is a fleeting reference, at the very end, to "Taps." The association:

Father/Civil War (Taps)/Thoreau/Walden Pond . . .

*In The Cage*, for oboe, English horn, timpani, piano, and strings, was the result of a walk in Central Park one hot summer's afternoon, Sunday July 28, "with Bart Yung (one-half Oriental) and George Lewis (non Oriental)":

> Sitting on a bench near the menagerie, watching the leopard's cage and a little boy (who had apparently been a long time watching the leopard)—this aroused Bart's Oriental fatalism—hence the text in the score and in the song ((no 64 of *114 Songs*)). Technically this piece is a study of how 4ths and 5ths may throw melodies away from a set tonality. The main line in 4ths had two lines of inverted counterpoint going with it. Whether this was intended to increase the fatalism or reduce it I don't know. It was left out of the printed score ((*New Music*, vol 5, no 2, 1932)) and the song copy—I can't exactly remember why, except that it's hard to play (and for some lady-boys to listen to) . . .

((*In The Cage* at once became the first movement/Theater Orchestra Set, with *In The Inn* (drawn from ragtime pieces that went back to New Haven days, with George Felsburg at Poli's), and *In The Night* (based on the lost *Hymn-Anthem* of 1901).))

*The Unanswered Question* and *Central Park In The Dark* are something else. They were designed as a pair:
 (1) "A Contemplation of a Serious Matter" or
       "The Unanswered Perennial Question"; and
 (2) "A Contemplation of Nothing Serious" or
       "Central Park in the Dark in 'The Good Ole Summer Time' "

And they are Charles Ives's first pieces to derive clear benefit from the use of two conductors. *The Unanswered Question* is scored for solo trumpet, 4 flutes, and a "distant choir" of strings:

The strings play *ppp* throughout, with no change of tempo. They are to represent "The Silences of the Druids" who speak, see, and hear nothing. The trumpet intones "The Perennial Question of Existence" and states it in the same tone of voice each time. But the hunt for the "Invisible Answer" undertaken by the flutes and other human beings becomes gradually more active, faster and louder through an *animando* to a *con fuoco*. The "Fighting Answerers," as time goes on, seem to realize a futility, and begin to mock "The Question"—the strife is over for the moment. After they disappear, "The Question" is asked again for the last time, and the "Silences" are heard beyond in undisturbed solitude . . .

Quite another question: *Central Park In The Dark*, for piccolo, flute, oboe, clarinet, bassoon, trumpet, trombone, percussion, 2 pianos, and strings:

> . . . a portrait in sound of the sounds of nature and of happenings that men would hear, sitting on a bench in Central Park on a hot summer's night. The strings represent the night sounds and silent darkness—interrupted by the sounds from the Casino over the pond—of street singers coming up from the Circle, singing— in spots—the tunes of those days—of some "night owls" from Healey's whistling the latest hit or the Freshman March—the occasional elevated, a street parade or a "break-down" in the distance—of newsboys crying "uxtries," of pianolas having a ragtime war in the apartment house "over the garden wall," a street car and a street band join in the chorus—a fire engine—a cab horse runs away, lands "over the fence, and out"—the wayfarers shout—again the darkness is heard—an echo over the pond . . .

*Central Park In The Dark* was started July, finished December 1906. A footnote on the second sketch:

> . . . runaway horse smashes into fence—heard at 65 CPW
> with Julian Myrick   July/Dec 1906 . . .

The Armstrong Committee had concluded its hearings, after 57 sessions, on December 30 1905. All the major figures in New York Life & Trust, Mutual Life and Equitable had been examined and found generally culpable. But while New York Life and Equitable had made fairly genuine attempts to put their own houses in order before the investigation began, Mutual Life had done nothing. Its President, Richard A McCurdy, had agreed to a 50% cut in his salary the day the investigation started, but that was all. He claimed "eleemosynary" motives for the life insurance business, and remained uncooperative to the last. Apart from evidence of nepotism that inevitably came to light, and the exaggerated salaries—worth, today, perhaps 5 times as much as then, so that McCurdy had effectively been earning $1.5 million a year—it was found that Mutual's Treasurer, Frederick Cromwell, had been personally involved in a syndicate financed with policyholders' money, and that George F Baker, a Vice President, had been living up to his title running a high-class brothel near Albany, and that members of the State Legislature had been among his clientele. The only member of Mutual's senior executive staff to come through the investigation with honor was their senior actuary, Emory McClintock. On January 3 1906, all but he resigned, and a new board elected Charles A Peabody President, McClintock 1st Vice President, W W Richards Vice President in charge of Real Estate Management, George T Dexter Vice President in charge of Agencies. Dr Granville White, great-grandson of Col Nelson White and a cousin of Charles's, was appointed Mutual's medical officer. Col Raymond resigned, and Robert McCurdy, manager of the Raymond Agency since 1903, was dismissed.

The Armstrong Report was submitted to the State Legislature on February 1906 and became law in April, with effect from January 1 1907. One of the major provisions was to limit all insurance companies with more than $1 million of policies in force to a 3% expansion per annum: this, of course, involved the "Big 3," but also most of the larger agencies, including the Raymond Agency. Another provision was to limit all salaries, without the prior consent of the Boards of Trustees and the State Inspector of Insurance, to $5,000 per annum. By the end of 1906, Charles Ives and Julian Myrick had resolved to set up in business on their own, and during 1907, George Dexter reported, "half the real insurance men left Mutual Life."

Charles and Julian spent Christmas 1906 together at Old Point Comfort/Virginia, discussing plans. They had approached John Tatlock, who had been head of Mutual's actuarial department when

Charles first went to work there, and now was President of Washington Life, and Tatlock had agreed to finance them. On their return to New York, he invited them to set up a general agency for his company, and offices were found at 51 Liberty Street: IVES & CO, it said, when they put the notice up. But even Myrick was skeptical of Charles's far-ranging ideas. Competitors gave them a year . . .

Harmony Twichell had occupied Charles's mind increasingly since the summer of 1905. Since then, there had been some slight correspondence between them. Now, as head of his own agency at the age of 32, he had the chance of doing something about it. But he had little confidence she would ever accept him. ((He wrote her father later: "I have always felt unworthy of her but don't think it best for her to let myself think too much about that . . .")) Keyes Winter had been engaged for some time, insisted Charles should be best man at his wedding—at some unspecified date in the future. Feeling the strain of his own personal affairs, Charles grew progressively more grumpy as the months bore on. Finally the wedding of "Mr Keyes Winter to Miss Marie Mosle" was announced, in *The Times*, for "Tuesday, April 2 1907." On a rejected page of sketch for the 1st Piano Sonata, the note:

C E I    Keep eyes on Keyes/get Keyes wedding present!

The wedding-eve bachelors' party—April Fools' Day—was celebrated up at the cabin on Pine Mountain. Charles graced the occasion with a spontaneous, something less than sober *Hallowe'en* —later scored for Piano Quintet . . .

At the start of June, Harmony Twichell returned to the Henry Street Settlement as a nurse—she had spent a month there in August 1905, just before meeting Charles again. On June 7 and 11 she went with him to two of Kaltenborn's concerts at the St Nicholas skating rink on West 66th Street, a few doors down from Poverty Flat. On June 21, with him to *Twelfth Night*, at the Garrick Theatre. Then, in August, for two weeks' vacation with her family at Elk Lake. There, on August 14, she wrote "Spring Song," which she sent to Charles at Saranac Lake, anxious to please him:

> Across the hill of late, came spring,
>    And stopped and looked into this wood,
>       And called and called.

> Now all the brown things are answ'ring,
>> With here a leaf and there a fair blown flow'r;
>>> I only heard her not, and wait and wait.

Anxious to please her, Charles looked out a straightforward piece written four years earlier, but discarded, and adapted it to her words. Meanwhile:

Sketch    Concord Sonata    Saranac Lake    Sept 1907

The exchange of letters grew more frequent. On October 28, another poem, "Autumn":

> Earth rests! Her work is done, her fields lie bare,
>> and 'ere the night of winter comes
>>> to hush her song and close her tired eyes,
> She turns her head the sun to shine upon,
>> and radiantly, thro' fall's bright glow,
>>> he smiled and brings the peace of God!

((( Here again, CI looked out some earlier music, now lost. The ink MS of his setting (in G major) of Harmony's words has the note: "Autumn in D♭ sung by Dr Griggs—Thanksgiving—65 Central Park West   1902 . . ." A later version, after June 1908, is in F major. Final version ((no 60 of *114 Songs*)) in D♭ . . . )))

On Saturday November 16, Harmony and Charles went to the Yale-Princeton Football Game in New Haven. Next day, at 125 Woodland Street, Hartford, Dr Joseph Twichell found them waiting to see him. Like many fathers of intelligent and beautiful daughters, he kept his own counsel about her relationships—if he noticed them at all. Among his very elaborate diaries, the entry for Sunday November 17 is his first mention of Charles:

> Going up to my study in the afternoon, I found Harmony and Charley Ives there. In response to my look of enquiry for the reason for it, they explained that they wanted my "Blessing" . . . I found later in the day that Charles had already made his confession to H ((Harmony's mother, Mrs Harmony Cushman Twichell)) . . . We have known him a good while: he is a classmate of David's who has loved him fondly. We were prepared to sanction the en-

gagement, which seemed to us suitable and auspicious in its promises
for us all . . .


## ADDENDA

*March 17 1907:* The Silent Panic. New York stock market
collapses. Bank of England dispatches $10 million in gold
specie in the SS *Lusitania,* to bolster the American econ-
omy . . .

*May 1:* Metropolitan Opera announces $10,000 opera competi-
tion. Closing date, June 1 1910 . . .

*May 10:* first of an exchange of letters between Charles and
Harmony about the adaptation of Gilbert Parker's *The
Red Patrol* as an opera libretto . . .

*Sept 21:* Poverty Flat moves downtown to more salubrious, less
extensive quarters at 34 Gramercy Park: Charles Ives,
George Lewis, Bartlett Yung, and his older brother Morrison . . .

*Oct 13:* October Panic. Second collapse of New York stock
market, precipitated by the failure of Heinze speculators
to corner United Copper. Banks stop specie payment . . .

*Oct 17:* Julian Myrick, 27, elected secretary of the New York
Underwriters Association . . .

*Dec:* President Roosevelt, blamed by businessmen for causing
the panics, denounces as "dangerous criminals" those cap-
italists responsible for "swindling in stocks, corrupting
legislatures, making fortunes by the inflation of securities,
by wrecking railroads, by destroying competitors through
rebates . . . "

# Ricercar II

Much of New England, still today, is wilder, harsher, more rugged than the old country, its dense flora and granite outcroppings closer kin to the Scots Highlands, the Argonne, or the Black Forest, than the pleasant country lanes and tidy hedgerows of the Midlands and southern England. Closer kin to Old England *c* 1620, maybe. Underneath, nothing much is changed. Nor readily arable land, this, as the Plymouth Brethren found. The sudden, technicolor resplendence of the New England fall comes with a single-minded vividness, a purism of nature that is mirrored in the white-painted New England churches, their tall spires pointing to an unequivocally Puritan heaven. And the light: supernatural, unnatural. Not a painter's light, this, though softening at its edges—Hancock, Nantucket, New Bedford—to an echo of the delicate light you get over Dartmoor or the Sussex Downs.

The fishing villages of New England wear a surface likeness to their picturesque ancestors of Devon, Cornwall, Wales, and the Fen country. Yet they bear right on the Atlantic, are the same the New England whalers put out from, before Standard Oil put the whaling industry out of business—*Essex, Acushnet,* Melville's *Pequod.* For North Sea, Irish Sea, English Channel *read* Atlantic & Pacific, and you have a measure of the New England seafarer's grasp of SPACE.

West of New England, across Lake Champlain into upper New York state, the land grows wilder still—once you leave the modern highways. Higher too. The Adirondacks around Keene Valley rise to a height of 5,000 feet and more—the highest, Mount Marcy, "Tahawus," is near 5,400 feet. Gray/brown cousins, these, to the White Mountains of New Hampshire, clad in pine, spruce, hemlock, yellow birch, beech, balsam fir, and around the myriad lakes, tamarack. Below the peak of Tahawus, the secret lake, "Tear-in-the-Clouds," sister to the lost lake of Hawthorne's Great Carbuncle. This was trapping country—elk, bear, panther, sable, mink—in the days when trapping meant survival, and a buckskin sold for a dollar. Verplanck Colvin told it, the year Charles Ives was born:

> Few fully understand what the Adirondack wilderness really is. It is a mystery even to those who have crossed and recrossed it by boats along its avenues, the lakes; and on foot through its vast and silent recesses, by following the ghastly lines of blazed or axe-marked trees, which the daring searcher for the fur of the sable or the mink, has chopped in order that he may find his way again in that deep and desolate forest. In these remote sections, filled with the most rugged mountains, where unnamed waterfalls pour in snowy tresses from the overhanging cliffs, the horse can find no footing; and the adventurous trapper or explorer must carry on his back his blankets and a heavy stock of food. His rifle, which affords protection against wild beasts, oftentimes replenishes his well husbanded provisions, and his axe aids him in constructing from bark or bough some temporary shelter from storm. Yet, though the woodsman pass his lifetime in some section of the wilderness, it is still a mystery to him  . . .

When Charles Ives went up to Keene Valley, the summer of 1896—and again over Labor Day weekend 1903—he took the Rensselaer & Saratoga Railroad from Albany to Westport, by Barber's Point, on the lower reaches of Lake Champlain. Then west by stagecoach, 10 miles to Elizabethtown, stopping overnight. Next morning, west again by stage, between Giant-of-the-Valley Mountain and Hopkins Peak, 10 miles to Keene Valley and the east branch of the Au Sable River. 25 miles north-west by stage, past the grave of

John Brown at North Elba, lie the Saranac Lakes, where David Twichell was assistant medical officer at Dr Trudeau's sanatorium, with its staff of Catholic nuns—Robert Louis Stevenson one of Trudeau's earliest patients, in 1887. 10 miles south of Keene Valley, through Elk pass by Nippletop Mountain, lies Elk Lake, one of the northernmost headwaters of the Hudson river, sheltering beneath the forests of Beech Ridge: Elk Lake, isolate, mysterious, where moose and giant elk came once upon a time. On its southern shore, since 1902, has been Pell Jones's Elk Lake Camp, the hostelry where the Twichells stayed in 1907, and after their marriage, Charles and Harmony Ives. The studio Ives had is gone now, but the other buildings, renovated, are still there. In the fall of 1915 Charles and Harmony and Edith stayed at Keene Flats—Keene Valley Plateau—which lies 2 miles north of Keene Valley, and took the house that had its own tennis court. Anna Brode was a girl then and used to take in their wash—used to take in the Woods' wash, too, during the summer, when they came up to the cottage, "Waldruhe," where the Twichell family stayed the summer of 1896. But that was before her time . . . . .

. . . . . And Gramercy Park, with its private garden that you had to have your own key to, its center fountain and dogwood tree with white flowering cups, and gardeners tending the beds of scarlet tulips. Shortly after Poverty Flat moved there, in September 1907:

(1) *On the Campus—Calcium Light Night! (A Take-Off)*—— "approved by Yale Club of 34 Gramercy Park . . ." ((based on sketches of Fraternity songs, made at the 1901 Yale triennial reunion));

(2) *A Lecture* (by Arthur Twining Hadley: "Some Influences in Modern Philosophic Thought")——"approved of by Bart & M Yung, Geo Lewis, 34 Gramercy Park . . ." ((designed as part of an extended orchestral piece, which has been lost; adapted, in 1909, to words by Kipling that Hadley had quoted in his lecture, as *Tolerance* (( no 59 of *114 Songs*)) ));

(3) first movement/2nd Violin Sonata—"July '03/Oct '07 . . ."

(4) second movement/2nd Violin Sonata—"1902/1907 Nov Gramercy Park . . ."

(5) second movement/1st Violin Sonata—"1903, finished Feb 1908   34 Gramercy Park   N Y . . . "

The pedigree of the Violin Sonatas is the devil. What you really have is this:

(1) a "First" Violin Sonata—"written in college (now dead)." Certainly lost. Adaptation as a 'Cello Sonata unfinished and destroyed.

(2) the *"pre-First" Violin Sonata*—started 1901, finished Nov 1903:

> (i) 1st movt "partly from an Organ Postlude   Centre Ch New Haven   '97." Ten measures near the end of the movement developed into the Trio section, second movt/ 2nd Violin Sonata (finished Nov 1907, Gramercy Park);
>
> (ii) 2nd movt (first version) "played at Organ recital Central Pres Ch   Dec 16 1901—Wm Haesche soloist" ((Later became *Largo,* for clarinet, violin & piano, a probable movement from the lost Clarinet Trio));
>
> (iii) 2nd movt (second version). Original music < 2nd movt/final "First" Violin Sonata (finished Feb 1908, Gramercy Park);
>
> (iv) rejected Scherzo = Ragtime Dance for Theater Orchestra (not the piece played at the Globe Theatre, Nov 1905, but perhaps a piece that CI refers to elsewhere, played at the Globe *December* 1905) < main body of second movt/2nd Violin Sonata (finished Nov 1907, Gramercy Park);
>
> (v) 3rd movt. Original music. ((CI was guarded about this as the source of a later Violin Sonata movement. On the title page of the 2nd movement (first version)—"3rd movement never completed . . . " On the title page of the 1st movement—"3rd movement non est NON EST . . ." But definitely EST. Became the 1st movt/2nd Violin Sonata (finished Oct 1907, Gramercy Park))).

(3) final, actual *First Violin Sonata,* finished February 1908, revised *c* 1909:

> (i) 1st movt. Original music, written in 1906.

(ii)  2nd movt. From second version, 2nd movt/"pre-First" Violin Sonata (see above).

(iii)  3rd movt. From the song sung by Annie Wilson at the Central Presbyterian YMCA concert, November 21 1901: "Return all parts copied to C E I   26 Liberty Street   2nd floor Charles Raymond & Co"—i.e. before the end of 1906, when CI left the Raymond Agency.

(4)  *Second Violin Sonata*, finished November 1907, revised 1909/10:

(i)  1st movt: *Autumn.* From third movement/"pre-First" Violin Sonata (see above).

(ii)  2nd movt: *In The Barn.* From rejected Scherzo and part of the first movement/"pre-First" Violin Sonata (see above).

(iii) 3rd movt: *A Revival.* Original music, written in 1906, though an elaboration of the movement *later* included as the fourth movement/4th Violin Sonata.

(5)  *Third Violin Sonata*, finished December 1914:

(i)  1st movt: "1st verse & 2nd & 3rd verses & Refrains from Organ Preludes, played at C P Church   Nov 1901 . . ."

(ii)  2nd movt: from *Ragtime Dance* (Globe Theatre, Nov 14 1905, "note to Mr Ross"), originally from *Toccata*, Central Presbyterian Church, May 8 1901 . . .

(iii)  3rd movt: from Organ Prelude, played at Central Presbyterian Church, Nov 1901—"flute stop & choir." ((On page 2 of the MS: "Richy Wagner is a soft-bodied sensualist = pussy . . ."))

(6)  *Fourth Violin Sonata*, assembled from earlier music *c* 1915:

(i)  1st movt: from Sonata for Trumpet & Organ, 1900, played at Central Presbyterian Church, Jan 1901.

(ii)  2nd movt: original music—but before *In The Night*, 1906.

(iii)  3rd movt: from cornet & strings piece, "Aug 1905, with Dave Twichell   Saranac Lake . . ."

(iv)  4th movt: original (earlier) version of *Revival* movement/2nd Violin Sonata.

## MISCELLANEA

(1) Dates of marginalia generally construable from their contexts, especially where they contain instructions for copyists that give his office adress . . .

(2) CI Sobriquets: "Arthur, Eddie, Rollo," &c. Rollo was a 19th century character out of Jacob Abott. Eddie may have been Edward Carrington Twichell, or CI himself (recalling his father's talk to him after his infant cousin's baptism). Arthur is probably Arthur Bodansky, and does not make an appearance in CI's marginalia till after April 1920 . . .

(3) CI's "basset-horn" period. Not a period, really, since only about six or seven works are involved. But it is intriguing what an affinity he felt for Mozart's favorite instrument . . .

# STRETTO

# New York III

Charles Ives and Harmony Twichell were married by her father, in
Hartford, June 9 1908. For their honeymoon (spent mostly with
Rocket, the horse given them as a wedding-present by David Twichell), they struck north on a 16-day walking tour of the Great Bar-
rington area, including Stockbridge, returning to New York (70 West
11th Street) Thursday June 25—"our first night at home." Then
back again to Stockbridge by train (Housatonic RR) for the weekend, taking the Sunday-morning walk along the river, and returning
to New York early June 30: "first meal at our own table—breakfast."

The Sunday-morning walk became *The Housatonic At Stockbridge*—third movement/1st Orchestral Set (*3 New England Places*).
But the first sketches went back six years, to 1901, soon after Robert
Underwood Johnson's poem appeared—soon after President Mc-
Kinley's assassination. Even before then, the idea for the piece may
have been there. On the verso of a Tenor Aria, dated "March 1898
76 South Middle," the note:

River mists, leaves in slight breeze, river bed—all notes and phrases
in upper accompaniment should interweave in an uneven way—
riverside colors, leaves & sounds—NOT come down on main beat . . .

After their return to New York at the end of June 1908, Ives began a new sketch, for flute, organ, and strings:

> This is to picture the colors one sees, sounds one hears, feelings
> one has, of a summer morning near a wide river, the leaves, waters,
> mists &c all interweaving in the picture & a hymn singing in church
> way across the river . . .

((The Stockbridge Congregational Church lies on the west bank of the Housatonic—about 50 yds wide at this point. The hymn—Zeuner's *Missionary Chant*—had close associations in CI's mind with the opening of Beethoven's 5th Symphony in tragic/lyrical transfiguration (*cf* The Alcotts movement/*Concord* Sonata). *The Housatonic At Stockbridge,* in its final scoring, for large orchestra, was not finished till the summer of 1914—the same time CI was finishing the fourth movement/4th Symphony. The two movements have important features in common.))

On September 25 old Uncle Joe died in Danbury, at the age of 75. The premonitions that Charles had experienced when Uncle Joe's son died, September fourteen years earlier, a few weeks before the death of his own father, now manifest themselves in a material way. Washington Life sold out to Pittsburgh Life & Trust, who did no business in New York. After less than two years in operation, Ives & Co ceased to exist. When he told his wife, "she didn't seem to mind," he said later. Nor would Charles himself, under different circumstances. But now, on the available evidence, a child was on the way, and cause for concern.

*((((September 30 1908:*
>       *David Stanley Smith appointed organist of Centre Church,*
>       *New Haven . . . ))))*

October was spent revising the first movement/1st Violin Sonata —"finished Oct 19 '08   6 PM   Saranac L   with Dave & Ella" ((David Twichell and his wife)). Next day was Charles's 34th birthday, and someone gave him a copy of Browning's "Paracelsus." On November 24, the sketch of *Adagio cantabile* was completed, for string quartet & piano—arranged, in 1916, to words of his own, as *The Innate* ((later, no 40 of *114 Songs,* with the footnote: "For the most part, use both pedals. If played on an organ, use chiefly the lighter string-stops, on an enclosed manual. Hold all notes their full value, regardless of dissonance.") )

On December 23, Ives received a letter from George Dexter, vice-president of Mutual Life, appointing him co-manager, with Julian Myrick, of a new general agency at 37 Liberty Street, effective January 1 1909—ten days hence. Salary: $5,000 per annum—the maximum payable under the Armstrong Laws. Ives's immediate reaction was to go to his desk and sketch 33 measures towards a *Robert Browning* Overture. Below:

> Chromatic leap around the block. Steppin' nice, backwoods &c—
> but now to serious purpose   Dec 21 1908   70 W 11 St . . .

The passage starts straight in with the triumphant string passage that later became measures 107/140, ending with the tumultuous sustained 12-tone chord that Ives first intended should lead into the coda. The same page of sketch ((made on the title page, ink copy, third movement/"pre-First" Violin Sonata!)) has, at the top:

> onto coda   Tone Poem No 2   Browning—end of march to coda

Though the piece must have been formulating in his mind, at least since October 20, this is the first evidence of written material—except for the cryptic "Chas E Ives   26 Liberty St   2nd flight up   60 John" that appears at the bottom of page 1 of the (later) MS full-score. This the address—and floor—of the Raymond Agency, which Ives left at the end of 1906; straightway contradicted by "60 John" —short for "John 3660"—his current telephone number at Ives & Myrick, 37 Liberty Street . . .

Businessman ?  Or Composer ?   Anything—but present business—could have invoked the association of ideas with the address of his former employers, Charles H Raymond . . . On page 12 of the MS full-score are copying instructions for Price, and his home address: "70 W 11 St."

*Other music from 1908:*

> (1)  The unfinished—or lost—*Emerson* Overture, for piano & orchestra. ((One of its four "centrifugal cadenzas" became Piano Study No 9—*The Anti-Abolitionist Riots*— already mentioned in connection with the *Browning* Overture sketch of Dec 21 1908 . . . ))

(2) *The Waiting Soul* ((later no 62 of *114 Songs*)), adapted
to William Cowper's text from earlier music—probably
for Harmony, a singer of modest pretensions.

(3) *Nature's Way* ((later no 61 of *114 Songs*)), adapted, to
CI's own words, from earlier music—same probable reason.

When Ives & Myrick was established, on January 1 1909, Ives
was 34, Myrick 28. George Dexter had remembered them largely
through Myrick's activities as secretary of the New York Underwriters Association. This established the format of their partnership:

> We were blazing a new field and it responded—estate planning and
> all that sort of thing. We had brokers who were general insurance
> men, and we taught them how to sell life insurance, and we built
> up a big agency through them, and it was very successful. I joined
> all the organizations and did all the outside contact work for the
> agency. Charlie belonged to all of them but took no active interest
> —I did that. That's the reason, I think, that I'm generally speaking
> better known in the business . . .

In July, Julian Myrick joined the West Side Tennis Club at Van
Cortland Park, and got engaged to Marion Washburn.

Since January, Ives had been working behind the scenes to get
the agency on its feet and had no time to compose. On April 20 Harmony was rushed to St Luke's Hospital for an emergency operation
and her gall bladder removed. There were complications that suggest
the termination of a pregnancy. On April 29, Ives sketched the song,
*Like A Sick Eagle*, to the opening lines of Keats' Sonnet "On Seeing
the Elgin Marbles." At the top of the MS title page:

> H T I in hospital   Sally singing   70 W 11   Apr 29 '09

Sally—Susan—was Harmony's second sister, come to keep house
while Harmony was in hospital. A letter from their mother on May
10, five days before Harmony was discharged:

> My heart is full of joy and gratitude over you, over Sally, and I
> must say over Charlie with his great loving heart. I thought myself
> so happy in my trust in him, but now, after the revelations of ten-
> derness in him through the great trial that has come to you, I feel I
> did not half appreciate what was in him. With him to protect you,

life cannot bring you anything you cannot bear—and still have in your heart abiding happiness . . .

The child, then, if there was one, lost. Anyway a hysterectomy—an operation fraught with very real peril 65 years ago. No other construction is possible.

Though the crisis must have been past by then, *Like A Sick Eagle* reflects Charles's, Sally's continuing distress. And Keats' words:

> The spirit is too weak—mortality
> Weighs heavily on me like unwilling sleep,
> And each imagined pinnacle and steep .
> Of godlike hardship tells me I must die
> Like a sick eagle looking at the sky . . .

The music:

> Draggingly . . . Voice intones words with English horn (not like singing) . . .

and the footnote:

> The + + over and between the notes means that between ½-tones a slide through a ¼-tone may be made, and between whole tones, through a ⅓-tone. This, done in a certain way, gives a more desolate sound . . .

(((Three years later, for *Pierrot Lunaire*, Schoenberg coined the word "Sprechgesang" . . . )))

The original setting of *Like A Sick Eagle* is for voice and/or English horn—later changed to basset-horn—flute, strings & piano. The 1920 arrangement for voice & piano ((no 26 of *114 Songs*)) gives no clue to the tonally complex flute, 'cello and double-bass counterpoints in the second half of the song.

On August 20, Charles and Harmony left for 3 weeks' vacation to Elk Lake—she for the final stage of convalescence, he to "mend fences": a final revision (as he thought) of the 3rd Symphony; the sketch of an orchestration of the opening fugue from the 1st String Quartet (towards the third movement/4th Symphony, now taking definite shape in his mind); and a revision, for full orchestra and later inclusion in the 2nd Orchestral Set, of the ragtime Theater Or-

chestra piece—that "Franz Kaltenborn wouldn't play! then . . . "
This was the first completed movement of the 2nd Orchestral Set,
titled *The Rockstrewn Hills Join In The People's Outdoor Meeting*—
a recollection from his youth, and the Camp Meetings among the
rockstrewn hills around Redding, when "some of the boys would rush
out and throw stones on the rocks in the river . . . "

((On the verso of one page of the MS there is the beginning of a
sketch for a "take-off" on Haydn's "Surprise" Symphony—certainly
generated by the start of the ragtime movement itself, which starts
out as though it were going to be an almighty take-off on the Haydn.
CI abandoned the sketch when he saw that the Haydn itself was a
"take-off"—something self-apparent to a European, no doubt, but
not to an American of Ives's generation, at a first hearing. (How
many of Haydn's audience, at the symphony's first performance, got
the joke ? The REAL joke, which knocked an entire cultural attitude ?)))

### A Moment's Exegesis:

Ives's hostility to the music of Mozart & Haydn—"nice little easy
sugar plum sounds" (to the opening phrase of Haydn's *Andante*)
. . . he knew these composers—especially their chamber music—
well. Somewhere he writes of spending the afternoon playing Mozart
violin sonatas with Reber Johnson, assistant concertmaster of the
New York Symphony:

> Reber had his good points. He had a beautiful tone on the strings,
> and played Mozart to perfection. I'll have to admit I enjoyed play-
> ing Mozart with him. But a whole afternoon of Mozart is a whole
> afternoon of Mozart (I was going to say something worse, which
> I occasionally know how to do) . . . He did occasionally have a
> good word to say for some mild new music—a nice piece by
> Massenet, with a G$\sharp$ in it somewhere . . .

Somewhere else he writes of hearing the Kneisel Quartet playing
Haydn—he had tickets to their winter chamber-music series even
as a freshman at Yale, heard them again at Mendelssohn Hall in
New York. And always walked out. It was the preciosity of their
playing that turned him off, and his contempt transferred itself to

the music. However "nicely" played, it wasn't possible to "emasculate" Beethoven or Bach or Brah:.is altogether.

Many composers have had blind-spots for other composers—Weber for Beethoven, Brahms for. Wagner, Britten for Brahms—but they all belonged to the same cultural heritage. America didn't, and it angered Ives to see expert musicians striking European postures that didn't suit them. "He may have been nearer right than we think . . ."

Back in the City, Ives started on the sketch for *Washington's Birthday*—now as the first of *4 New England Holidays*—for flute, horn, bells, strings, and a chorus of jew's harps:

> I've always been a good Jew's harp player regardless of consequences, but I didn't know exactly how to write for it—its ability to play a diatonic tone is more apparent than real. And in this piece, from half a dozen to a hundred Jew's harps are necessary—In the old barn dances, about all the men would carry Jew's harps in their vest pockets or in the calf of their boots . . .

Of the *Washington's Birthday* movement, he wrote:

> "Cold and Solitude," says Thoreau, "are friends of mine. Now is the time before the wind rises to go forth and see the snow on the trees." And there is at times a bleakness, without stir but penetrating, in a New England midwinter, which settles down grimly when the day closes over the broken hills. In such a scene it is as though nature would but could not easily trace a certain beauty in the sombre landscape—in the quiet but restless monotony! Would nature reflect the sternness of the Puritan's fibre or the self-sacrificing part of his ideals?

> The older folks "sit the clean wing'd hearth about,
> > shut in from all the world without,
> > content to let the north wind roar
> > in baffled rage at pane and door . . ."

> But to the younger generation, a winter holiday means action!—and down through "Swamp Hollow" and over the hill road they go, afoot or in sleighs, through the drifting snow, to the barn dance at Brookfield Centre. The village band of fiddles, fife and horn keep up an unending "break-down" medley, and the young folks "salute their partners and balance corners" till mid-

night;—as the party breaks up, the sentimental songs of those days are sung, half in fun, half seriously, and with the inevitable "adieu to the ladies," the social gives way to the grey bleakness of the February night . . .

In November, Ives began two other new orchestral works; and, on November 11, went to a symphony concert at Carnegie Hall—the Boston Symphony Orchestra under Max Fiedler in a program of Reger, Brahms, and Richard Strauss.

Concert-going was rare for Ives. He was jealous of the time taken away from his own writing, and found listening to unfamiliar music tended to confuse his own musical ideas:

> Hearing the old pieces that I'd been familiar with all my life (e.g. the Beethoven and Brahms symphonies, Bach, or even the *William Tell* Overture, &c) did not have this effect. But I remember hearing something by Max Reger ((*Symphonic Prologue to a Tragedy*))— and when I got back to what I was working on, I was conscious of a kind of interference or lapse—something as you feel when writing a letter and someone butts in and reads their letter to you while you're trying to write yours . . . At any rate, I found I could work more naturally and with more concentration if I didn't hear much music, especially unfamiliar music . . . if I'd had more time for my own music, quite probably I wouldn't have felt this way. But when people take it as a matter of course that I know such and such music, such and such a symphony, and I tell them I don't, they seem so surprised . . .

The two new pieces Ives was working on when he went to that Carnegie Hall concert:

(1) *An Elegy To Stephen Foster*, originally conceived as an independent overture, then as the first movement/2nd Orchestral Set, retitled *An Elegy To Our Forefathers*.

((The music is proliferate with the alternating minor-third figure— "I'm coming"—from Foster's *Old Black Joe*. CI found a natural association between the Founding Fathers of New England—and/or First Fathers of Virginia—and Stephen Foster as the Founding Father of American music.))

    (2) *The Black March: "St Gaudens"*—conceived and executed as the first movement/1st Orchestral Set (*3 New England Places*). The subject of the music is the statue, by Augustus St Gaudens, of Col Shaw and the 54th Regiment of Black Contrabands, on Boston Common.

((This is also proliferate with the "I'm coming" figure. CI first intended the middle movement of *3 Places* to be a musical portrait of Wendell Phillips, a prominent Abolitionist, and "the mob at Faneuil Hall . . ."))

Although the first dated sketches of the *Black March* are not until the summer of 1911, Ives must have started work on it in November 1909, or very shortly afterwards. A few months later he had to "yank back a page of the *Black March*" before showing Walter Damrosch the score of his 1st Symphony. It was very typical of him to have new music tucked in among the pages of an old score.

    On March 19 1910, Damrosch devoted his Saturday-morning rehearsal with the New York Symphony to reading through the last three movements of the 1st Symphony—"not the first movement," said Ives, "which went through too many keys . . ." ((Parker's criticism, and he sensed that Damrosch would be of like mind.)) Ives found Damrosch's praise—to Mrs Ives—the right words coming from the wrong person. As such inacceptable. "This instrumentation is remarkable, and the workmanship is admirable . . ." But Damrosch had already given himself away, in Ives's estimation:

> He started with the slow movement—*Adagio*—an English horn tune over chords in the strings. When he heard the pretty little theme and the nice chords, he called out "Charming!" . . .

Yet Ives sent him the newly copied score of his 2nd Symphony. And Damrosch supposedly mislaid it. It has never since come to light. ((A later score of the 2nd Symphony, reconstructed from the orchestra parts and published in that form, contains several mysterious "improvements" certainly never sanctioned by Ives. The greater mystery: why the original MS, in Ives's possession, or the photostat copies were never consulted when a new score had to be made . . . ))

    The rehearsal reading of the 1st Symphony under Damrosch

had another aftermath. Reconstructing the available evidence, what must have happened is this . . .

A member of the New York Philharmonic had been moonlighting at the Saturday-morning reading by the New York Symphony, was impressed with the Ives, and told Gustav Mahler, the Philharmonic's conductor. Mahler, on the look-out for new American music, telephoned Mrs Ives, who directed him to Tams' Copying Bureau on West 28th Street. The score of the 2nd Symphony had already been sent to Damrosch, the score of the 1st had not yet come back. Mahler saw the newly copied score of the 3rd Symphony (revised version), and asked to take it. William Tams, overawed that someone of Mahler's reputation should take an interest in his liberal but eccentric client's work, let it go without a murmur. The score went, that summer, back with Mahler to Munich, where he was giving concerts, including the first performance of his own 8th Symphony. At some juncture there was at least a reading of the Ives 3rd. And the "lost score" may be in Munich to the present day.

In the fall of 1954 I went to a concert at the Deutsches Museum, Munich, with a Bavarian ancient, Messerklinger by name. He was a retired timpanist who, in his youth, had played under Mahler at the Museum concerts. The program, given by an American conductor, included an *"erste Ausführung"* of the Ives 3rd Symphony. ((German makes a distinction between *"erste Ausführung"*—first performance in a specific locality—and *"Urausführung"*—first performance anywhere. The *Urausführung* of the 3rd Symphony was at Carnegie Chamber Hall, New York, April 5 1946 under Lou Harrison.)) As we left the concert, old Messerklinger kept shaking his head at the program in his hand, muttering *"das stimmt nicht"* ("that isn't true")—*" 's war keine erste Ausführung"* ("it wasn't a first performance at all"). So he said, the old man had played the symphony under Mahler in the summer of 1910. I suggested it might have been another, similar work, but he held his ground. The performance we had heard was from the published score and orchestral parts—no timpani (though there is an optional timpani part), the part for bells (marked *ad libitum* in the published score) omitted. I taxed him by asking if he had played timpani. *"Nein, nein!"* he shouted. *"Ich 'rinnere mich ganz klar—i' hab' Glocken g'spielt— ganz am Schluss—Dreiklänge waren's, gegen 'was vollkommen an-*

*der's i' Streicher* . . ." ("No, no!—I remember perfectly well—I played the bells—right at the end—triads they were, against something completely different in the strings . . .") *"Unheimlich war's"* ("it was uncanny") he added quietly. Then grinned, *"jede meinten i' hab' falsch g'schlagen!"* ("everyone thought I was playing the wrong notes!"). Old Messerklinger's knowledge that an optional bells part even existed, that it was "right at the end," that its effect was "uncanny" and his colleagues thought he was playing "wrong notes"— all this seems conclusive evidence that a performance—or at least a reading—of the Ives 3rd took place under Mahler in Munich.

If this was true, it meant that the individual parts of the symphony had to have been copied out. Mrs Sidney Cowell—who is wholly skeptical—has said that an account of the copying expenses would certainly have come to light among Ives's papers. Whether this is so certain, seeing the disarray his papers and MSS were found in after he died, Mrs Cowell would certainly know. What is quite certain, a practicing musician's sense of philanthropy in 1910 extended to assuming the expense of having parts copied for an unknown American colleague. In the absence of an interested publisher, it was, and is, often the only way of bringing an unknown work to performance—short of sending the composer a copying bill, which Mahler would not have dreamt of doing. Copying fees were minimal in those days, in any case, and the 3rd Symphony is a work of modest proportions. More important, copyists in those days were—still are— impoverished composers themselves, for the most part. Schoenberg, Berg, and Webern all did copying in their younger days. And in copying out the parts of his 3rd Symphony, Ives's style would have been disseminated among unknown composers in the heart of reactionary central Europe—something that would have appealed immensely to Ives's sense of humor, could he have known it . . .

*Jan 1 1910:* Julian Southall Myrick marries Marion Washburn. Charles Ives is best man.

*April 21:* With the return of "The Mysterious Stranger"— Halley's Comet—which had heralded his birth, Mark Twain dies, aged 74, at Stormfield, his house in Redding.

*April 22:* Harmony's mother, Harmony Cushman Twichell, aged 66, dies suddenly the night after Mark Twain's funeral.

Summer vacation—again at Elk Lake, at Pell Jones's—was "filled with silences." Harmony wrote the poem "Mists," which Ives set to music: "Low lie the mists, they hide each hill and dell . . ." ((later no 57 of *114 Songs*)), adding the marginalia:

last mist at Pell's    Sept 20 1910    H Poeta

((CI later referred to this setting for the mist-like opening of *The Fourth of July.*))

Also at Elk Lake, the preliminary sketches of the first movement/4th Symphony and the Hawthorne movement/*Concord* Sonata. And—the revised version now in Munich, with Mahler—the labor of getting out a third version of the 3rd Symphony, based on the original 1904 score . . .

((After they moved to Redding, in 1913, Ives wrote on the title page:

Symphony No 3 ("The Camp Meeting") (Score-sketch) Three
movements 1. "Old Folks gatherin'" 2. "Children's Day"
3. "Communion"   return if lost (eternally or not) to Chas E Ives
Redding/Conn. written between 1901/12   finished summers at
Elk Lake 1910/11   rescored copy 1909—see ink copy 1910 in safe
51 Liberty Street . . .

But 51 Liberty Street had been the address of Ives & Co—left when it folded in 1908. Munich had become 2 years' distant, in Ives's mind . . . ))

All copied, in 1910—the First Piano Sonata:

What is it all about—Dan S asks. Mostly about the outdoor life
in Conn villages in '80s and '90s. Impressions, Remembrances, and
Reflections, of Country Farmers in Conn Farmland. Fred's Daddy
got so excited he shouted when Fred hit a Home Run & the school
won the baseball game but Aunt Sarah was always humming—
Where is my wandering Boy—after Fred an' John left for a job
in Bridgeport—there was usually a sadness—but not at the Barn
Dances with its jigs, foot jumping, & reels mostly on winter nights.
In the Summer times, the Hymns were sung outdoors; Folks sang—
as ole Black Joe—& the Bethel Band—Quickstep Street March, &
The People liked things as they wanted to say and things as they
wanted to do in their own way—and many old times there were
feelings, and a spiritual Fervency . . .

This, then, the impetus that urges Ives's later works. Not a childish relay of cornball images—that is what they have become—but a childlike observance of vernacular ritual, of the reality of fantasy, the reality of free association and its power of invocation . . . It was inevitable that he should be drawn, at the last, to Hawthorne, "the greater artist."

The idea of the *Concord* Sonata had first been conceived at Saranac Lake, summer of 1907. First mention of the Hawthorne movement—together with the projected second movement/4th Symphony, and the unfinished/lost *Hawthorne* Piano Concerto—had been the summer of 1910. In April 1911, Ives began in earnest:

> Piano Sonata No 2 "Concord Mass 1850" 2nd movt "Hawthorne" (sketch of Concerto in safe 37 Liberty Street) started Apr 1911 70 W 11

In February, he had still been working on the *Emerson* Overture. One leaf of MS from the *Concord* Sonata has the marginalia:

> to Cadenza 6 of Feb 22 '11 ((Washington's Birthday . . . ))

The association between the *Concord* Sonata, *4 New England Holidays,* the 4th Symphony, and the 1st Orchestral Set grew more pronounced. In March he finished the third (fugal) movement/4th Symphony. By the beginning of April he was back working on the 1st Orchestral Set:

> Bass Brigham, Yale '97 and a violinist ((former member of the New Haven Orchestra, under Parker)) called on us at 70 West 11th Street sometime before the spring of 1911. I was then working on *The Housatonic At Stockbridge* and played it for him. He said, "well, that's a funny-sounding collection of sounds—your tonality and your chord relations are more wobbly than Cesar Franck's, which are bad enough." I got him to play over the first violin part of the third movement of the Third Symphony. He got all mixed up and called it NG, but he seemed to like some of the Second Symphony, which we tried over. (Compare these two scores, and you can easily see why . . .

On May 2 1911 Charles and Harmony Ives left the apartment at 70 West 11th Street that had been their bridal home, and rented a small house in Hartsdale, near White Plains/N Y, from Edward Hamilton Whitman. The same day, the Metropolitan Opera announced the award of their $10,000 opera prize to Dr Horatio William Parker, for his opera *Mona* . . .

# Hartsdale

60 years ago, Hartsdale was a village of less than 500 people, its oldest inhabitants the giant elm and cedar trees, ash, maple, locust and spruce, that had stood there, aloof and undisturbed, since before the coming of white men. Today, blight, and the pollution of a town grown to more than 20,000 have taken most of the elms, industry the maple and spruce. But dense woods of cedar still abound along Ridge Road, and crowd Hillcrest Road down to Hart's Corners. Ives's first Hartsdale house stood on Ridge Road, near the house of the Odell family, loyalists, which was confiscated and used as Rochambeau's headquarters during the Revolutionary War. Below the ridge, south of Hart's Corners on Central Avenue, is the farmhouse used by Rochambeau's chief-of-staff. And to the west, down by the Hudson River at Dobb's Wherry, the house used as Washington's headquarters during the planning of the Yorktown campaign. Also by Dobb's Wherry—Indian Hill, camping ground, till the late 18th century, of the Wiequeskek Indian. And back near Hart's Corners, crouched below the cedars on Hillcrest Road—Scilly Rock, site of the old Methodist Church built in 1832, and the rockstrewn meadow where the Camp Meetings were held, "Methodies" coming from as far as Tarrytown, Yonkers, Turkey-ho, and New Rochelle.

Ives had known of Hartsdale since Poverty Flat days at 65 Central Park West—perhaps even at West 58th Street. Thomas Healey, who had the restaurant on Columbus Avenue at 66th Street, owned a chicken farm on Old Army Road, Scarsdale—just south of Hartsdale—and later opened a high-class caravanserai, "The May/November Farm," on Central Avenue. His brother John was Poverty Flat's landlord at their first address, 317 West 58th Street.

Hartsdale—and more especially its railroad station—has its name from Eleazar Hart, a substantial landowner whose family had lived in the area for generations. In 1843 the New York & Harlem RR proposed extending its tracks to White Plains, and when Hart learned that they planned to cross his property, he sent word to the company's officers that he would deed them the land *gratis*, wholly satisfied the railroad would benefit the community at large. It was from Hartsdale Station that Charles Ives left, each morning, by the 7.59 train for the City. Harmony used to drive him there in their light-green surrey, drawn by Rocket, and meet him off the 6.17 in the evening.

After the move to Hartsdale, the copying instructions on Ives's MSS all carry the office address of Ives & Myrick—this, for clear practical reasons, and because he did not want the business side of music to intrude on his seclusion at Hartsdale. Though he enjoyed telling William Tams, and business colleagues, that he was living in "Whitman's house," and letting them think he meant Walt Whitman. But with the years at Hartsdale—May to November 1911, April 1912 to June 1914—came the emergence of the grand design in his composition: all but one of his greatest works were started and/or finished there.

*State of Ives's Works from May 1911, Aged 36:*

(1) *Decoration Day*. First mention. Completed in score-sketch, May 1911—probably on May 30, Memorial Day: CI had a penchant for starting or finishing pieces on appropriate anniversaries or holidays. Designed as the second of *4 New England Holidays*, which he then saw as his "Fourth" Symphony:

II Decoration Day (in New England 1880) for Set of New England "Holidays" (Symphony No 4) . . .

and the program note:

> In the early morning the gardens and woods around the village are the meeting places for those who, with tender memories and devoted hands, gather the flowers for the Day's Memorial. During the forenoon as the people join each other on the Green there is felt, at times, a fervency and intensity—a shadow, perhaps, of the fanatical harshness—reflecting old Abolitionist days. It is a day as Thoreau suggests, when there is a pervading consciousness of "Nature's kinship with the lower order—Man."
>
> After the Town Hall is filled with the Spring's harvest of lilacs, daisies and peonies, the parade is slowly formed on Main Street. First come the three Marshals on plough horses (going sideways), then the Warden and Burgesses *in carriages*, the Village Cornet Band, the G A R, two by two, the Militia (Company G), while the Volunteer Fire Brigade, drawing the decorated hose-cart, with its jangling bells, brings up the rear—the inevitable swarm of small boys following. The march to Wooster Cemetery is a thing a boy never forgets. The roll of muffled drums and "Adeste fidelis" answer for the dirge. A little girl on the fencepost waves at her father and wonders if he looked like that at Gettysburg.
>
> After the last grave is decorated, "Taps" sound through the pines and hickories, while a last hymn is sung. Then the ranks are formed again and "we all march back to Town" to a Yankee stimulant— Reeves' inspiring "Second Regiment Quick-Step,"—though to many a soldier, the sombre thoughts of the day underlie the tune of the band. The march stops—and in the silence, the echo of the early morning flower-song rises over the Town and the sunset behind Pine Mountain breathes its benediction upon the Day . . .

((Among "the sombre thoughts" that intrude on the essential gaiety of the march, (1) a distorted phrase from the chorus of *John Brown's Body*, screamed out by oboes and E-flat clarinet; and (2) the continuing re-echo of "Taps" within the orchestral fabric. It is not so difficult to make either of these events audible in performance— if CI's dynamics are observed—but I have never heard them from any other conductor. In fact, they seem to be deliberately suppressed, as "compromising" and "subversive" elements . . . ))

(2) In June, two pieces for chamber orchestra—"with or without voices"—completed in sketch:

(i) on June 4, Harmony's 35th birthday, *The Last Reader*, for trumpet, 2 violas, and organ (later adapted to the words of Oliver Wendell Holmes, as no 3 of *114 Songs*)); and

(ii) *The Ruined River*, for 2 clarinets, 2 trumpets, trombone, percussion, piano, and strings:

Back from Zoar Bridge   Gas machine kills Housatonic!   June 9th 1911

This was towards a projected series of six pieces that was to form the 1st Chamber Orchestra Set, and already included *A Lecture* (September 1907), *Like A Sick Eagle* (April 1909), *Calcium Light Night* (September 1907), and *Allegretto sombreoso* (*c* 1909, later adapted to the words of Byron's "Incantation" ((no 18 of *114 Songs*))). Ives already had words for *The Ruined River* in mind when he sketched it, and later added them to the score, transferring the scene to the Connecticut Valley and underlining his ecological concern:

> Down the river comes a noise!
> It is not the sound of rolling waters
> It's only the sounds of Man
> Dancing halls and tambourine
> Phonograph and gasoline
> Human beings gone machine
> ta-ra-ra-BOOM-de-ay . . .
> KILLED is the blare of the hunting horn
> The River Gods are gone . . .

((later arranged for voice & piano, under the title *The New River*, as no 6 of *114 Songs*.))

(3) *The Fourth of July*, begun July 4 1911, as third of *4 New England Holidays*. On page 1 of the score-sketch, the title:

IV Symphony (or Set no 1 for Orchestra)
III "Fourth of July" (a boy's "4th of July" in these here you Knighted States) . . .

((NB The *3 New England Places* which ultimately made up the 1st
Orchestral Set were none of them complete, though all had been
started in sketch. CI was beginning to have second thoughts about
the viability of calling the *4 New England Holidays* a symphony,
and so toyed with the idea of calling them his 1st Orchestral Set. On
a page of sketch for *Decoration Day:*

> Orchestral Set . . . Holiday Symphony—
> but not called Sym as 1st theme is not in C
>                    & 2nd   *"*   *"*   *"*    G    So Rollo!

Also on page 1 of the *4th Of July* score-sketch, above, right, added
later:

> Started 1911 from chords in "Cage" *c* 1905 . . .

((*In The Cage*, first movement/Theater Orchestra Set))

> . . . in Whitman's little house   Hartsdale—Sally came out one
> hot 4th of July—Rocket sick . . .

Above, left, later still:

> Mr Price: Please don't try to make things nice! All the wrong notes
> are *right*. Just copy as I have—I want it that way . . .

and on page 5 of the score-sketch:

> Band-stuff—they didn't always play right & together & it was as
> good either way   For instance—above is just harmony—a "take
> off" of a country boy's "4th"   Here the main key is B♭ but out
> in B♯—viola A♮ up & down . . . Cornets get B♭ & A shanks mixed
> up, off notes *p*—right notes *ff* . . . be sure cornet & any brass
> playing off-key to mark *p* for off notes & *ff* for on notes . . .

The descriptive notes came later—much later—after CI revised
the score again in 1920:

> . . . it's a boy's "4th"—no historical orations, no patriotic gran-
> diloquences by "grown-ups"—no program in his back yard! But
> he knows what he's celebrating—better than most country politi-
> cians. And he goes at it in his own way, with a patriotism nearer
> kin to nature than to jingoism. His festivities start in the quiet of

the midnight before, and grow raucous with the sun. Everybody knows what it's like—if everybody doesn't, they should—Cannon on the Green, Village Band on Main Street, fire crackers, shanks mixed up on cornets, strings around big toes, torpedoes, church bells, lost finger, fifes, clam-chowder, a prize-fight, drum corps, burnt shins, parades (in and out of step), saloons all closed (more drunks than usual), baseball game (Danbury All-Stars *vs* Beaver Brook Boys), pistols, mobbed umpire, Red, White & Blue, runaway horse,—and the day ends with the sky-rocket over the Church steeple, just after the annual explosion sets the Town Hall on fire. All this is not in the music—not now . . .

((A boy's "4th," yes—but a small boy exceeding wise, versed in the music of nuclear physics, the sound of a bursting nova a thousand light years ago. And the marvelous sudden silence of the secret ending, that "only children are old enough to understand . . .")）

    (4) *Concord* Sonata:
      (i) *Emerson* movement, in progress;
      (ii) *Hawthorne* movement, in progress;
      (iii) *The Alcotts* movement, already existing in the form of the *Orchard House* Overture (1902/04), transcribed for piano—"but a page"—between 1912/14;
      (iv) *Thoreau* movement, begun at 70 West 11th Street, continued at Hartsdale—some sketches on the verso of sketches for *The 4th Of July*—finished May 30 (Decoration Day) 1915:

      from some ideas—Walden sounds, Ch bells, flute, Aeolian harp— to go with Harmony's Mist (Elk Lake 1910) . . .

    (5) 1st Orchestral Set ("3 New England Places"):
      (i) *The Black March* ("St Gaudens"), in progress;
      (ii) *General Putnam's Camp*, in progress since 1908:

      Wanted in these you-beknighted states! more independence election day    1908 . . .

      (iii) *The Housatonic At Stockbridge*, in progress . . .

    (6) 2nd Orchestral Set:
      (i) *Elegy To Our Forefathers*, completed;

(ii)  *The Rockstrewn Hills,* completed;

(iii)  third movement not begun till May 7 1915 . . .

(7)  *Robert Browning* Overture, nearing completion in its first state, which lacked a middle section, reprise of main section, and extension of coda:

> Browning was too big a man to rest in one nice little key, in his inward toughness & strength he walked on the mountains, not down a nice proper little aisle . . . R B is called obscure, indefinite, &c just because his system of contemplation and thinking didn't jibe with the usual—his mental workmanship is as sound, logical & strong as easier plans Rollo likes . . . His mind has many roads, not always easy to follow—the ever flowing, changing, growing ways of mind & imagination—over the great unchanging truths of life & not death . . .

September 16/October 6 1911 was spent, once again, at Pell Jones' hotel on Elk Lake. At the foot of page 3, score-sketch, first movement/4th Symphony:

> The "Eternal Question" Watchman What of the Night Pells Sep 24  1911

((This, the Prelude of the 4th Symphony, was the "Horns & Strings Piece" started "at suggestion of DCT Saranac Lake 1905 . . ."; also derived from the "organ & soprano song" done at the Central Presbyterian YMCA service in 1901—used again in 1907, in the third movement/1st Violin Sonata . . . ))

And below measures 141/150, *Browning* Overture sketch:

> Pells  Oct  1911

They returned from Elk Lake via Pittsfield/Mass, calling on Harmony's "Uncle Albert"—Albert Sprague—and his daughter, Mrs Sprague Coolidge. Here Ives made the acquaintance of Edgar Stowell, a violinist who was conductor of the school orchestra at the Mannes Music Settlement, on West 3rd Street. Harmony discreetly took Mrs Coolidge for a drive, and Ives played Stowell part of the *Black March*—now almost complete. But Stowell wouldn't let him finish—"said it sounded awful . . . " He did like some of the

Second Symphony, though, and later played the first movement at one of his school concerts.

((Stowell must have performed this from the copyist's score—the score that has mysteriously vanished—so Walter Damrosch had returned it after all . . . ))

Back in Hartsdale, Ives finished the Hawthorne movement/ *Concord* Sonata on October 12—Columbus Day. On the title page of the sketch:

Piano Sonata No 2   "Concord   Mass   1850"
Hawthorne movement started April 1911, ended Oct 12 1911

and at the end of the ink copy:

Finet    Oct 12    1911    to celebrate

The weekend before Thanksgiving, the Iveses moved back to New York City, renting an apartment at 118 Waverly Place, just down the street from where Harmony's father had lived, back in 1859, after his graduation from Yale. There, and at Waverly Place, his roommate had been Edward Carrington, killed fighting with the Confederate Army in the early days of the Civil War. He occupied a place in young Twichell's affection equal to Mark Twain's in later life, and his first son—Harmony's eldest brother—had been named Edward Carrington Twichell. He, in turn, was a character who had appealed immensely to Ives ever since their first meeting, at Yale, in 1897, when he came over to see his brother David. The score of *Thanksgiving* is dedicated to him:

"Thanksgiving or Forefathers Day"
IV movement N E "Holidays" (this is a nice piece
of turkey—Eddy!)
& dedicated to E C T    Centre Church    New Haven
Thanksgiving 1897    put in this piece Aug 1904 . . .

Thanksgiving had always been observed in the Ives family as a return to the first meaning of the holiday—America's Forefathers giving thanks for their first fruitful harvest at Plymouth Plantation, August 1622. It was inherent in the state motto of Connecticut—*qui transtulit sustinet* ("which being transplanted, sustains")—as much applying to the first seed that was sown as to the first settlers themselves. For Thanksgiving 1911, Ives wrote *Requiem*, a setting of Robert Louis Stevenson's text:

> . . . Home is the sailor, home from the sea,
> And the hunter home from the hill . . .

((This was before CI read Stevenson's attack on Thoreau . . .

Christmas 1911 was spent in Danbury, and here Ives finished writing *The Gong On The Hook And Ladder*, for chamber orchestra:

> . . . The Annual Parade of the neighborhood Volunteer Fire Company was a slow marching affair—for the Hook & Ladder was heavy, and the Gong on the hind wheel "must ring steady-like"—and coming downhill and holding backward fast, and going uphill out of step, fast and slow, the Gong sometimes seemed out of step with the Band, and sometimes the Band out of step with the Gong—but the Gong usually got the best of it . . . another nice joke, which most everybody can see except a nice, routine conductor (near musician), who plays the notes "right" and beats time serious and nice, but doesn't place the music at all . . .

((A "nice joke"—of course. But the joke over, there is still an undercurrent instinct with fear, an association with *From The Steeples*, when fire had descended from Pine Mountain . . . ))

At the head of the first page of MS sketch:

> Space or Duration Rhythm measure of this space = $\frac{7}{8}$ = 1    a gong or bell or drum may strike this all through . . .

*En Passant:*

> *March 12 1912:* première of Horatio Parker's opera, *Mona*, at the Metropolitan. Runs for five performances and is dropped.
> *March 23:* official banquet for Parker at Sherry's, *c* 80 guests, acknowledges Parker's gain of a pawn with a pawn . . .

Charles and Harmony Ives moved back to Hartsdale on April 5, now renting a larger house from Mr Edward Hamilton Whitman. During their absence, they learned later, Commander Evangeline Booth, daughter of General William Booth of the Salvation Army, had taken a house nearby . . .

Ives was now working on the final, extensive revision of the *Browning* Overture. The first extant page of sketch—written December 21 1908, the day Mutual appointed him senior partner of Ives & Myrick—had the marginalia: "steppin' nice, backwoods &c (but now to serious purpose) . . ." At that time, every prospect of a family, and the desire to have some backwoods of their own. He had been living in rented houses and apartments ever since Yale—following Thoreau's dictum, that it is simpler to get milk from the dairy than own your own cow. Now, with no prospect of a family, Ives, with Thoreau, was aware of the peculiar enslavement that accrued to the property-owner, was wary and chary of getting into it. Still, if the daughter of the Salvation Army evangelist could build herself a house in Hartsdale, a successful insurance agent might buy some land somewhere, against his own retirement.

The middle section of the *Browning* Overture was already written, now involving a reprise of the main section. This, in turn, involved an extension of the existing coda. The inspiration for that —measures 312/320 in the final score—came as the result of a Sunday-afternoon walk with his youngest nephew, Moss White Ives, aged 7, along Ridge Road, down to Sprain Brook and over to Saw Mill River:

> "The Forest joins the Services and lifts its Voices and marks its choruses of waving limbs by its many rhythms" after a walk with Moss White   Hartsdale   July 1912 . . .

and below the same measures in the full-score sketch:

> "The Forest ends its Communion with men
> The Elms & Cedars end their songs . . ."

Finally, the second week of August, Ives bought some property on Umpawaug Road, by West Redding—14¾ acres of undeveloped hillside—from a local farmer, Francis Ryder. But he still was cautious, and building was not put in progress till the following spring.

By the end of August, the Emerson movement/*Concord* Sonata and the *Black March* were finished. In September they joined David Twichell and his wife on Saranac Lake. Below measure 53 of the full-score of the *Black March*:

Franklin Carter Esq asked me to whistle this measure—no smile Saranac Lake NY Sep 12 1912 . . .

The *Black March* complete in full score, *The Housatonic At Stockbridge* in an advanced state of sketch, Ives saw that they formed the outer panels of a New England triptych—that *Putnam's Camp,* started "election day 1908" (("wanted—in these you-beknighted states—more independence")), was the clear central panel. By Columbus Day 1912, the full-score of *Putnam's Camp* was finished, and he now came to regard the three pieces as his 1st Orchestral Set.

Ives's sense of social, musical, and political indignation—never far from flashpoint—was roused by three incidents in October/ November 1912. They shared common ground, for him, in reflecting three facets of the establishment, THE SYSTEM:

(1) the murder trial, in October, of Harry Horowitz, alias "Gyp the Blood";

(2) a visit to Hartsdale by Max Smith, a classmate of CI's at Yale, now music critic for the New York *Press;* &

(3) the three-cornered Presidential Election.

Horowitz had been charged with the sensational murder, on July 13 1912, of Hermann Rosenthal, sent for trial, convicted, and sentenced to death. Somehow Ives contrived to sketch some music, intended for band, under the title *"Gyp The Blood" or Hearst ? Which Is Worst ?* Later he said he could make out the reason for this piece politically, socially, better than musically . . . " Below the few extant measures of sketch:

Gyp, a prominent criminal, (legally) gets the gallows—Hearst, another prominent criminal, (not legally) gets the money. Hearst's newspapers make Gyps. He sells sensational bunk to the soft-eared soft-headed, and headlines and pictures that excite interest in criminal life among the weak-brained and defectives. An old-fashioned horse-thief is a respectable man compared to Hearst. When the American people put Hearst with the horse-thief, "on the rope," American history will have another landmark to go with Bunker Hill, and perhaps a new song to go with *The Battle Cry Of Freedom* . . .

The music, then, abortive; the sentiment, acknowledged or not, universal: Hearsts and their ilk wear a haunted, soulless look. Here, both music and sentiment were sublimated into a piece, sketched on the verso of "*Gyp The Blood*," rich in social/political overtones —*Largo: "The Indians*," for basset-horn, bassoon, Indian drum, piano, & strings. A miniature masterpiece of greater stature, even, than *The Pond*—greater, because its nostalgia is neither personal, nor national, but universal. Ives followed the text of Charles Sprague's poem, written in 1838, for the instrumental setting, later arranged for voice & piano ((no 14 of *114 Songs*)):

> Alas! for them their day is o'er,
> No more for them the wild deer bounds,
> The plough is on their hunting grounds,
> The pale man's axe rings through their woods,
> The pale man's sail skims o'er their floods;
> Beyond the mountains of the west,
> Their children go to die . . .

The second incident—Max Smith's visit to Hartsdale with his wife Mary . . . Ives played him some of the 3rd Symphony, the *Black March, Putnam's Camp*, the Hawthorne movement/*Concord* Sonata, part of the second movement/4th Symphony:

> After I'd finished, Max, who had gone out on the stoop, said, "That first one was bad enough, but these were awful! How *can* you like horrible sounds like that ? And it's even worse than you were 10 years ago . . . "

Max Smith and David Stanley Smith were good friends of his, of long standing—so long as they kept off the subject of music. Here, Ives classed them with Clara Mannes and Elizabeth Sprague Coolidge:

> Their motto: "All things have a right to live and grow, even babies and music schools, but not *music* . . . "

The third incident—a source of negative indignation, prompting the sketch *Vote For Names:*

> After trying to think what's the best way to vote—I say—just walk right in & grab a ballot with eyes shut & walk right out again!

> Vote for Names! Names! Names! all nice men!!! 3 nice men Teddy Woodrow & Bill   $ame $ame $ame

Same chord hit hard over & over   Hot Air Election Memo   This, this or this ???   A sad chord—a hopeless chord—a chord of futility—$ame 3   After leaving polls on Nat'l Election Day 1912 walking back over Healey Chicken Farm . . .

Social/political issues continued to preoccupy through December:

(1) "Men of Literature" Overtures   No 3 "Matthew Arnold" (for orchestra & unison voices)

7 night job!   Dec 9/15   1912
(1 week Job Done—Good or Bad ? But not all done . . .)

((This has been lost, but seems to have been complete in the score-sketch state, with "1st part a London street band . . ."))

(2) *Lincoln, The Great Commoner*, for orchestra & (((mostly))) unison voices, a setting of Edward Markham's poem. Stands beside *General William Booth* as Ives's greatest chorus & orchestra piece. Dedicated to David Twichell.

((The last 7 measures of the *Lincoln* music are used again at the end of one of CI's last works—*An Election: "Nov 2 1920"*—against the words:

"O Captain, my Captain! a heritage we've thrown away . . ."))

At the end of January 1913, Ives and his wife took her father up to a mental sanatorium in Brattleboro/Vermont for a month's observation. Joseph Twichell had retired from Asylum Hill Church, Hartford, a few months earlier, at the age of 74, and now his mind was beginning to disintegrate. Harmony stayed there with him the whole month—"the longest I was ever away from Charlie"—and Ives took the train up to see them whenever he could. He recalled that William Tams sent some of his pieces up there for proofreading, "and by mistake one of them was opened by a patient, who looked quite worried . . ." But most of the month, for Ives, had to be spent at the office, commuting, as usual, from Hartsdale. One Saturday afternoon—February 22—he took himself to Carnegie Hall, to hear Karl Muck conducting the Boston Symphony in a program of Bach, Beethoven, Brahms, and Mozart—Symphony in G minor K550, his father's favorite work . . .

In April, a piece for piano quintet, with optional bass drum—*In Re Con Moto Et Al.* On page 1 of the MS sketch:

Studies in Space, accent & pulse Rhythms
Mr Greinert    Copy only from sign    Will come up Monday about
5 & explain

on page 2:

> . . . personally I wouldn't have the bass drum played except at
> rehearsal—listeners ought to be able to keep time fundamentals in
> mind . . .

on page 3:

> gets faster & *fff* as possible to end:     end Bang!
> Hartsdale NY    Apr 13    1913

In May, a piece for trumpet, clarinet, alto horn, piano, and drums, *Scherzo: "The Se'er"*   designed as the first of the series of six (the other 5 already written) forming the 1st Chamber Set. As usual, Ives had a text in mind when he wrote the piece, and later arranged it for voice & piano ((no 29 of *114 Songs*)).

And in August, the first sketch of the Piano Phantasy, *"The Celestial Railroad,"* based on material from three sources: (1) the Hawthorne movement/*Concord* Sonata; (2) the second movement/ 4th Symphony; and (3) the lost *Hawthorne* Piano Concerto. A leaf of sketch for *"The Celestial Railroad"* has:

> from Piano Concerto    Aug 20    1913
> see copy in safe    I & M    38 Nassau

((The offices of Ives & Myrick moved from 37 Liberty Street to 38 Nassau Street on February 1 1914, and stayed there till the end of April 1923. By that time, there was no trace of the *Hawthorne* Concerto . . . ))

Also in August . . .

*Two Slants—Christian & Pagan*

. . . this the result of hearing Daniel McCurry preach a guest sermon on the contrast between Christian and Stoic ideals, at Hartsdale Methodist Church, August 17 1913:

> (a) *Duty,* for male chorus & orchestra, a setting of two lines
>     from Emerson—"quoted by Rev Mr McCurry in sermon
>     this AM . . ."

(b) *Vita*, for unison chorus & organ—"using 32′ stop"—a setting of a line from Manlius' "Astronomica": "Nascentes morimur finisque ab origine pendet . . ."

*Between August 1913 and February 1914:*

(1) At least the sketch of a *Walt Whitman* Overture, as the next in the "Men of Literature" series. On the pencil sketch of the 1921 setting, for voice & piano, of lines from *Song Of Myself* ((no 31 of *114 Songs*)), the note:

Sec XX page 49    Leaves of Grass    Redding shelf
Orchestra Score 1913    see score in 38 Nassau safe

and added later:

can't find score—not with papers in office or in Redding . . .

(2) *December*, for unison chorus, piccolo, 2 clarinets, 2 horns, 3 trumpets, 3 trombones, tuba, and basses, to the Rossetti translation of a text by Folgore di San Geminiano. On the title page:

"A Winter Orgy    Rossetti    Baccanalia    December"
(by 101 drunken mobs)
Mr Price: Please copy Picc clar etc on separate lines as I telephoned today. Will come up Saturday & explain    C E Ives    37 Liberty

(3) *The Masses*, for chorus & orchestra—at least as far as the state of the 1st page of full-score:

Mr Greinert: Please copy up to end of measure 4    will send up more tomorrow PM    C E Ives    4th floor    37 Liberty Street

But by page 9, the date: "Dec 28 1914 . . ." By then, Europe was at war, and the near-Marxist expression of Ives's own text had found a sudden, desperate sanction. On page 11:

The Masses are on the blink!    Eddie!
They get it in the NECKO!!

On January 12 1914, *The Independent* printed a review of Vachel Lindsay's "General William Booth Enters Heaven"—the Salvation Army evangelist had died the year before—and Ives at once got to work on a setting, for solo baritone, chorus, and brass band. This, together with *The Housatonic At Stockbridge* and the last movement/4th Symphony, occupied him till the summer. In June, they left Hartsdale, and West Redding became their permanent address. A month later, Sarajevo . . .

## ADDENDA

*May 30 1914:* CI plays Piano Study No 5 for Max Smith:

Decoration Day at Hartsdale—Max sidesteps . . .

*June 4:* CI completes *The Rainbow*, for basset-horn, flute, celesta, organ, and strings:

to H T I   on her first birthday in Redding . . .

*July 3:* CI plays Piano Study No 4 at a concert in Redding, the audience including his next-door neighbor, Francis Ryder, who has become an ardent champion of his music:

—the audience then goes out & breaks or rocks—by Sky Rocket to Danbury!—

*July 4:* Jan Sibelius, 49, conducts the first performance of *Oceanides* at the Norfolk Festival—the Yale Summer School of Music, given on the Battel estate—stays at Whitehouse, and receives a Doctorate of Music *honoris causa* from the hands of Dr Horatio W Parker . . .

# Redding I

Charles Ives calls to mind one of those big, gruff, good-natured
sheep dogs you find in the Scottish highlands. On the job he's quick
as a flash. Off it, he knows where his dinner is, or his bed, but he'll
walk around them for hours, checking them out, before he sets to
or settles down.

The house in West Redding was finished in July 1913, but it
was nearly a year before they moved in permanently. Sometime that
July, Ives took the train up from Hartsdale to see it. On the voice
& piano arrangement of *The Ruined River*, the marginalia:

Redding July 1913    Piano & voice arranged from "The Saugatuck/
Housatonic River" (one Sunday with Amelia . . .

((Likely Amelia Merritt Ives, cousin Howard's daughter, now 28—
it had been after her baptism, back in 1884, that Ives's father
gave him the "Eddy/Thoreau/marriage/keep-away-from-music-as-a-
living" talk in the front parlor. Or it might have been Aunt Amelia
—at age 76, inquisitive as ever . . . ))

Then, on August 2, back up from Hartsdale for 10 days, putting
the house in order. And again in September, for a two-week vacation
spent fixing things up. That was the time of the infamous visit by

Mrs Sprague Coolidge, when she stopped by with her parents on their way home to Pittsfield. 20 years later, Ives recorded the story:

> After dinner, before going, daughter says to writer: "Are you still keeping up your music ?" Writer says: "Well, yes." So former asks writer to play some of it, and came into the little room with the piano, behind the dining room. I happened to have on the piano the score of the Black March, and started to play a little of this—daughter's face grew sour. "Do you really like those awful sounds ?" she said. So I stopped and played something that I thought might be a little less rough on her—the first part of *Washington's Birthday*. That made her walk out of the room . . .

Now, the ill-bred, studied offensiveness:

> . . . In getting into the car, headed toward Pittsfield, she said: "Well, I must say your music makes no sense to me. It is not, to my mind, music. How is it that—*studying as you have with Parker*—you ever came to write like that ?  You ought to know the music of Daniel Gregory Mason, who is living near us in Pittsfield—he has a real message. Good-bye . . ."

(((CI had the last laugh, could he have known. His MSS—the Ives Collection—now are housed in the music library of Sprague Hall, donated to Yale University by Elizabeth Sprague Coolidge in memory of her father. But the laugh came too late. Back in 1913, all he could do was go back to his kennel and lick his wounds. What chance did a grand old sheep dog have, against a superior bitch who was only out to castrate him ?)))

The Elizabeth Sprague Coolidges of this world are a perennial curiosity. Their presumable ancestors, the Charles Spragues, poets of awareness and sensitivity, beget descendants who inherit an awareness and sensitivity for business—like the Albert Spragues, close friends of the Joseph Twichells, who make fortunes in the wholesale grocery trade. Fine. The world needs wholesale grocers. Then the Albert Spragues beget daughters who inherit (a) their money, and (b) a vague, uncomprehending awareness of who rather than what their ancestors have been—*viz*, "artists." That, plus daddy's money, gives them a sense of power: wealth *plus* art = "culture." They will become patrons of the arts. And the lady-bird artists respond, patronizing the patrons . . .

And what do the Charlie Iveses do ? When they're through licking their wounds, they go meekly out, their tails between their legs, and buy Daniel Gregory Mason's Violin Sonata in G minor, Opus 5. And having played their own 2nd Violin Sonatas and 1st Violin Sonatas with the Edgar Stowells, they play Mason's Violin Sonata—"with a nice theme like *Narcissus*"—and the Edgar Stowells tell them that Mason's sonata is better than theirs because it's real "Geigermusik"—real "fiddle-music," in fiddlers' parlance, that "lies under the hand." And the Charlie Iveses believe them. For the time being.

Meanwhile, back at Umpawaug Road, West Redding—Charles and his wife finally settled in there in June 1914. By the end of the summer *The Housatonic At Stockbridge* and the fourth movement/ 4th Symphony were finished. By September 26, the full-score, ink copy, of *General Booth*, for baritone solo, chorus & brass band ((lost: only the sketches survive—and the 1935 reconstruction, for chamber orchestra, by John Becker)). Then, on October 12— Columbus Day—the abortive sketch of a piece for voices and chamber orchestra called *Sneak-Thief*:

People of the World! rise and get the Sneak Thieving Kaiser . . .

Two days later—6 days before Ives's 40th birthday—Professor Franz Milcke paid them a visit.

There is a traditional male superstition about the age 40. It's the age when you're supposed to have made it or you're never going to. Ives had made it in the insurance business by then—he was already a rich man. But we're less concerned about his business activities than his music, and so was he. No one knows much about his activities in the business world now—or wants to, especially. His partner, Julian Myrick, by the time he retired, a much richer man than Ives, was known throughout the insurance world as "Mr Life Insurance." But Ives, with his first training school for insurance salesmen, his pioneering in the field of real estate insurance, his unfailing supply of new ideas and fresh ideals, endless high-minded memoranda to his salesmen, blazed a trail in business that was harder to follow than the trail he blazed in music. Harder to follow, because businessmen just aren't as bright as musicians—artists in general—when it comes to anything less obvious than making a fast buck. And nothing could be more obvious. Jotted on a leaf of MS from *4 New England Holidays,* Ives's candid comment:

> He doesn't know much,
> *But*—he thinks he knows a lot.
> Oh, *doesn't* he think he knows an awful lot!
> But—what he knows everybody knows,
> And what he doesn't know everybody knows too.
> And when it comes to talkin',
> He's there with both his jaws,
> An' the sounds you hear are the sounds you hear
> When crows get going their "caws";
> Yes—he's a busy, buzzin' business man,
> Talkin' glib and continual . . .

But Milcke! That was something else. Ives's marginalia in the 3rd Violin Sonata tell it. In the right-hand margin of page 1:

> This Sonata No 3 is not much good. It was finished just after a famous German Virtuoso violinist, Milcke by name, was here in Redding Oct 1914 to play the 1st Sonata . . . no resemblance to music, he said (politely) . . . So many similar complaints about and before that time I began to think there must be something wrong with me to like this & get so much fun out of it, &c . . . so I tried to make a nice piece for the nice ladies. Har 'tis. N G . . .

On the title page of the ink copy:

> 1st movement—3rd (last) movement—from Organ Preludes 1901 middle part after lost MS score for small orchestra 1904   the whole finished & emasculated 1914 after Prof M got off his regular stuff . . .

At the end:

> . . . ended (not Fine) Dec 20 1914 (This, most of it, is a backward step—the result of a visit from a "know it all" soft eared professional Prima donna violinist . . .

And on the sketch of a later song, *Tom Sails Away* ((no 51 of *114 Songs*)):

> Sketch for a Violin Sonata—Milcke looked at it—when on a visit to us in Redding Oct 1914—was to be put in 3rd ((as an additional

movement))—Didn't—too much for Milcke—put into this song
Sep 1917 . . .

Nearly 20 years later—too late—Ives's anger found just articulation in a much-quoted passage:

> Generally speaking, this sonata was a slump back, due, I am certain, to a visit from a typical hard-boiled, narrow-minded, conceited, prima donna solo violinist with a reputation gained because he came to this country from Germany with Anton Seidl as his concertmaster. Mrs Ives knew him in Hartford, and as I had had so much trouble with musicians playing my music, we thought it would be a good plan to get one of the supposedly great players. Before finishing the Third Sonata, I wanted to have the First and the Second played over.
>
> The "Professor" came in and, after a lot of big talk, started to play the first movement of the First Sonata. He didn't even get through the first page. He was all bothered with the rhythms and the notes, and got mad. He said "This cannot be played. It is awful. It is not music, it makes no sense." He couldn't even get it after I'd played it over for him several times. I remember he came out of the little back music room with his hands over his ears, and said, "When you get awfully indigestible food in your stomach that distresses you, you can get rid of it, but I cannot get those horrible sounds out of my ears by a dose of oil."
>
> I remember Milcke, the Professor, in looking over some of the other music, came across a part of the *In Re Con Moto Et Al* for chamber group (which I didn't intend to show him), and also the church bell piece called *From The Steeples*, and a Chamber Set, &c. He jumped back, mad. Then I thought I shouldn't treat him so rude and gave him a copy of the second movement of the First Symphony. He looked and felt better and smiled—"Now that's something like" —&c, &c. But then came a joke for both of us, for in it were some pages of the *Tone Roads* and part of the Piano Trio (the college days Scherzo, I think, or the first movement). He stared at, then threw it and went out of the room—and went home the same afternoon.
>
> After he went, I had a kind of feeling which I've had off and on when other more or less celebrated or well known musicians have played

or tried to play some of my music. Said I to myself: "I'm the only one, with the exception of Mrs Ives and one or two others perhaps—Mr Ryder, Dr Griggs—who likes any of my music, except perhaps some of the older and more or less conventional things. Why do I like these things ? Why do I like to work in this way and get all set up by it, while others only get upset by it and it just makes everybody else mad, especially well known musicians and critics—for instance Dave Smith and Max Smith—nice boys! Are my ears on wrong ? No one else seems to hear it the same way. Perhaps I'd better go back to Mr Jadassohn."

These depressions didn't last long, I'm glad to say. I began to feel more and more, after seances with nice musicians, that if I wanted to write music that, to me, seemed worth while, I must keep away from musicians . . .

But by now it was almost finished. The works still to be completed were all in an advanced state of progress—all but one, that never was finished, and another, the greatest, not yet even conceived, and a handful of minor pieces. And Ives kept out of the way of musicians.

The weekend before Thanksgiving they moved into New York for the winter, renting an apartment at 27 West 11th Street—less than a block from their first married address. Here, over the holiday, Ives finished The Alcotts (third movement/*Concord* Sonata), on December 20, the 3rd Violin Sonata, and early in the New Year, *The Masses.* Ives's text:

> The Masses! The Masses! The Masses have toiled,
> Behold the works of the World!
> The Masses are thinking,
> Whence comes the thought of the World!
> The Masses are singing, are singing, singing,
> Whence comes the Song of the World!
> The Masses are yearning, are yearning,
> Whence comes the Hope of the World!
> The Masses are Legion;
> As the raindrops falling together make the Rivers
>                         and for a space become as one,
> So men seeking common life together for a season
>                         become as one,

> Whence come the Nations of the World!
> As the tribes of the ages wandered and followed the stars,
> Whence come the many dwelling places of the World!
> The Masses are dreaming, dreaming,
> Whence come the visions of God.
> God's in his Heaven,
> All *will* be right with the world  . . .

The marginalia in the full-score discuss the design of the music:

> The plan of this in the orchestra parts is to have each group, in a
> different rhythm, complete the 12 notes (each on a different system
> & end & holding last (of 12) as finding its star). Occasionally  . . .
> ((the remainder torn off))

and straightway dismiss it:

> . . . Something in this calculated, diagram, design way may have
> a place in music, if it is primarily to carry out an idea, or part
> of a program subject matter as in the above, but generally or too
> much or alone as such, it is a weak substitute for inspiration or
> music. It's too easy, any high-school student (unmusical) with a
> pad, pencil, compass & logth table and a mild knowledge of sounds
> & instruments (blown or hit) could do it. It's an artificial process
> without strength, though it may sound busy & noisy. This wallpaper
> design music is not as big as a natural mushy ballad  . . .

((So, 10 years before Arnold Schoenberg assumes credit for discovering the principles of 12-tone composition, CI has rejected
them. But not quite rejected. He had experimented with them in
1893, again in 1904, when he kept Bill Maloney awake one St
Patrick's night, used them, in 1908/09, in the *Browning* Overture.
And he was using them right now, in the "Universe" Symphony,
based on the 1904 piece—used them again, in the 1915 *Tone
Roads* No 3, and the few 1919 sketches toward a 3rd Orchestral
Set . . . ))

On May 8 1915, they moved back to West Redding. The day
before, the SS *Lusitania* had been torpedoed and sunk off the south
coast of Ireland—114 Americans among the 1,198 who lost their
lives. The news was reaching New York by 9.30 AM, and a morning

"extra" rushed off the press. Ives read it at the breakfast table, before leaving for the office:

> I remember, going downtown to business, the people on the street and the elevated train had something in their faces that was not the usual something. Everybody who came into the office, whether they spoke about the disaster or not, showed a realization of seriously experiencing something. That it meant war is what the faces said, if the tongues didn't. Leaving the office and going uptown about six o'clock, I took the Third Avenue L at Hanover Square Station. As I came on the platform, there was quite a crowd waiting for the trains, which had been blocked lower down, and while waiting there, a hand-organ or hurdy-gurdy was playing in the street below. Some workmen sitting on the side of the tracks began to whistle the tune, and others began to sing or hum the refrain. A workman with a shovel over his shoulder came on the platform and joined in the chorus, and the next man, a Wall Street banker with white spats and a cane, joined in it, and finally it seemed to me that everybody was singing this tune, and they didn't seem to be singing in fun, but as a natural outlet for what their feelings had been going through all day long. There was a feeling of dignity all through this, and the hand-organ man seemed to sense this and wheeled his organ nearer the platform and kept it up *fortissimo*, and the chorus sounded as though every man in New York must be joining in it. Then the first train came in and everybody crowded in, and the song gradually died out, but the effect on the crowd still showed. Almost nobody talked—the people acted as though they might be coming out of a church service. In going uptown, occasionally little groups would start singing or humming the tune . . .

This became *From Hanover Square North The Voice Of The People Again Arose*—third movement/2nd Orchestral Set, Ives's most exalted work. The piece was sketched, completed, and scored within a few weeks during the fall of 1915—his last great movement to be started and finished.

Meanwhile, the Thoreau movement/*Concord* Sonata had been finished on May 30—Memorial Day—at West Redding, and the Sonata was complete. The implications of the *Lusitania* sinking must still have been occupying Ives's mind—yet they were so analogous,

Uncle Isaac and Aunt Emily outside the family house at 167/169 Main Street, Danbury. In 1887, the house was renumbered 210.

The room where Charles Ives was born on October 20 1874.

Centre Church, New Haven, where Charles Ives was resident organist from September 1894 to July 1898. The white paint-work on the belfry was removed in 1915.

The Stobart, Worcester & Dunham piano purchased by Charles Ives's grandfather, George Wilcox Ives, in 1849. Charles's father, George Edward Ives, gave lessons on it to the children of Danbury and to Ives himself. George Ives's Civil War trumpet lies on top.

Ives, aged 20, sits by the Franklin stove in his room at 76 South Middle—now Connecticut Hall—with his Yale roommate, Mandeville Mullaly. The photograph was apparently an accidental double-exposure.

59th Street, looking toward Columbus Circle, in 1898. Facing these buildings was the house where Dick Schweppe lived; it backed onto the rear of
Poverty Flat.

A turn-of-the-century view of Broadway, from Liberty Street, where Charles
Ives was sent to work for the Raymond General Agency in February 1899.

*Above:* June 9 1908—the wedding picture of Charles and Harmony, with the Twichell family, at 125 Woodlawn Street, Hartford. From left, first row: Mrs Willis Wood (Judy Twichell), Miss Susan (Sally) Twichell, Miss Louise Twichell, Willis Wood Jr, the Rev Joseph H Twichell, Mrs Joseph Twichell, Miss Helen Wood, Miss Sarah Dunham, Mrs David Twichell (Ella Cooke). Second row: Edward Twichell, Willis Wood, Joseph Hooker Twichell, Charles and Harmony Ives, Burton Twichell, David Twichell.

Charles and Harmony at Umpawaug Road, West Redding, a few days after his retirement from Ives & Meyrick in 1929.

The Housatonic at Stockbridge "... the colors one sees, sounds one hears, feelings one has, of a summer morning near a wide river, and a hymn-singing in Church way across the river ..." Ives' description of a Sunday morning walk with Harmony, June 28, 1908.

Elk Lake, with a view of Nippletop Mountain to the north, from Pell Jones's. The Fugue from the 4th Symphony was "started at Pell's, summer 1909 ..."

The old Methodist Church, Hartsdale Road, where
Charles and Harmony heard the Rev Daniel McCurry
preach a sermon on Sunday August 17 1913.

Keene Valley Plateau—"Universe Symphony," October 1915.

Charles Ives with his adopted daughter Edith. A passport photograph taken in July 1924.

in spirit, to the circumstances that led up to the Civil War, to
Thoreau's own position in relation to those circumstances, that Ives
experienced no sense of conflict. And when, in the fall, he came
to write the *Hanover Square* movement, he found, perhaps for the
first time in his life, all his vast compositional resources ready mar-
shaled for his use.

((The movement is not hugely difficult, technically speaking, for
the individual instruments involved. But the maze of cross-rhythms
makes the ensemble, in rehearsal, as formidable as any of Ives's
works. Orchestral players often ask whether Ives could really hear
all these cross-rhythms—whether he wasn't simply "guessing":

> I have with much practice been able to keep five, and even six,
> rhythms going in my mind at once, so that I can hear each one
> naturally by leaning toward it, changing the ear in each measure—
> and I think this is the more natural way of hearing and learning
> the use of and feeling for rhythms, than by writing them and
> playing 'from them on paper, which shows the exact position of
> each note in relation to each other, in the eye. The way I did it
> was to take, for instance, in the left hand a 5—with the left foot,
> beat a 2—with the right foot, beat a 3—with the right hand, play
> an 11—and sing a 7. Various other rhythms can be held in the
> mind in this way, and after a while they become as natural as it is
> for Toscanini to beat down-left-right-up as evenly as a metronome
> for two hours steadily, and do it nice, with the ladies all tapping
> time with their feet . . .

So Ives *could* "hear what he wrote"—a not uncommon talent for
a composer. But, what some composers can't, he could also "write
what he heard"—what his inner ear heard, that is.))

At the start of World War I, in August 1914, there was a
growing awareness, inside the United States, that her own house
was not in order. With the congressional investigation of 1913,
Wilson had forced through the Federal Reserve Bill, big business
had acquired an outward vestige of decorum, but in many areas
of social reform America was still in the early 19th century. This
had begun to change with the turn of the century, and by 1914
the American social conscience had made a number of inroads into
the established system—designed, if not to eradicate, at least to

alleviate some of the more manifest misery of the "under-privileged."

One of these inroads was the Fresh Air Fund of New York, a scheme for sending families from the ghettoes on a two-week paid vacation to the country. Harmony Ives was one of the Fund's founders and patrons—indeed, she had conceived the idea at the Henry Street Settlement, 7 years earlier, when she found 10-yr-old millhands working a 60-hour week for the $2 essential to their families' survival. And so, on July 31 1915, there came to Umpawaug Road, West Redding, the Osborne family and their children—the youngest, 15-month-old Edith, weakly and dark-eyed from squatting beside her mother 10 hours a day in an ill-lit New York sweatshop. When, two weeks later, the Osbornes had to go back to the city, they left Edith behind, at the urgent appeal of Harmony, for the baby girl was beginning to respond to the fresh air and a wholesome diet. And two months later, when Charles and Harmony took their own belated vacation at Keene Valley, Edith went with them.

June and July had been spent reworking the second (Hawthorne) movement/4th Symphony, September writing the *Hanover Square* piece, and at Keene Valley, Ives returned to the sketches of the "Universe" Symphony, begun over two years earlier:

> Thoughts for 5th Symphony   Medium Orches (Oct 1915) Redding & Keene Valley . . . The Battery Unit = lowest vibration of & basis of each cycle—& stands as the representation of the eternal pulse & planetary motion of the earth & universe . . .

and a diagram of 1 measure containing the metric subdivisions:

> . . . 11/13/17/19/23/29/31 . . . 11 is taken as the last (highest) of the indivisible meters . . . the Rhythms may be kept, but the phrasing, even or uneven, may constantly change . . . the Orchestra Units, from 3 up, are the varying pulse . . .

> Plateau, Keene Valley, Oct 1915 . . . Universe Symphony . . . for Section B . . . upper orchestra representing the Heavens . . . 5 groups of chordal counterpoint . . . lower orchestra representing Earth . . . 4 groups . . .

> 2nd Prelude (Univ Symph) Birth of the Waters . . . A striving to present—to contemplate in tones rather than in music as such—

that is—not exactly within the general term or meaning as it is so understood—*to paint* the creation, the mysterious beginnings of all things known through God to man, to trace with tonal imprints the vastness, the evolution of all life to the spiritual eternities, from the great unknown to the great inknown . . .

. . . chord for 1st Rigid-theme (Earth created) . . . of various formations but in endless cycles = the relentless processes of nature, of all time, of the universe . . .

Universe Sym 3rd section Foreground Harmonic basis, 24 different chordal scales . . .

. . . as the eternities are unmeasured, as the source of universal substances are unknown, the earth, the waters, the stars, the ether, yet these elements as man can touch them with hand & microscope . . . they are not single & exclusive strains, but incessant myriads, for ages ever & always changing, growing . . . of life & death & future life . . . the only known is the unknown . . .

Ives was already a rich man—not yet in the millionaire's class, but near—could well afford to quit business and devote himself full-time to composition. But he didn't. What stopped him ? Did the inspiration stop, dry up ? Was it already flagging, right here, in his "thoughts for a 5th Symphony" ?

At the beginning of November, they rented a New York apartment for the winter, at 142 East 40th Street—on Saturday afternoon, November 13, went with Mark Twain's daughter to a piano recital given by her husband:

. . . Clara Clemens (Mrs Ossssssipy Gabrilowitsch) invited us to go with her to an all-Beethoven recital in Aeolian Hall, New York, played by Ossssssip. After two and a half hours of the (perhaps) best music in the world (around 1829), there is something in substance (not spirit altogether) that is gradually missed—that is, it was by me. I remember feeling towards Beethoven—a great man, but Oh for just one big strong chord not tied to any key . . .

Early in 1916, the second movement/4th Symphony was finished in score, and the whole symphony sent to Tams to be copied. Meanwhile, they had been negotiating with the Osbornes to adopt Edith legally, and took her with them when they moved back to West

Redding at the end of April. Finally, on October 18, Harmony could write in her diary: "Edith now our own . . . " Two days later—his 42nd birthday—Ives celebrated by writing a little piece for himself, for basset-horn, flute, 3 violins, drums, and piano— *Luck & Work* ((later adapted, to Robert Underwood Johnson's text, as no 26 of *114 Songs*)).

It was finished. The rest is silence. Except for a few pieces of empty patriotic rhetoric in 1917, five or six staidly conventional songs in 1919/20, two or three faint echoes of vanished genius up until 1926. Plus the sheer labor of getting out the voice & piano arrangements for *114 Songs*, between 1919 and 1921. And *Essays Before A Sonata*, of course.

Ives started writing these in 1916. The political climate was getting too tense for writing music in any case—just endless revisions to masterworks that already were complete, the nervous actions of a man whose mind was elsewhere. Starting the *Essays* gave an outlet to his nervous energy, the stability of 60 and 70 years' perspective, back into the world of Emerson and Hawthorne and Thoreau, back to his roots, what his music had all been about in the first place.

And, in 1916, Ives must have started to play the stock market. No man can accumulate the kind of wealth that he had, by 1919, without. Maybe he had played it before, in fun, but 1916 seems the likely date that he started in earnest. European markets had been closed to America for two years; the domestic market, forced into higher production, was booming. Booming, too, with the production of war materials for the Allies, war materials for Germany. No ethical problem here, so long as America remained strictly neutral . . .

And with the boom came tighter controls on industry, improved working conditions, more safeguards, disability and retirement pensions—all a potential market for insurance. Ives & Myrick were among the first to corner that market, sold $14,793,437 in policies between May and December, as compared with $3 and $4 million sold by their nearest competitors. Not that there was any real competition. The Morgan group held a monopoly of New York's "Big 3" —Mutual Life, New York Life, Equitable—had held, since 1910. It may be true that Ives & Myrick continued to bring a sense of integrity to their work. It is certainly true that a lust for wealth overwhelms every other lust and the finest of human emotions. It has overwhelmed many other men of integrity. There is no reason to suppose that Ives was immune. And there has to be a better reason for him stopping composing than simply having written himself out.

And perhaps the faintest shadow of estrangement between Ives and his beloved Harmony. There is no marriage in the world, between intelligent people, that can survive a total absence of friction. Both had wanted children—Charles's brother, Moss, now had six children, Harmony had been one of a family of eight. For Harmony's part, a faint, inarticulate resentment that had grown with the years, and now transferred itself to her husband—a common psychological phenomenon. Then reason would take over. All right, they couldn't have children of their own, so let them adopt one. And, after seven years, they had. But why not earlier ? Why not that first summer, back in 1909 ? Why not in Hartsdale ? But Charles would not settle down. Always these rented apartments, rented houses, his reluctance to being pinned down. And then, at last, a place of their own, at West Redding. And still he had wavered, for two more years.

For Charles's part, a resentment too. Initially, the sense of having been cheated, a primitive instinct that assails any man when he learns that his wife cannot give him a child. Then, a typical male reluctance to adopting a child, because it seemed an admission of failure, a reflection on his male ego, his masculinity. All unreasonable, all understandable. And then, Harmony's friends and acquaintances, and their friends and acquaintances—Elizabeth Sprague Coolidge, Clara Mannes, Edgar Stowell, Franz Milcke, Clara Clemens and Ossip Gabrilowitsch. Harmony's faith in her husband's genius was implicit, complete and utter. She understood nothing of his music, from a technical standpoint, and in her quiet way, would try and bring it to the notice of people "who knew." It was always disastrous, but still she persisted. And because these people were Harmony's friends, Charles would listen to them, swallow their criticisms, meekly follow their advice—for the time being. The anger only came later, with the realization that, in music too, they were trying to emasculate him, make him conform to their own effeminate posturings. His own friends—Max Smith, David Stanley Smith, Reber Johnson, Howard Starr, even Bass Brigham—

these were different, he had a working arrangement with them, made allowances for them, basically liked them. Only for Harmony's friends, ultimately, unbridled contempt. And the silent resentment grew, like corn in the night . . .

All this, on both sides, unspoken, unseen, largely unconscious, the more dangerous for being unspoken, unseen, unconscious. And Ives stopped composing—for the time being—and turned his musician's hands to making money—for the time being. With an adopted daughter, best make her future doubly secure financially. Or so he reasoned to himself.

All this time, America was moving nearer to war. Wilson stood for peace, a "peace without victory" in Europe urged by ideals too high-minded for most of the electorate. His re-election, in November 1916, had been narrow—his defeat, by Hughes, already conceded by the New York papers, before the final results came in and swung the balance. Only evidence of Ives's political preference is the scribbled note:

Redding   Nov 8   1916   W W elected!

((This on the leaf of MS sketch "for a Violin Sonata" that he had shown to Milcke in 1914, didn't use—"too much for Milcke"— put in the song, *Tom Sails Away*, September 1917 . . . ten months later.))

But within two months of Wilson's re-election, the United States had broken off diplomatic relations with Germany. On April 6 1917, declared war. And America went wild.

It had been the same in Europe, summer of 1914. Goodness knows, after centuries of war, over every inch of her own soil, Europe should have learned her lesson. Yet still she had to go through all the stereotyped motions of blind patriotism, the ridiculous ritual solemnity of overgrown schoolboys playing with tin soldiers. But this time the soldiers weren't made of tin. They got hurt, maimed, killed, mutilated by the millions. This wasn't "the war to end all wars" at all. It bred only a bitter, bestial, terrible hate. By 1917, Europe was utterly disillusioned.

Not so America. She had only the lesson of two wars on her own soil to go on, but they had both been charged with some sense of purpose, of idealism. Now that America was graduating into a World War class, she brought to it the same sense of purpose, idealism. It was the only model she had. (Three years back, it had been the only model Europe had had.)

And so the parades, the banners, the flag-waving, the "dollar-a-year" men, the Liberty Loan drives, the Red Cross rallies, the ticker-tape processions for "our boys" going off to training camp. And the spy hysteria—Karl Muck among several thousand German nationals interned—the stigmatizing of pacifists, lynching of innocent citizens with foreign-sounding names. All desperately sincere, desperately earnest, schoolboys' make-believe. A make-believe "over there" with make-believe St Georges going to make-believe kill the make-believe German dragon. On Memorial Day 1917, Ives finished a distressing medley of patriotic jingoism, for chorus & orchestra, *He Is There!*—a rehash of his 1914 *Sneak-Thief:*

> . . . after last Bugle call—march may end—or if you want to—2
> whoops blows bangs cuffs whacks ( ("smiles, scolds, smirks") ) on
> Kaiser's Jaw—not on his head! He hasn't got any . . .

( ( (cf the 1899 *Yale/Princeton Football Game*) ) )

Nearly a year later—April 24 1918—American troops were in their first real engagement, at Seicheprey. As the casualty lists started reaching home, America began to realize, with Europe, that there was no game, no joke, no make-believe, that this was total war, and war was not healthy for children and other living things.

By June 1918, Ives's identification with the war had become absolute. He was determined to join the Volunteer Ambulance Corps in France, had failed his first medical, and spent the first three weeks of July working on Frank Ryder's farm, to build up his physique. He was entirely confident of passing his medical the second time round, and returned to New York City on September 15 in a blaze of fitness. On September 20 Aunt Amelia died, at the age of 81. Ives went back up to Danbury for her funeral, and decided to stay on in Redding and do a few more days' farm work. On October 1, the day before he was due to take his second medical, he collapsed, complaining of giddiness, fever, pains in his chest. The preliminary diagnosis was Spanish influenza. A more thorough examination showed a coronary thrombosis with suspected extensive cardiac damage, and his doctor ordered him complete rest for at least three months. Six weeks later—November 11 1918—the Armistice was signed in Versailles. The war was over. So, too, Ives's creative life as a composer.

# Ricercar III

Go back a little. Back two years. Back to November 1916 . . .

I have said I can see no other reason for it, that CI quit composing sometime in 1916 to make money. A lot of money, by ordinary standards. I don't believe he thought his creative powers impaired at that time, though the last big pieces—*Thoreau, Hanover Square*, the second movement/4th Symphony—had hurt him.

Then, in November 1916, the note, "W W elected!" Scribbled, not on any work in progress, because there wasn't any, but on a leaf of MS that had been rejected two years earlier, after Milcke's visit to Redding, and not used again till September 1917. But why there ? There are marginalia about Milcke all over the 3rd Violin Sonata, 18 years later he still recalls the man's visit with near paranoid clarity. It had aroused in him such a distaste for the fabric of music-making he never wanted to write another note, the more he thought about it. And he must have been thinking about it in November 1916. "W W elected!" Was this to efface a bad memory, exorcise Herr Milcke's phantom with a clean-blooded American sentiment ? Of wholehearted enthusiasm ?

It has to have been enthusiasm. Woodrow Wilson's brand of idealism matched too closely his own. Four years ago, at Hartsdale, it hadn't seemed that important—Wilson, Roosevelt, Taft: "3 nice boys $ame $ame $ame . . ." And four years ago he was nearing the crisis of his own writing. Now, for the time being, it had passed, and he had energy to spare for political sympathies. And consider the alternative. Wilson's opponent, Charles Evans Hughes—counsel, 11 years back, for the Armstrong Investigation. CI had been working for the Raymond Agency seven years by then, and though he broke with them soon after, the loyalties still were fast. Hughes had brought out a lot of Mutual Life's dirty linen, and even 11 years later, CI's New England sense of privacy can have held no brief for him.

So enthusiasm over Wilson's re-election. Peace without victory in Europe meant, to most Americans, continuing peace for the USA. CI could go along with that. Then, within weeks almost, the abrupt about-face. CI could go along with that too. Now go to April 1917 . . .

Just over a week after America's entry into the war, a big convention of Life Insurance men was held at the Waldorf-Astoria. For this, CI had put together a hurried setting of John McCrae's poem "In Flanders Fields." It was performed by an indifferent singer with a tenth-rate pianist. And it fell flat. And no wonder.

To begin with, nothing was more calculated to anger a group of businessmen than having to stop talking and listen to music—any music, short of a floor-show; and particularly unfamiliar music, badly performed, that was supposed to have a "message."

Secondly, the news had just reached them that Wilson was going to set up a Federal War Risks Bureau, threatening their own monopoly with democratic competition, and they were furious anyway.

Thirdly, aside from the standard of performance, the song just wasn't any good.

This—apart from the 1914 *Sneak-Thief*—was the first time CI had made a serious blunder. Even *Sneak-Thief* wasn't really a blunder—just misplaced enthusiasm. And it never got off the ground in any case. But *In Flanders Fields* was, a fearful blunder.

Because here, his magic touch, in recycling old music, failed him. A day or two before the convention, Julian Myrick learned that the author of "In Flanders Fields" had been medical officer to one of Mutual Life's Canadian agencies. With an eye to the main

chance, he persuaded his partner to get out an overnight setting of
the poem. The speed was no problem, because CI could always use
old music. But he looked out, of all things, the 1899 *March For
Dewey Day*, which had made much of *The Red, White & Blue,
Battle Cry Of Freedom, America, Reveille*, &c, &c. No doubt he
figured that, because the tune of *America* was the same as the British
national anthem, their two texts carried identical sentiments. First
miscalculation. Then you get, against the words:

> In Flanders fields the poppies blow . . .

the music to:

> ( ( ( *"O Columbia, the Gem of the Ocean . . . "*
> Between the crosses row on row,
> That mark our place; and in the sky
> The larks still bravely singing fly . . .
> ( ( ( *"God Save Our Gracious King . . . "*
> Scarce heard amidst the guns below . . .
> ( ( ( *"The Union for ever!*
> *Hurrah, boys, hurrah . . . !"*
> We are the dead . . .
> ( ( ( *"You've got to get up, you've got to get up,
> You've got to get up in the mor-ning . . . "*

McCrae's text goes on:

> Take up our quarrel with the foe!
> To you from falling hands we throw . . .

to the vocal line of the *Marseillaise:*

> ( ( ( *"aux armes, Citoyens . . . "*

O.K. Better. But, in the accompaniment, in appalling counterpoint, double octaves, *fortissimo:*

> ( ( ( *"God Save Our Gracious King,*
> *Long Live Our Noble King,*
> *God Save The King . . . "*
> The torch! Be yours to hold it high,
> If ye break faith with us who die . . .

((( ("*Send Him Victorious,*
        *Happy and Glorious* . . .
        We shall not sleep though poppies grow . . .
((( ("*Columbia, the Gem etc* . . .
        In Flanders fields

Had this been a Civil War poem, Ives would never have made such a miscalculation. He knew all the Civil War tunes, and all the Independence War tunes, with all the subtlest shades of irony that history had invested them, like the back of his hand, part of his national heritage. The mistake Ives made was in supposing that the sentiment of one national tune for one nation was good for all national tunes and all other nations. But America wasn't the only country with a national heritage, and these weren't her dead McCrae was writing about. Not yet, anyway.

Ives sensed the song was going to be a flop, and wanted to call the performance off. But Myrick wouldn't hear of it. Then, during the convention, he had to listen to all these angry insurance executives talking about Wilson's War Risks Insurance . . . federal life insurance . . . incipient socialism . . . what about when the war was over ? . . . the next thing they'd have would be social security, socialized medicine, federal pension schemes, and where would that leave *them* ? It was the same thing all over, even in business. Just a game. A dull, senseless, academic, game. No one ever got hurt—they did, of course, but you didn't actually see them, so it didn't matter . . . Then, two weeks later, May 2 1917, Pittsburgh Life & Trust crashed, the biggest individual scandal in Life Insurance history. Pittsburgh Life—the company that had bought out Washington Life nine years ago, and put him out of a job.

General Pershing had asked for 3 million troops. By March 1918, there were still only 291,000 American servicemen in Europe. By June, that number was being sent over every month. Everybody who was anybody was going to Europe. Ives felt it was time he went too. Failing his first medical only made him all the more determined.

Did he really want to go ? Did he, as a creative artist, really identify himself with the cultural aberration that was taking place in Europe ? Or was it a Byronic gesture, like Stephen Crane ? Byron had left England, thoroughly disenchanted—died, years later, in Greece, searching for a soldier's grave.

   Because that's what you really have. Disenchantment. Ives had
lost out all along the line. His music had been rejected out of hand.
His parenthood compromised because he could not father a child
of his own. His manhood—physical fitness, 100% American—
called in question. His business activity become meaningless. Four
aspects of the established system no go. Europe offered an honorable
escape. But it was too late.


          Of all men, saving Sylla the Man-Slayer,
              Who passes for in life and death most lucky,
          Of the great names which in our faces stare,
              The General Boone, back-woodsman of Kentucky,
          Was happiest among mortals any where;
              For killing nothing but a bear or buck, he
          Enjoyed the lonely vigorous, harmless days
          Of his old age in wilds of deepest maze.

          'Tis true he shrank from men of his nation,
              When they built up unto his darling trees,—
          He moved some hundred miles off, for a station
              Where there were fewer houses and more ease;
          The inconvenience of civilization
              Is, that you neither can be pleased nor please;
          But where he met the individual man
          He shewed himself as kind as mortal can.

          So much for Nature:—by way of variety,
              Now back to thy great joys, Civilization!
          And the sweet consequence of large society,
              War, Pestilence, the despot's desolation,
          The kingly scourge, the Lust of Notoriety,
              The millions slain by soldiers for their ration,
          The scenes like Catherine's boudoir at three-score,
          With Ismail's storm to soften it the more.

                    from Byron: *Don Juan*, Canto VIII

# PEDAL POINT

# Second Ending ...

> I long ago lost a hound, a bay horse, and a turtle-dove, and am still on their trail. Many are the travelers I have spoken concerning them, describing their tracks and what calls they answered to. I have met one or two who had heard the hound, and the tramp of the horse, and even seen the dove disappear behind a cloud . . .
>
> HENRY DAVID THOREAU: *Walden*

Ives was laid up for a while, first in hospital, till the immediate danger was past, then at Umpawaug Road, till he had replenished strength enough to move south for the last weeks of convalescence. They were due to leave in mid-December, when Harmony was summoned to Hartford. Her aged father was dying. Amelia Van Wyck—Amelia Merritt Ives, that was—took her place at Charles's bedside. They finally got away on January 15 1919, to Asheville/North Carolina, a health resort east of the Great Smoky Mountains, were there nine weeks, and came back to New York City on March 19. Harmony's journal: "Amelia waiting for us . . . " ((Dear woman, she had waited for Charles for many years, earlier on; and he, dear man, had never noticed. The urge for cousins to marry cousins, like many genetic phenomena, skips a generation, they say.))

During his illness, Ives had resolved on 3 things:

(1) The war was over. There was no reason why he shouldn't get back to his music now. He was worth almost $2 million, knew, he said, that all this money had been honestly earned—"though the blacksmith who earns $8 a week is probably more honest . . . " He decided to limit his

personal income to his actual needs—some said $10,000 a year, some $20,000. This to cover all expenses incurred by his music.

(2) He found an immediate return to creative musical thinking impossible—the attempt, in January 1919, to sketch a 3rd Orchestral Set had been an utter failure. So, as a continuing therapy, he would confine himself to copying up some of the old music, writing simple new pieces that made no demand on his creative/emotional resources, and try to work himself back into a more productive frame of mind.

(3) As the first fence-mending project, he would copy up the *Concord* Sonata, finish writing the prefatory essays, and get both published. Then get photostats of all the other music done, so there should be duplicates.

By February 5 he had finished the final (Thoreau) essay and started on the Epilogue. By February 20, finished copying the Emerson, Alcotts, and Thoreau movements of the Sonata and sent them off to New York to be engraved. For the next month, he worked on the Hawthorne movement, which was still being troublesome, still needed revision. Then back to New York, and into light business harness.

For May 29—Edith's fourth birthday—Harmony wrote a poem, which Ives set, nursery style. That same month: *Cradle Song*, a harmonization of a tune by Elam Ives of Meriden, which he had found in his father's copy of the 1846 "Musical Spelling Book," together with a text by Elam's daughter, Augusta.

On June 25, when they moved back up to Redding, Ives's doctor advised him not to try and commute. So he tried seeing if the creative faculties would work again, and wrote the song *Afterglow*, to an indifferent poem by James Fenimore Cooper's grandson. The music looks interesting, at first glance. But it goes down the same blind alley Skryabin went, 10 years earlier. Still, it was a start.

September 25 they returned to New York—120 East 22nd Street, rented from Henry Sedgewick—and Ives went back to the office full time. After all, these were his friends, even if they were not incorruptible. And there was more work to be done than ever.

That fall an announcement appeared in the New York *World*,

soliciting new scores for a rehearsal reading by the New Symphony Orchestra, at Carnegie Hall, late April 1920. "For the fun of it"— though seriously enough to go to the trouble of having the parts copied—Ives sent in *Decoration Day,* one of his easiest orchestral works. On April 20 he had a letter from Paul Eisler, the assistant conductor: " . . . after reading . . . *most* carefully . . . absolutely impossible for us to play . . . much too difficult for us to play at sight . . . inasmuch as our rehearsal time would not allow . . . " &c, &c. Ives wrote back the next day and suggested paying for extra rehearsal time. This brought Eisler hurrying over to their apartment, and Ives took him through the score. Eisler was astonished—"but you play *like an artist!*" ((what on earth had the boy expected ?))—and agreed to do the piece:

> . . . Mr Bodansky was the conductor of the orchestra, but did not conduct this piece, and I don't think he saw the score. It was picked out by a committee of the orchestra, but I don't know who they were. I'm pretty certain that, had Mr Bodansky seen the score, it would not have been played. At the concert, Mr Bodansky's head was sitting right in front of us. He looked as though he didn't know what it was all about (that is, the music), and always smiled at the wrong time . . .
>
> Mr Eisler, an Assistant Conductor of the Metropolitan Opera, stood up and started them off with a nice baton in his hand. At the end of each section, one little violinist in the back row was the only one playing, all the others having dropped by the wayside. Then when they got to letter B, they all started together, and the backline violinist was again the only survivor reaching C. Section C was started in the same way, and so on till the march at the end came. I doubt if there was a single measure that was more than half played. As a player would get off and stop, he'd usually turn round and smile (one always spit in his handkerchief)—the same kind of smile a fat lady has when she runs for a trolley, half mad, half embarrassed, and half something else. After the "performance," at which some of the audience laughed, some of them cussed, and some of them did something else, Mr Eisler was mad, came up, and handed me back the score saying, "There is a limit to musicianship." But I didn't tell him, as I wanted to, the greatest limitations to musicianship are *your* limitations.

Sometime next month—May 1920—Ives sketched a list of "things to be done":

1. Article for Eastern Underwriter "Small Policies" (by Aug 1)
2. Prefaces & Sonata for Schirmer (by July 25)
3. Finish & copy *Circus Day Band* (as soon as possible)
4. After 1 & 2 are finish work daily on correcting "Majority"
5. Score no 3 N E Holidays "4th of July" (anytime before Oct 1)
6. correct Presentation—Torts (Insurance)
7. send "20th Amendment" paper to magazines (anytime)
8. Address List for "Musical Courier" of names to send Sonata (after Oct or Nov)
9. Select & correct 25 or 30 songs for printing—also set English words for some of the German (Oct or Nov)

Ives's elaborate memoranda, usually in the form of marginalia on his MSS, cover a deal of extraneous matter: politics, social commentaries, sport, economics, domestic responsibilities—"Rocket sick," "seed for next planting," &c, &c. Many of the MSS carry his current business address, for the benefit of his copyists. But items 1 & 6 in the list above are his first—only—reference, in the context of "other business," to the substance of insurance. After 20 years in the business . . .

*Nos 2 & 8:* the *Concord* Sonata was being engraved by Schirmer Inc, *Essays* printed by The Knickerbocker Press—deadline for corrected proofs, July 25; for delivery of printed copies, "after Oct or Nov." They were finally ready January 18 1921. And Harmony sent one to Mrs Sprague Coolidge . . .

My Dear Harmony:
 In accordance with your request I sent a copy of your husband's music to a friend in Boston, who is very interested in new work and modern ideas, and who has given up writing in the European Idiom, and has recently been studying Asiatic music.
 I sent it to him because I did not in the least understand your husband's work myself, and I thought that I could not judge of anything which to me was so foreign. I must confess that I found nothing in it which I liked, but there is so much nowadays that I do not like because I do not understand it that I did not wish to express my opinion about it.

I have today a response from this gentleman, and it is not encouraging to Charlie's work. I do not want to quote him because I think it would hurt you, but you see I am trying to be honest in responding to your request, and feel that it is more friendly to write in this way than not to write at all . . .

Ives's reply:

Thank you for your letter to Harmony. If it isn't asking too much, I would like to hear all your Boston friend has to say about my music (I still call it that). He can't hurt my feelings—I've been called all the names in the criminal code. Favorable comment, to a great extent, is negative—that is, in effect—it sends one up too many blind alleys. If I could see some of this man's music, any that is fairly representative of his main beliefs, I could probably tell whether his criticism will be of value to me, as far as future work goes. But whatever he says won't be discouraging—that can come from only one source—you forgot that . . .

*Nos 3 & 5:* new revisions of old pieces—*The Circus Band,* finished just before his father died, and *4th Of July,* finished 1913. But Ives could not leave them alone . . .

*Nos 4 & 7:* his old hobby-horse, now to see service as a war-horse. The "20th Amendment" found its way to the *Atlantic Monthly* and *Outlook* in May/June, then became the Old Father William footnote to a tired, sterile, tub-thumping affair, *An Election: "Nov 2 1920,"* for chorus & orchestra:

The assumption, in the text, that the result of our national election in 1920, was a definite indication, that the country, (at least, the majority mind) turned its back on high purpose is not conclusive. Unfortunately election returns coming through the present party system prove nothing conclusively. The voice of the people sounding through the mouth of the parties, becomes somewhat emasculated. It is not inconceivable that practical ways may be found for more accurately registering and expressing popular thought—at least, in relation to the larger primary problems, which concern us all. A suggestion to this end (if we may be forgiven a further digression) in the form of a constitutional amendment together with an article discussing the plan in some detail and from various aspects,

will be gladly sent, by the writer, to any one who is interested enough
to write for it . . .

" . . . allow me to sell you a couple . . . " But how do you express such an idea in music ?   Like this . . . ?

". . . we've got enough to eat, to hell with ideals!"
All the old women, male and female, had thier day today,
And the hog-heart came out of his hole;
But he won't stay out long, God always drives him back!
"O Captain, my Captain,

                    ( ( (this, against music lifted wholesale
from his great *Lincoln* music) ) )

                                 a heritage we've thrown away;
          But we'll find it again, my Captain, Captain, O Captain . . . "

. . . CI, like very many Americans, was distraught because
Harding's victory meant the final collapse of Wilson's ideal, a
League of Nations. That day, Wilson had told his cabinet: "You
need not worry. The American people will not turn Cox down and
elect Harding. A great moral issue is involved. The people can and
will see it. In the long run, they will do the right thing." They didn't,
and CI's one phrase was accurate—a heritage *had* been thrown away.

But the rest of *An Election: "Nov 2 1920"* is wide. Not like
this. Not even in the "Soliloquy of an old man, whose son lies in
Flanders Fields . . . he is sitting by the roadside on the day after
election, looking down the valley towards the station"—CI's tear-
jerking stage directions. And this was the man who twice thought
seriously about writing AN OPERA. It's as bad as Walt Whitman,
ACHING WITH AMOROUS LOVE. CHUFF, CHUFF, CHUFFFFING up the
valley past the old man and his ridiculous soliloquy.

And especially not with the Boston police strike, the Palmer
Raids, with Debs, that same election day, polling nearly a million
votes from Atlanta jail. Those weren't League of Nations issues.
They weren't even majority issues. But they were fundamental to
mankind. Like the League of Nations. Compare CI's "Majority"
essay:

If you—THE MAJORITY—want the minority to say what you shall
do, to direct every move you make, to run the world for you, to run
your affairs for you, say so—and you'll have that privilege.

If you—THE MAJORITY—want peace on earth, you can have it.

If you—THE MAJORITY—want war, it's yours for the asking.

If you—THE MAJORITY—want a few murderers to take charge of your government and turn your daughters over to the state to breed public families, you can have them.

If you—THE MAJORITY—want to turn the murderers over your knee, say so, and it is done.

If you—THE MAJORITY—want middlemen to make your laws, they can't, unless you say so.

If you—THE MAJORITY—want medieval national prejudices, high tariffs breeding race jealousies, hatred and war, and standing armies and mass murder—just say so and you can have it, it's yours for the asking.

$$. \quad . \quad . \quad . \quad . \quad ))))$$

*Lastly, No 9:* "select & correct 25 or 30 songs for printing . . ."

By the fall of 1921, 25 or 30 songs had grown to 114. Of these: 64 old songs "selected & corrected," 14 new ones written, 36 earlier orchestral/instrumental pieces adapted or transcribed—the whole done, by Schirmer's engraver again, proofs sent, read and returned during May/June 1922, published, bound in dark blue buckram, at the end of August. Silly reviews, "offense to several musical pussies," &c, &c—esp. some of the paladins of the musical establishment. Ives shot back, in May 1923, with a clever song satire, *The One Way.* Full title, on page 1 of the MS:

The One Way   The True Philosophy   Of all nice Conservatories of Music—& nice "Mus Doc's"—IMA/SEEDY/GODAM/LILY . . .

and the footnote, bottom of page 2:

. . . tack a little "french" on . . . you're liable to get a little money from the American Ladies (Patrons) or a nice job in a nice music college—a PPB   a nice Degree   OG GD (always Class— quote from the Classics or French!—"They ain't no nice poetry or music in America") Help Keep Music an Emasculated Art! & make a living. Prof Gumbo—for $12400, will give you a thorough course in the art of imitating & arresting, dwarfing, emasculating the minds & souls of nice young American Music Learners . . .

The arrow was silent, flew out of sight, and no one heard it fall. Till 40 years later, when the song was published (short title, emas-

culated footnote). At the time, savagely vindictive—one side. Other
side—a deepening sense of desolation. 50 years later, *114 Songs*
has become a collector's item, unquestioned, largely unsung, monument to one aspect of Ives's creative genius. For Ives, at the time,
*114 Songs* was the final abdication of his creative powers. A 1925
memo on an old Ives & Myrick letterhead found him still fumbling
through the pages of the songbook, looking for something to rewrite,
adapt, transcribe:

Suggested song-groups & about this order of preference

"Three Poets & Human Nature"
page   71 Browning—"Paracelsus"   Trumpet & Trombone Solos—
           1st 2 pages for full chamber orches & piano
  "    74 "Walt Whitman"   Chamber   Orches   Piano   Trumpet
           for voice
  "   244 Matthew Arnold "West London"   Woods, strings, piano,
           perhaps a little brass occasionally—1st part a London
           Street Band

"The Other Side of Pioneering" or "Side Lights on American
Enterprise"
  "    13 "The New River"   Trumpet Solo, Sax, 2 V's, Piano
                                                    have score
  "    29 "The Indians"   Oboe Solo, & Trumpet Solos (Strings),
           Piano                                    old score
  "    19 "Charlie Rutlage"   Eng Hr or Oboe, Trumpet, Strings,
           Piano   Tuba or Trombone ?               score lost
  "    59 "Ann Street"   Trumpet Solo, mostly Piano (occasional
           Violin, Viola, Sax)

"From The Side Hill"
  "   131 "Mists"   Flute Solo, Strings (harmonic chords ?), Piano
           Piano, Celesta at end ?
  "    16 "The Rainbow"   fuller scoring at beginning. Strngs, Piano,
           (Clar & Bassoon ?), Trumpet & Flute Solos
  "    86 "Afterglow"   Strings, Harp, Flute & Oboe Solo—occas
           Celesta   Piano ?
  "     6 "Evening"   Oboe & Flute Solos, 2 or 3 Strings, Piano—
           occas Celesta or Bells

"Water Colors"
>     ″    10  "At Sea"  Flute Solo, Strings (mute *all*), Piano—
>               Celesta or Bells—6 notes only
>     ″    62  "The Swimmers"  (Rather full orches Strings, wood,
>               piano, Trumpet (& piano) Solo, Trombone, Tuba, Drum,
>               Tymp
>     ″    27  "The Pond"  Flute, horn, 1 or 2 Violins, Piano—There
>               is an "echo" effect . . .
>               "Full Fathoms Five"  not in book
>               I have this somewhere, but can't find it here . . .

This list was sometime after January 1925. Back in the summer of 1924, they had been to England—Charles and Edith for the first time; Harmony had been there before, with her father. While they were staying at the St James's Palace Hotel, London, they heard of David Twichell's death, by suicide, on August 12, in New York. Ives wrote him the curious epitaph:

> Music is one of the ways God has of beating in on man—
>     his lifes, his deaths, his hopes, his everything—
> an inner something, a spiritual storm,
>     a something else that stirs man
>         in all his parts and consciousness and "all at once"—
>     we call these parts (as a kind of entity) "soul"—
>
> it acts thro' or vibrates, or couples up human sensations
>     in ways (or mediums) a man may hear or know:
>         that is, he knows he hears them
>             and says (or thinks or feels) he knows them—
>
> further than this,
>     what this inner something is which begets all this—
>         is something no one knows—
>     especially those who will define it
>         and use it *primarily* to make a living—
>
> all this means almost nothing to those who will think about it—
>     music—that no one knows what it is—
>         and the less he knows he knows what it is
>             the nearer it is to music—probably

David Twichell was 49. Ives himself 49. His father 49 when he died. The father-fixation reasserted itself—became, with the sea voyage home (Ives's first), *A Sea Dirge*, to lines from Shake-speare's *Tempest* (((idea, Melville's, of *The Tempest* as 1st "Amer-ican" play—"O Brave New World!")))

> Full fathom five my father lies . . .

On the MS:

> Jan 19—cold    120 E 22    1925    NG ?    Whether worth keeping ?
> H says yes    Edith & Moss say no & also Moss White . . .

Summer of 1926 he tried again—the unfinished song *Sunrise*, set to words of his own. On page 2:

> . . . better for strings—NG here! Arthur!

page 3:

> . . . taken from chords & parts of a II S Q & put into this song
> Aug 1926—but not a good job—the words are NG but better than
> the music . . .

One day soon after, he came downstairs from his studio at 164 East 74th Street—their eighth and last New York address—and Harmony found him with tears in his eyes, saying he couldn't seem to compose any more—nothing went well—nothing sounded right. He was 51, the age when an artist, if he is still alive, should be reaching his fullest maturity.

Ives went through the motions of composing twice more. Spring of 1932, aged 57, he was back into the "Universe" idea. After 17 years. "I want to work this out completely this summer." And the marginal note: "Think advisable stay on job another year if pos-sible." In 1942, aged 67, he had out his box of tin soldiers again, *He Is There!* refurbished as *They Are There!* (("Fighting for the People's New Free World . . . ! "))

And that was it. Nothing more. Finit.

This is the way the world ends.

# Fermata

## 2 For the Record . . .

. . . Charles Ives died, May 19 1954, in Roosevelt Hospital/New York, aged 79, of a relapse following the successful operation, 14 days earlier, of a double hernia.

Three years earlier, the New York Philharmonic did a first performance of the 2nd Symphony, at Carnegie Hall. Harmony Ives went down to New York with the Cowells to hear it. Charles Ives didn't. And he didn't listen to it on the maid's kitchen radio and do a little jig to himself afterwards either. He listened on the Ryders' radio next door, with evident and growing distress. When the last movement went on one measure longer than he'd written it, he leapt to his feet, mad, and wrenched the program off. Then went over to the fireplace and spat in it.

## 52 Years Earlier . . .

*Worcester, England*

. . . Parker's *Hora novissima* at 3 Choirs this AM   Good, well made work   American composer   Met him at lunch at M's   Brisk little chap . . .

—H E WOOLDRIDGE: *Diary for Sept 8 1899*

Henry Ellis Wooldridge Esq D Mus
Slade Professor of Music
Oxford University                                              June 5 1902

My dear Harry:

Am to receive my Honorary Doctorate from "the other place" next Tuesday. Leave Cambridge Thursday morning & can be with you "in time for tea." The train gets to Oxford at 3.27 PM—by some conspiracy, there seems no direct connection between the two towns.

Munich was v pleasant & shall have much to tell you. We return there later this year. Saw Richard Strauss—an absolutely splendid fellow—but not your friend Mahler I fear.

Our best wishes to you—and to Ellen for her speedy recovery,
                                  Yours in haste,
                                       Horatio W Parker


*. . . sollten die Stimmen fertig sein, dann würde ich das Stück ja gerne schon am Dienstag probieren. Die Titel rühig auf Englisch lassen!*

(("  . . . if the parts can be ready, I would like to start rehearsing the piece on Tuesday. Keep English titles . . . "))

                    —*Unsigned note, in Mahler's hand, to Music Librarian,*
                              *Deutsches Museum / Munich, summer 1910*


. . . Mahler's 8th in Munich! Unforgettable   M looks so ill we hardly knew him   Alma says bad heart   prognosis poor
            —H E WOOLDRIDGE: *Diary for September 12 1910*


. . . Your query baffles me. There was a Charles Ives in my class when I first came to Yale, but I can not think he is the same. Mahler, indeed! Dear me . . .

                    —H W PARKER: *letter to H E Wooldridge, Oct 4 1910*

# ...First Beginning

The Mexicans also practiced a similar purification
at the end of every fifty-two years, in the belief
that it was time for the world to come to an end.
HENRY DAVID THOREAU: *Walden*

Stubborn. It was pretty much all over for him, as a composer, but
he wouldn't let go. Pretty much all over, back in 1917, but he
wouldn't let go, to himself, till the fall of 1926. Then, within a
few months, two movements from the 4th Symphony, one of his last,
greatest, and most complex works, were given their first hearing,
under optimum performance conditions, before an excited audience
and enthusiastic press, at Town Hall, New York.

It was the price the Gods demanded in propitiation. He had
played their Muse false; only by renouncing her could they acknowledge him as a composer. The double irony, that it should
have been this work, when so many of his earlier, simpler pieces
had been declared "unplayable, NOT MUSIC." And within twenty
minutes, the American musical world he had been born into, 52
years earlier, was ended, the old order changed. But New York
1927 was not Paris 1913, and the American musical world knew
it not.

For itself, and for the events it set in train, this was the real
FIRST BEGINNING. Its prehistory/third irony/went back to the end
of World War I, and the mass exodus of American creative artists
in Europe. Living was cheap, European cultural values impover-

ished. On both counts, Americans could afford to live high on the
hog. Many stayed, professional expatriates, Gertrude Stein's "lost
generation."

Meanwhile . . .

European composers were starting to come to America—not
for their health, not (yet) for their wealth, but for ARTISTIC SUR-
VIVAL, to get something built could no longer be built in Europe.
Among them:

> (1) in 1915, the 30-yr-old French/Italian composer and con-
> ductor Edgar Varèse . . .

. . . in 1915 his American contemporary Wallingford Riegger
was conducting opera in Germany; he returned home in 1917, when
America declared war . . .

In 1919, Varèse forms the NEW SYMPHONY ORCHESTRA, conducts their first concert April 11 . . .

. . . his radical policies over new music force him to resign;
by 1920 he has been replaced, as conductor, by Artur Bodansky.
But Varèse was on the committee that accepted Ives's *Decoration
Day* . . .

> (2) also in 1919, the 30-yr-old French pianist Eli Robert
> Schmitz, on a recital tour of the United States; stays on,
> to found, in 1920, the FRANCO-AMERICAN MUSIC SO-
> CIETY . . .

> (3) in 1921, Varèse is co-founder, with his French-born con-
> temporary the harpist and composer Carlos Salzedo, of
> the INTERNATIONAL COMPOSERS' GUILD . . .

. . . in 1921, 20-yr-old Aaron Copland leaves for Paris, to
study with Nadia Boulanger . . .

((Between 1921 and 1927, when it was disbanded, the International
Composers' Guild sponsored some notable first performances: Ruggles, *Men & Angels* (December 17 1922), *Men & Mountains* (December 7 1926); Copland, Symphony for Organ & Orchestra (January 11 1925); Varèse, *Intégrales* (March 1 1925), *Amériques*
(April 9 1926); works by Berg, Webern, &c, &c . . .

. . . Carl Ruggles, two years younger than Charles Ives, was
born in 1876—founder and conductor, in 1912, of the Winona

Symphony/Minnesota. *Men & Angels,* written in 1922, was his first of a total of only 6 compositions. He died, aged 95, in 1971 . . . ))

(4) in 1923, the FRANCO-AMERICAN MUSIC SOCIETY is incorporated as the PRO MUSICA SOCIETY, Robert Schmitz its first president; on October 4, he writes a letter of enquiry, about insurance, to Ives & Myrick . . .

(5) in 1924, the 38-yr-old Spanish composer and conductor, Pedro Sanjuan, moves to Cuba and founds the Havana Philharmonic; his concertmaster, and former composition student, is 24-yr-old Amadeo Roldan . . .

. . . 30-yr-old Walter Piston, a naval officer during World War I, graduates *summa cum laude* from Harvard in 1923, goes to Paris to study with Nadia Boulanger . . .

In September 1925, Schmitz writes to Ives—"I am most interested in the piano transcription from the Hawthorne movement (4th Symphony) . . . "

. . . 28-yr-old Virgil Thomson, from Kansas City/Missouri, goes to Paris to study with Nadia Boulanger . . .

. . . 33-yr-old Adolf Weiss, from Baltimore, goes to Vienna to study with Arnold Schoenberg . . .

((Weiss, at the age of 18, was 1st bassoonist of the New York Philharmonic under Gustav Mahler, of the New York Symphony under Walter Damrosch, from 1923, 1st bassoonist of the Rochester Philharmonic under Albert Coates and Eugene Goossens. His first orchestral work, *The American Life* ("Scherzo Jazzoso"), was written in 1927, first performed February 21 1930, in New York . . . ))

(6) also in 1925, the 31-yr-old Russian conductor Nicolas Slonimsky comes to America as opera coach at Eastman School of Music/Rochester; in 1927, forms the Boston Chamber Orchestra . . .

In March 1926, the PRO MUSICA SOCIETY meets to discuss the program for their projected First International Referendum of Contemporary Music, to be held early the next year . . .

. . . 29-yr-old Roger Sessions receives the first of two Guggenheim Fellowships; leaves for Paris, to study with Nadia Boulanger . . .

(7) in 1928, Varèse founds the PAN AMERICAN ASSOCIATION
OF COMPOSERS . . .

. . . the 22-yr-old Cuban composer Alejandro Caturla, a student of Pedro Sanjuan in Havana, leaves for Paris to study with
Nadia Boulanger . . .

(((( Finally, in 1937, American composers got something going on
their own—the AMERICAN COMPOSERS' ALLIANCE . . . ))))

                                    . . . But back to March 1926. According
to the minutes of the Pro Musica meeting, Schmitz was anxious to
secure the American première—a concert performance—of Milhaud's chamber opera *Les malheurs d'Orphée,* shortly to go into
production at the Théâtre de la Monnaie, Brussels, for its world
première on May 7. Other than that, the Pro Musica program should
perhaps reflect a New World bias—either American music, or
European music on an American subject. Debussy had been discussed, in the context of some rumored music for an opera on *The
Fall Of The House Of Usher;* but his publishers, Durand & Cie, had
written from Paris to say it was a chimera—nothing had been found.

It was evident from the start, that Ives's 4th Symphony was a
natural; together with the Milhaud, it would make up a complete
program—there was no need to look further. Ives, though a member
of the committee, was not at the meeting, and Schmitz proposed
that investigation be made at once, to see if the material could be
available in time for the concert. The date was fixed for January
29 1927, at 3 PM, Town Hall booked for rehearsals the entire week
before.

After finishing the 4th Symphony, sometime in 1916, Ives had
given the score to the copyist Greinert, a huge, sad, bear of a man.
Like Hawthorne's Giant Transcendentalist, he was German by birth,
and as America moved nearer inevitable war with his fatherland,
Greinert grew more and more upset, couldn't concentrate, made
incessant mistakes, finally gave up and passed the score to George
Price to complete. Since then, it had lain in Ives's office safe—first
at Nassau Street, after May 1923, at 46 Cedar Street. Now, three
years later, the chance of a performance had become palpable, Ives
looked it out and found Price had done his usual thing of making
arbitrary "improvements." He gave it to Reiss, his most reliable

copyist, to do over from the beginning, and get out the complete set of orchestra parts.

Leopold Stokowski—the obvious choice—had been approached as conductor of the Ives, but was not free. On May 27, the 33-yr-old English conductor Eugene Goossens gave a concert at Lewissohn Stadium. He had made a reputation for himself conducting *Le sacre du printemps*—with the London Philharmonic in 1923, Berlin Philharmonic in 1924; recently, with his own orchestra, the Rochester Philharmonic. Schmitz went to see him, learned he would be free the last week of January 1927, and confirmed the arrangements in writing on June 1. In 1961, Goossens recalled the Ives:

> . . . It was a terribly difficult work—much more difficult than *Sacre*—and more rewarding, I should say—I don't know—I only did it that one time. I wanted to do it again, in Rochester, later in Cincinnati, in Australia, Berlin—but the material was never available. That's publishing enterprise for you. If Ives had been European, publishers would have been falling over each other to publish him.
>
> Henry Cowell sent me a copy of the movement that was printed in *New Music*—marvelously engraved—but NO PARTS! What's the use of a marvelously engraved score—and marvelous music—without PARTS—for the orchestra? We used PARTS for the Pro Musica concert—hand-copied, I remember, but very well done—so they must be around somewhere. But that's the only performance there's ever been, as far as I know.
>
> I well remember the first time I saw the score—I was staying at the Chelsea, and Ives and Robert Schmitz brought it over. I remember that I was particularly impressed by the last movement—it had an almost Shakespearean power and inevitability to it—and majesty. It called *King Lear* to mind, and I said so. Charlie Ives made a funny face and didn't say anything, but that's how the Debussy *King Lear* music got into the program. We decided, for a number of reasons—NO PARTS was one—that the last movement couldn't be done, and that left the program a little on the short side. So we had to find another piece to put in its place. Schmitz suggested the Debussy—he had a thing about Debussy. So did Ives. So did I. But a dreary little work it turned out to be.
>
> We had 10 rehearsals altogether—Milhaud took six, for his

opera; three would have been enough. I rehearsed the first three movements of the Ives in some detail—the Prelude and the Fugue sounded magnificent—God, how that man knew how to write. He knew every trick in the business. But after we got to the Debussy, we realized the program was now a little on the long side, and Milhaud was worried that the critics would leave before his piece. I wanted to cut out the Debussy and do the whole Ives symphony, but Schmitz wouldn't hear of it. Besides, there were NO PARTS for the last movement. I'd just finished a very trying first rehearsal on the Hawthorne movement, and everyone was feeling a little on edge. So it was decided to cut out the Fugue. Rehearsals went better and better, and we probably could have done the Fugue at the concert —but for Darius, worrying about his newspaper critics. I don't believe they stayed to hear his piece anyway.

The first rehearsal on the Hawthorne movement was a lesson to me—I used a second conductor after that, a student of mine from Eastman, young Paul White, I think. I'd never used a second conductor before—outside the opera house—but it was very needful here. It wasn't so much the complexity of the score—without a second conductor there was no element of conflict—conflict of temperament, as much as anything else. Ives's conducting note on that second movement was an object lesson in practical musicianship, which every composition student should be made to learn by heart.

After one rehearsal, we all went over to Ives's house, and he showed me a piece for chamber orchestra where he'd used a BASSET HORN! I suggested he might get a few more performances if he changed it to bass clarinet, or bassoon, and he gave me a 10-minute lecture on the merits of the basset horn's tone qualities. Mozart would have been in ecstasies. Then he went over to the piano and solemnly reproduced the sound of a basset horn on the keyboard. It was the most amazing thing—you could have sworn there was an actual basset horn in the room. Like Thurber's Seal in the Bedroom—it was so uncanny—so *unlikely*—you wanted to laugh. Robert went over to the door and looked outside, to see whether he hadn't hired a basset horn player as a practical joke. It would have been very like him.

He and his wife sat in the green room during the rehearsals of his piece. You couldn't hear anything for the steam pipes—it was a cold winter—and a leaking water closet next door. Every time I came in there to see him—he wouldn't come out—she would get up and leave, so "Mr Ives" could be "alone" to talk with "the Conductor" about "the Symphony." She always called him "Mr Ives" —even to close friends. Rather lower middle-class clerical, I thought. After the last rehearsal, the orchestra had come to like the music and gave him an ovation of clattering bows and shuffling feet—a very high compliment. But he wouldn't come out of that d—— green room, even after I went and fetched him. The players were a bit miffed in the end—thought he was a snob. But he was a charming and delightful man when he chose to be—and as shrewd as the devil . . .

## En Passant

. . . The night before the Pro Musica concert, Copland's Piano Concerto received its first performance, in Boston, with the Boston Symphony Orchestra under Koussevitzky, the 26-yr-old composer as soloist . . .

On Sunday, January 30 1927, Olin Downes, for *The New York Times*—the only extensive American review Ives's music ever received, till his last years:

> The International Referendum Concert, given by the Pro Musica Society yesterday afternoon in Town Hall, offered a program that consisted wholly of works new in America or played for the first time anywhere. To this latter class belonged the "Symphony for Orchestra and Pianos," by Charles Ives; to the former, Debussy's incidental music written for an Odeon performance of Shakespeare's *King Lear* in 1904, and Darius Milhaud's chamber opera, *Les malheurs d'Orphée*. This work was conducted by Mr Milhaud in person. The other conductor was Eugene Goossens.
>
> At the risk of appearing provincial, chauvinistic, this writer records that his preference among the works of the afternoon was for the music of Mr Ives. This music is not nearly as compact, as finished in workmanship, as smart in tone, as that of Mr Milhaud, but it rings truer, it seems to have something more genuine behind it. There are ineptitudes, incongruities. The thing is an extraordinary hodge-podge, but something that lives and vibrates is there. It is not possible to laugh this music out of countenance.

Mr Ives began his symphony in 1910 and completed it about ten years ago. The symphony has four movements, a prelude, a fugue, a third movement in a comedy vein, and a finale, according to the program notes of Henry Bellamann, "of transcendental spiritual content." The prelude and the lively movement were the ones heard yesterday. The esthetic program of the "symphony" is less explicable than the music—"the searching question of What ? and Why ?  which the spirit asks of life." The prelude, apparently, is supposed to propound these questions and the three later movements to supply diverse answers. Be all this as it may, the principal characteristic of the prelude is a New England hymn sung in full harmony of mixed voices *(((???)))*, with orchestral commentary of a nature rather groping and incongruous with the choral material.

There is the thought of a New England Sabbath—Mr Ives is a New Englander—when the soul turns in upon itself and questions the infinite. Then, the fugue being omitted, comes the "lively movement," a kind of insane scherzo, in which Mr Ives thinks of "comedy," but "comedy in the sense that Hawthorne's Celestial Railroad is comedy. Indeed, this work of Hawthorne's may be considered as a sort of incidental program in which an easy, exciting and worldly progress through life is contrasted with the trials of the pilgrims on their journey through the swamp . . ." There is much more explanation of Mr Ives's music in the program, but the music is more illuminating.

There is something in this music, real vitality, real naivety, and a superb self-respect. The lachrymose hymn, reappearing in the fast movement *(((where?)))*, is jostled out of existence for whole periods, only to bob up again here and there, as homely and persistent as Ned McCobb's daughter. And then Mr Ives looses his rhythms. There is no apology about this, but a "gumption," as the New Englander would say, not derived from a "Sacre du Printemps," or from anything but the conviction of a composer who has not the slightest idea of self-ridicule and who dares to jump with feet and hands and a reckless somersault or two on his way to his destination.

And the picture of the Concord Fourth of July is really amusing, really evocative of the spirit of that time and day. These were not safe and sane Fourths; they were Fourths that some survived when patriotism was more than jingoism, and a stirring thought; when the nation was in its childhood and firecrackers took off the ear or put out an eye. The scrabble of war songs and brass band tunes that all the villages knew, the noise of the circus, the blare of the band, are in this eccentric symphony, with its holier-than-thou hymn tunes, its commotion, its rowdiness, blaze and glare. There is a "kick" to this piece, regardless of the composer's philosophic or moral purpose. It is genuine, if it is not a masterpiece, and that is the main thing.

The Pro Musica Society is to be thanked for bringing this and other music of the afternoon to a hearing permitting the public to listen to it and form an opinion of its own. The performances were of a high order. Mr Milhaud conducted with the authority and clearness of intention expected of him. Nor should the prowess of Mr Goossens go without praise. He accomplished the dangerous task of the conductor of Mr Ives's music with remarkable authority and control . . .

Lawrence Gilman, for *The Herald-Tribune,* Monday, January 31:

Of the two movements from Mr Ives's symphony, we must say that we wished we might have heard the other two movements that were omitted. Mr Bellamann, in his admirable program notes, tells us that Mr Ives was employing what are now known as typically "modernistic" devices a good many years ago; and this is not hard to believe, for his writing in this symphony has a sureness of touch which is not that of a neophyte learning a new technique.

Mr Ives is an American, and his symphony is the musical testament of a New Englander; but in this instance he has no need to ask us (in the biting phrase of Philip Hale) to "cover mediocrity with the cloak of nationalism." This music is as indisputably American in impulse and spiritual texture as the prose of Jonathan Edwards; and, like the writing of that true artist and true mystic, it has an irresistible veracity and strength, an uncorrupted sincerity.

This Fourth Symphony of Mr Ives is evidently built upon a far-reaching spiritual plan. It has, as Emerson said of Whitman, a long foreground. We repeat that we should like to hear the entire score . . .

It took close on 40 years for Gilman's wish to be granted. By then, both he and the composer were dead.

In the summer of 1927, Ives met Henry Cowell for the first time. From their meeting came the collaboration, to publish, at Ives's expense, the Hawthorne movement. It appeared in the January 1929 issue of *New Music* (vol 2/no 2), wonderfully engraved by Hermann Langinger of the Golden West Music Press/Los Angeles—former top engraver to Universal/Vienna, publishers for Mahler, Schoenberg, Webern, and Berg. T Carl Whitmer, for *The Musical Forecast*, March 1927:

> . . . One of the most stirring, stunning pieces of rhythmic polyphony in contemporary music. Technically, the involved combination of effects is a marvel of inner hearings, to say nothing of adroitness of management. Ives has cast aside as altogether unworthy, all prettiness of effects and gets down to the bottom of elemental man—of you with your social superficial self lifted away. You are now primitive in force and not sophisticated. This innerness-plus-machinery of the man-from-Mars makes great music. Here and there sophisticated technique elbows the roughest themes, and frantically expressed emotions bump a finesse of taste and silken hair-splitting effects. Glissandos in double-basses and cellos slide down, giving you the effect of dropping elevators plunging you down to Gehenna. And all so logically—if such a word can be said to apply to the sub-emotional depths . . .

On July 14 1929, the historic letter:

Dear Mr Slonimsky:

> Last spring Henry Cowell told me that you had been kind enough to ask for a score of mine which your orchestra might play. I should have written before but have been laid up for some months back and haven't been able to attend to things—even correspondence; and also was not sure I could get anything ready by next fall, as all my longer scores are for larger orchestras. But I have one which I got out the other day and played for Henry Cowell who liked it and thought it should and could be done, with some revision reducing it to your chamber group . . .

(( . . . This, Slonimsky's Boston Chamber Orchestra; the score, Ives's 1st Orchestral Set—*3 Places in New England* . . . ))

The same month, Ives wrote his partner in New York to say he had decided to retire. Since last year, when Myrick came out strong for Hoover, Ives for Alfred E Smith, the tension between the two men had grown into an active dislike. Ives found the direction the insurance world was moving in more and more distasteful; Myrick, his partner's scruples more and more irritating. Julian Myrick, who never even graduated from high school, had made it to the top with his smooth, slick, back-slapping, "talkin' glib and continual"—president, now, of the National Association (of Underwriters), chairman of the Davis Cup committee, rubbing elbows with the elite of Forest Hills. But the civilities were preserved. Myrick delivered the ritual coup de grâce, "What the Business Owes to Chas E Ives," for *The Eastern Underwriter*. Ives, to Henry Bellamann, the gelded speciousness about "existence's fabric weaving itself whole . . ."

His decision to retire was well timed. In October, the New York Stock Exchange collapsed, and away in West Redding, he was spared the spectacle of Bank Presidents brawling on the open streets of Gotham. On December 29 he wrote Slonimsky again:

> The copy. of the score is being photographed and will be sent you this week. I hope you may like it. It adapted itself more readily than I supposed to the smaller orchestra. There are some places where the woodwind may be too heavy for the strings—for instance, at the end of the 3rd movement there is a rather mean, off-rhythm, inner part for oboe, which may be omitted, letting the oboe play along with the trumpet on the main tune—there were originally 3 trumpets here. However, do anything you like.
>
> There will be a pianist and in the middle movement an extra drum player to be engaged, if you decide to play it; and I shall want to take care of this and any other expense you may be put to in playing it. I would also appreciate it if you will have the parts copied in Boston and get some careful person to correct them and send me the bill . . .

On February 16 1930, Slonimsky performed *3 New England Places* for the American committee of the International Society for Contemporary Music, in New York. Ives was at the performance, and wrote Slonimsky the next day to thank him . . . "You left your baton here—it feels rather ethereal . . . " His piece was recommended for performance at the ISCM Festival—to be held in Brussels that year—but turned down by the international committee. Now the Pan American Association of Composers stepped in, and sponsored a program of Ives (*3 New England Places*), Cowell (*Synchrony*), and Ruggles (*Men & Mountains*) to be given by Slonimsky and the Boston Chamber Orchestra at Town Hall, New York, January 10 1931 . . .

(( . . . CI was at this concert too. When someone in the row behind him starting hissing at the Ruggles, he nearly ruined the performance altogether by leaping to his feet and shouting: "You goddam sissy!—when you hear strong masculine music like this, get up and USE YOUR EARS LIKE A MAN . . . ")

By now, plans were well advanced for Slonimsky to give two concerts of American chamber music, under the auspices of the Pan American Association, at the Maison Gaveau, Paris. Ives wrote him on February 26:

> Now here is an important job for you. Mrs Ives wrote today to Mrs Prof Kingsley Porter about the Paris concerts, asking her & his help, saying you would call her up & try & see her—we hear they are going abroad shortly. They live at Elmwood, Cambridge, in the old James Russell Lowell house . . .

On April 26, Varèse wrote Slonimsky from Paris:

> Cowell writes me of a prospective concert in Paris. May I suggest—may I even insist—that you play *Intégrales* instead of *Octandre*. I have already written Cowell and Salzedo my reasons for it. *Intégrales* was played here only once two years ago—not under favorable conditions—and yet provided a sensation. There is a demand for a repeat performance, and I think that the announcement of *Intégrales* on your program would help fill your hall.
>
> I am looking forward to seeing you soon here in Paris—and having at last the pleasure of hearing you conduct . . .

On May 28, Ives to Slonimsky, already in Paris:

> We were glad to get your letters. Both came this AM. It's 'most mail time—& just a line to catch tomorrow's boat.
>
> That's quite alright about Varèse. I don't blame him for wanting something new played. Have arranged with the Chase National Bank to cable their Branch Office in Paris, a credit of $250 to you,

which you can draw on by your personal check whenever you need any. Do whatever is necessary to be done, please, & don't worry. Nobody can read by Roman Candles. I agree with Henry that now you are over there, there's no need of hurrying back if there are things to be done—for instance, the English concert. The concert will go alright. Just kick into it the way you did in the Town Hall —never mind the exact notes or the right notes—they're always a nuisance. Just let the spirit sail up to the Eiffel Tower and on to Heaven. Never mind the ladybirds, male & female, in the audience— they're dear & nice.

I hope you get enough rehearsals . . .

FIRST PARIS CONCERT, June 6 1931:

| | |
|---|---|
| Adolf Weiss | *The American Life* |
| Charles Ives | *3 Places in New England* |
| | |
| Carl Ruggles | *Men & Mountains* |
| Henry Cowell | *Synchrony* |
| Amadeo Roldan | Ballet Suite: *La Rembambaramba* |

SECOND PARIS CONCERT, June 11:

| | |
|---|---|
| Pedro Sanjuan | *Sones de Castille* |
| Carlos Chavez | *Energia* |
| Carlos Salzedo | *Préambule et Jeux* |
| | |
| Alejandro Caturla | *Bembé* |
| Wallingford Riegger | 3 Canons |
| Edgar Varèse | *Intégrales* |

Ives wrote Slonimsky next day:

We very much appreciated your thought in sending the cables. I sent the long one on to Henry. I hope all the composers will realize what you have done for them. A composer can say, no matter how it goes, "my music *is* my music"—regardless of what George says—but a conductor has to break it into the existence of others—some of them "nice-pussy-boys"—ta-ta—some job!

It will be fine to see you again, but I hope you feel justified in staying as long as you want. How about the English & other concerts ?

Please give my thanks to Varèse for all he has done. I hope his music went well & was appreciated . . .

On September 3 Slonimsky, back from Europe, gave the first performance of *Washington's Birthday*, first of the *4 New England Holidays*, in San Francisco. On October 12, Varèse wrote him from Paris:

Cowell wrote me from Hamburg immediately after his landing. He told me about your success in California, which does not surprise me but does not prevent me from congratulating you most sincerely . . .

*Orchestre Symphonique de Paris.* The February concerts must be made an immense success, and they must be given with all possible assurance of artistic results—with all necessary rehearsals, &c. I will occupy myself with the task of molding the orchestra—a labor of slow penetration which is of absolutely prime importance . . .

*Arcana.* There is a great deal to talk about it, and an atmosphere of great and sympathetic expectation is created around this score. It will be published within a fortnight and I will send you a copy at once. Do not forget to bring your own set of Chinese blocks for *Arcana*. If you find a good tamtam—deep—sonorous—warm—gargantuan—bring it along too . . .

On October 20, Ives from West Redding:

As I learn that it is my birthday, I will celebrate by sitting down in a moderately comfortable chair and writing to you. Last week *Ich hatte, morgen früh ein froehlich Blatt* (one of the best words in the English language) *vom liebe Heinrich, er sagt*—that (and you probably have already heard) the Berlin Philharmonic is to give two concerts of American music, and you are to conduct one of them and the regular German conductor the other—why don't you do both! Henry was here on the day before he sailed. He seemed quite in sympathy with your foreign plans—and also said that, thanks to you the San Francisco concert was more of a success than usual and I hope you felt the same . . .

Two concerts of American music with the Paris Symphony Orchestra, two with the Berlin Philharmonic. Both large—full-size—orchestras, experienced and critical. The Paris concerts were set for February 21 and 25. Slonimsky's concert with the Berlin Philharmonic was to be March 5. The other, conducted by Otto Klemperer, was canceled. Ives, at 57, was the eldest of the group of American composers—and the only one who wasn't composing any longer, hadn't now, for 14 or 15 years. Plus his reluctance to having any of his other works exposed. There was inevitable pressure from the younger men to ease him out. On November 17, he wrote to Slonimsky:

> I had a letter from Robert Schmitz, who is going to be in Paris after the 1st of the year, and who says he will be glad to play the piano at the Paris concerts. He knows that set of mine which I gave you (a semi-Piano Concerto). Schmitz is well known in Paris . . .

((This was the 2nd Orchestral Set, the second movement—*The Rockstrewn Hills*—the "semi-Piano Concerto."))

On Christmas Eve 1931, Varèse wrote Slonimsky from Paris again:

> OK for *Intégrales* in Berlin and Budapest. Please get a string-drum from Carl Fischer in New York—it costs only a dollar or two—and take it with you, as it is impossible to find one in Europe. They call it Lion's Roar, a stupid name, more suitable to describe the rumblings of a Methodist minister. OK also for Cuba to do *Amériques* after the fusion of the two orchestras in Havana. Merci. You and the score look like Siamese Twins on the photograph.
>
> *Arcana.* We will correct the mistakes in the score together in Paris. I am glad that you are beginning to study it and I will be happy to hear the première of the revised version under your intelligent and precise direction. Your progress does not surprise me. I have opened an unlimited credit in your future . . .

Four days later, Amadeo Roldan, concertmaster and assistant conductor of the Havana Philharmonic, gave the first public performance of Ives's *Decoration Day* in Havana. It was a sensation. The crisis was past. Ives wrote Slonimsky, early in January, with greater self-assertion:

> I was glad to hear that you feel better about the 3 other pieces of mine at the Paris concert. Good, clear parts are made.

It can be put like this: Three Pieces for (Large) Orchestra: I *The Cage*, II *The 4th Of July*, III *An Elegy*. Hoping to see you soon . . .

((This, of course, a composite of other things: *In The Cage*, first movement/Theater Orchestra Set (( Leopard's Cage/Lion's Roar)); *4th Of July*, third of the *4 New England Holidays*, third to receive a first performance; and *An Elegy To Our Forefathers*, to Stephen Foster, first movement/2nd Orchestral Set, what it had all been about in the first place . . . ))

The programs of the Paris concerts and the Berlin concert were the same: Adolf Weiss, *The American Life* ("Scherzo Jazzoso"), in its original full-orchestra version; Charles Ives, the composite "Suite II"; Amadeo Roldan, the suite from *La Rembabaramba* again, but now including the movement for a complete Cuban percussion section; Carl Ruggles, *The Sun-Treader*, symphonic poem on Robert Browning, for large orchestra, specially written for the Paris and Berlin concerts; Henry Cowell, *Synchrony* again; and Varèse, *Arcana* . . .

((Cowell had wanted to write a new piece, *Rhythmicana*, for Paris and Berlin, that would feature Leon Theremin's instrument, the Rhythmicon; *vide* CI's January letter to Slonimsky:

> I had a long talk with Henry the day after you left. I told him about the Rhythmicon situation—and we went into it from all angles. It relieved my mind to know especially that the new one would really be nearer to an instrument, than a machine. It wasn't so much the question of having another made—as I think it ought to—it will be improved, transformed, studied on—but the main question is whether it is yet time to present it in Paris—and if so how is the best way to do it. I sent the remitted check to Mr Theremin yesterday—and he's started building. It will be yours & Henry's—I just want to help—and sit under its "shadow" on a nice day . . . ))

. . . Varèse spoke of the Paris concerts as being crucial. Maybe they were, in the light of later things. But the Berlin concert, May 5 1932, had more crucial potential . . .

This was Berlin of the immediate pre Nazi years—vital, radical, sensual. The Berlin of Berthold Brecht, Lotte Lenya, Kurt Weill;

Marlene Dietrich and *The Blue Angel.* Of Erich Kleiber and the
Berlin State Opera, who gave the world première, two years earlier
to the day, of Milhaud's opera *Christopher Columbus*—the Metropolitan turned it down. Of the Kroll Theater—till 1931, when
reactionary elements, the seeds of Nazism, forced it to close—where,
in 1929, Klemperer had given the world première of Hindemith's
opera *Cardillac.* The Berlin, too, of Furtwängler's Berlin Philharmonic, jealous, proud, condescending. Furtwängler would never
have allowed Klemperer to conduct his Philharmoniker, even in
a program of American music. A young Russian/American conductor, yes—he would be moving on.

Klemperer went to Slonimsky's concert, that Saturday afternoon in the Beethoven-Saal, and was thunderstruck by Ives's *4th
Of July.* Too arrogant—or too shy—to go and see the younger conductor, he called the American Embassy on Monday morning. They
had no information to give him. They had had instructions from
Washington to boycott the concert.

Klemperer wanted to do *The 4th Of July* with the Los Angeles
Philharmonic, after he became their conductor, in 1933. "Good,
clear parts are made . . ." Again, in Pittsburgh, in 1937. "Good,
clear parts are made . . ." In Prague, in 1947. In Paris, in 1948.
In London, in 1953. "Good, clear parts are made . . ." Each
time, the same reply, the material was not available. Or no reply
at all. But Klemperer made the mistake of addressing himself to
a publisher, or a concert promoter, and not to the composer. "Good,
clear parts are made . . ." The history of American music publishing enterprise.

Back in the USA—May 1932—Yaddo Music Festival, organized by Aaron Copland; and Copland as accompanist to Hubert
Linscott in 7 Songs by Charles Ives. At one of the open forums,
Copland said that more attention was paid by the American press
to a modern music première in Württemberg/Germany than to an
entire festival of premières in Saratoga. And the once-forgotten/
twice-remembered: "Frankly, I consider newspaper criticism a men-
ace. We would be better off without it." By July, at least *Hound &
Horn* reviewed the Ives:

> . . . But in Mr Ives's SEVEN SONGS we heard the great work
> of a curious genius. One of the unforgettable things taken away

from Yaddo was CHARLIE RUTLAGE, with its distillation of the true flavor of the West; the false front of clapboards, the smell of dusty saddle and the clank of harness against a horizon of immense blue . . .

It was five years since the FIRST BEGINNING, back in 1927. With the early months of 1932, the performances of *4th Of July* and *Elegy To Our Forefathers* summoned a brief echo from the abandoned "Universe" piece. But it was momentary as a falling star. His health lapsed again, and, by May 12, on his doctor's advice, Ives and his family were on their way to England.

There remained one last FIRST THING to be done for the BEGIN-NING to be accomplished, the ritual complete. In 1935 it was achieved. The engraved score and complete set of ORCHESTRA PARTS of *Three Places in New England* was published by Birchard & Co, of Boston, a commercial music-publishing house.

# Indian Summer / Virgin Spring

*We have been in Westmoreland living*
*"slow with the sheep." The lakes and*
*mountains and country are beautiful. We*
*admire the English ways. When they get run*
*over, they smile & say sorry (C♯↗B♭)*
*to the taxy driver . . .*

To be in Mr Birchard's catalogue
is more of an honor to *me* than to
him—that is, I consider myself
the honored one—as he is the
only American publisher, as far
as I know, who has published
music he believed should be
published, yet knowing it would
bring him certain loss and the
ridicule, or at least "a nice
smile" from the trade . . .

*Our plans are indefinite — but we are*
*going to Germany (and will see Henry) and*
*probably to France. I will write a long and*
*a nice letter to you soon — when I can lose*
*the vibrato . . .*

> Please, tell him how much I appreciate
> his interest. You told him, I presume,
> that we wanted parts engraved and he
> should include this in his estimate.

*We are here on a side hill of limoni and*
*oranges — have you ever been in*
*Sicily? — that is, early in the morning? . . .*

> I don't know what to say about the
> score. The estimate is somewhat more
> than I had thought of "laying out" at
> the present time. The score, of course,
> will have to be engraved — but would
> this other process come out just as
> clearly as the engraved parts?

*The sun comes out of Greece over the*
*Ionian sea, and then a nice breeze over*
*Calabria brings it to the eye — but with*
*it lemons, and madamigelle to the other*
*eye!* "Mi manda un barbiere alle otto!" . . .

> Also, another point that I've heard
> about through Henry's troubles and
> others, is the question of "performance
> fees." It apparently often means a law
> suit and prevents a performance.
> Henry says Stokowski returned a
> score recently saying the Philadelphia
> Orchestra would not pay fees, &c . . .

*When the sun shines it is as our June — when*
*not, it is like "Election Day" & Republicans!*
*It is the color "buono mollo" — in everything*
*and everywhere that makes up the scenery*
*here . . .*

> I would be willing to make any business
> arrangement that Mr Birchard would
> suggest, so that "performance fee" could
> be *cut out*. If this can be done, I think I
> might as well go ahead and have the score
> made, on the estimate in the letter. (Have
> extra pencil — I revert to it — can steer it
> with less vibrato than pen . . .

*There are many artists here — no musicians.*
*"Lo voglio molto forte!" Will probably stay*
*here until the first part of March, then go to*
*some of the Italian cities for a while and*
*may sail from Naples — or possibly, a boat*
*to England, and back that way — "desidero*
un sigaro forte!"

> Am not sure I'd make any changes in the
> score — the drum part at the beginning of the
> second movement, I wrote that way so the
> "down beat" bass drum would go along as
> they play it, on main beats, not after-beats.
> On p 27 think it might be easier for the drum
> and piano to play it as written — would also
> keep 2nd Viola here. Generally speaking,
> I don't like to change anything after once
> finished. (Please excuse paper, pencil and
> ritin'. As you see, there is no "tremolo" with
> nice pencil . . . )

*Is Russia a musical nation — like Italy?*
*I mean is Russia a musical nation — or*

*do they just like nice voices? I hear from
Henry occasionally — he is now in
California and says that America is a
musical nation — out there . . .*

I've started going over the proofs — and ran
right into a "mess" that I thought was straight-
ened out when Hanke did the parts. I asked him
to both "up" and "down" stems on all strings
(except Bass) unless there were long passages
of a page or more where there is only one part,
then just one stem would do, if "unis" or "a due"
or "non div" was put . . .

Your conductor's note is "well put"—there are
some conductors that I'd send it to just as it
stands; but there are others who I wouldn't like
to have think (as it came ostensibly from me)
that I underrate their intelligence—for instance,
Goossens . . .

*I didn't mean to get this old subject into
this letter — but an article in an English
paper this morning — "Are we a musical
nation?" — brought it. I'm sorry. There is
nothing in a musical nation — not even
music — for a nation is only a nation — but
a good cigar is ET AL!*

Last measure p 19: have put Cello part in 1st
Bass (this is better I think — sometimes a Cello
sounds too loud and scratchy down there.

Opposite p 19 (last page of music of I): would
put verse in small print—would have these verses
at end and not beginning of movements. Rather
not feature the verses &c before the music.

Think that whatever conductor's instructions,
should go in a note printed on a separate sheet and
be sent out when parts are sent out and not in score.

I think your "note" about beating 2 rhythms is excellent and well put, even as it stands, if it got before men of your genius, brains & courage—but where are they ? Most conductors, if they should be told to beat 2 rhythms together, would fall down in a nice-looking swoon and give up the whole job —and it gives them another excuse for not playing anything. The 2 slight revisions I've made, would make it more optional and not sound quite so much as if I were laying the law down. And from some experience, asking most men to do a new way, only makes them do it worse . . .

*We have been settled in America for a few weeks, gradually getting our bearings and household Penates back into place. Have seen no one yet but the family &c, though have heard from Henry Cowell and Carl Ruggles — they're both well — one seething, and one cussing . . .*

Haven't started working on the III movement yet. My hands and arms have been bothering me again — it's hard to handle a pen — but the meanest part is not to be able to play the piano when I want. However — am better than I was last week. Will you please ask them to send me another proof of III in black & white (& charge it to me). After I look at those white notes on green for about 10 minutes, they all start to move around — like rice in green soup to my eyes . . .

*What concert is to be in March, that Varèse spoke to you about? It's very good of him to have you do something of mine. I might suggest 2 short but active songs (with orchestra) — and the quiet "In The Night" for orchestra . . .*

Have been rather slow in correcting the last movement, but now have got it cleared up and am mailing it to you today. On the last page, the quotation from the poem should be printed in small print, the way the other movements were done. Please tell the engraver that I want to see the last proofs of the whole thing, including verses, &c, before it goes to press. And please ask them to send the balance of the bill as soon as they know what it is . . .

*Weiss did the Theater Orchestra Set at a*
*school concert about 2 years ago — there*
*are good, clear parts for this. But "The*
*Ruined River" and "December" will have*
*to have the old scores copied and parts*
*made. As I remember, there are some*
*measures that are rather indistinct, but not*
*many. "The Ruined River" takes 2 Saxo-*
*phones, but one & a trombone would do it.*
*Good night.*

Atoms are indivisible — so are 32nd notes. From p 74 each 2 measures are put down as such, through p 80. In other words these "backwater" waves are put down in a prescriptive formula which exists only on paper — so when played exactly right — it's wrong — like Arthur Evans' cow. Don't read the above again but just tell the engraver I tried to make as little trouble as I could — and the attached sheet makes the lower staff Piano, from p 74 to p 80, clear, uniform, and nice. The real music is all put into the footnote to p 74.

*Since writing you we have had some low*
*days — Uncle Deac died — quite suddenly after*
*a stroke. You remember him living with us in*
*Redding — the oldest of our generation — and*
*one of the last of the old type, now quite*
*vanishing — and the world loses something*
*indefinable . . .*

You are right—let them take p 77 from the corrected copy (correct on paper, though you can't make me play it that nice way except Sat night) Am quite sure, in sending the copy back with these 2 measures, I explained to the engraver to go by these—if he had he would have saved us and himself trouble. When they send the I and III final proofs, if the former proofs with corrections in could be sent also, it would save time in checking up. The other engraver (Langinger) always did that . . .

*Weiss & Riegger came in—and also Varèse—they are full of plans—which I hope will work out. They told me first that Reiner was to conduct the Town Hall concert on April 15—that made me sore—but Varèse telephoned the other day to say that* you *were to conduct—which is* quite *right—very much quite alright!*

I don't care about the cover page—as long as the letters aren't = (are not) big, especially my name. Would just have *Three Places in New England* (an Orchestral Set) and the separate titles of each movement inside . . .

*I've been on the point of writing you for many days back—but I'll have to admit for some time I didn't seem to be able to keep in decent shape—and had to give up doing just about everything. It's humiliating and makes me mad. Mrs Ives has decided, backed up by all the family plus the MD, that the best thing to do now is to sail over to England and stay there for 2 or 3 months—anyhow, for good or otherwise, we're going to sail on August 10 . . .*

WEST REDDING
May 11 1935
Everybody at church—except the one who ought to be. I expected to send back a score from New York. Will do so soon. There's one item in it, that makes no

sense. "Don't play first measure
unless there are 3 trombones"—
now if it had said—"don't play
first measure unless there is a
good conductor"—that would
have been the most sensible note
ever written—the only conductor's note ever needed!

Please ask Birchard & Co to
send a copy of the score to the 2
names enclosed. And if they also
will send a half dozen (or more)
copies to me, I'll appreciate it.
Will also pay for the postage if I
should . . .

MRS CHAS E IVES
WEST REDDING
CONNECTICUT

July 6 1936

My Dear Nicolas—

We were glad to get a line from you and to know that you are
all well—I can imagine that Electra's conversation is most diverting.

We have been here since early May. Mr Ives isn't feeling very
well—I get a little discouraged about him tho' he got a very good
report from the doctor before we came away as to his physical symptoms—he says to send his love to you and to say that when he can
he will get the work you want—the violin sonatas. He has been

working over his Browning score—some of it was lost and much of it nearly illegible & it has been a lot of work to get it in shape even to be copied. He can work only for a short time as his eyes allow little strain. He would write you himself but his handwriting is so bad that he hesitates to. He really has so many trials and is very uncomplaining.

We were interested to see the excerpt from the French paper. Of course the writer had his own idea which he wanted to bring out. It wasn't lack of an audience & appreciation that made Mr Ives stop composing. It just happened—the War & complete breakdown in health. He had worked tremendously hard in his quarry all those years & exhausted the vein I suppose. I am always hoping he may open up a new vein & he may. His ideas are by no means exhausted but there are the physical disabilities to be contended with. He is such a wonderful person—he has such strength of *character* and will & sense. In all family troubles & decisions & problems he is the one they all come to.

Well, I didn't intend writing so much but you are a friend and I get rather pent up.

Please give my warm regards to your wife—we saw Mr Furness recently who says he sees her often—at the Library I think he said— and with best wishes from us both

   I am
    Yours as ever sincerely
     Harmony T Ives

# THREE PROTESTS,
# A VARIED AIR
# &
# VARIATIONS

# Three Protests...

> It seemed by the distant hum as if somebody's bees had swarmed, and that the neighbors, according to Virgil's advice, by a faint tintinnabulum upon the most sonorous of their domestic utensils, were endeavoring to call them down into the hive again.
>
> HENRY DAVID THOREAU: *Walden*

*The Danbury News,* July 6 1931

## HEARD IN PARIS
### WORK OF CHARLES IVES WELL
### RECEIVED IN FRENCH CAPITAL

Many Danbury friends of Charles E Ives, a former Danburian, now living in Redding, will be pleased to hear of the interest aroused and the deep impression made by two concerts given recently in Paris, under the auspices of the Pan American Association of Composers, which featured Mr Ives's New England Symphony. Mr Ives is a brother of Judge J Moss Ives, of this city, and is recognized as one of the outstanding American composers writing in the ultra-modern vein . . .

*The Boston Herald,* July 7 1931

#### MR SLONIMSKY IN PARIS

Nicolas Slonimsky of Boston, indefatigable in furthering the cause of the extreme radical composer, has brought out in Paris orchestral compositions by Americans who are looked upon by our conservatives as wild eyed anarchists. He thus purposed to acquaint Parisians with contemporaneous American music. But the composers represented were not those who are considered by their fellow-countrymen as leaders in the art, nor have they been so considered by the conductors of our great orchestras . . .

*The Danbury News*

> These Parisian concerts were conducted by Nicolas Slonimsky, conductor of the Boston Chamber Orchestra, who is now on his  way back to America and who will be Mr Ives's guest at his Redding home for a few days, soon after his arrival in America . . .

*The Boston Herald*

If Mr Slonimsky had chosen a composition by Loeffler, Hill; one of the Deems Taylor suites, Foote's suite, or music by some who, working along traditional lines, have nevertheless shown taste, technical skill, and a suggestion at least of individuality, his audience in Paris would now have a fairer idea of what Americans are doing in the art . . .

*The Danbury News*

> Leading French newspapers and musical critics have been loud in their praise, both of Mr Slonimsky as a brilliant young conductor of great promise, and of the talent of Mr Ives . . .

*The Boston Herald*

Are these Parisians to be blamed if they say that the American composers thus made known to them are restless experimenters, or followers of Europeans whose position in the musical world is not yet determined . . .

*The Danbury News*

> The critic Paul le Flem, for the Paris *Comoedia*, says: "One Charles Ives appears to have discovered, before *Le Sacre du Printemps*, a style which, in its boldness, places its author in the forefront of the *avant-garde* . . .

*The Boston Herald*

. . . men who show ingenuity chiefly by their rhythmic contrivance
and orchestral tricks; men who apparently have no melodic gift, or,
having it, disdain it for the tiresome repetition and transformation
of an insignificant pattern . . .

*The Danbury News*

". . . This is the orchestration of an artist. And it is a real
brainwave, to have imagined, in the second movement, this
encounter between two village bands, each one playing in its
own tempo, resulting in a conflict of color, key and rhythm
that are exhilarating to hear . . .

*The Boston Herald*

. . . who neglect the sensuous charm of stringed instruments and
put their trust for startling effects in combinations of wind and
percussion choirs . . .

*The Danbury News*

". . . Every instrument is employed for its solo quality and
not for its harmonic effect; with the bow, the reed, the em-
bouchure, and the keyboard, M Ives produces delicate half-
tones subtly touched, softly brushes a background against which
another instrument will begin to sing with poignant power . . ."

*The Boston Herald*

. . . followers, but with unequal footsteps, of Stravinsky, Prokofieff,
and certain continental composers of whom Hindemith is a prominent
example ?

*The Danbury News*

The following is the comment of *Les Beaux-Arts*, Brussels:
"Among the Americans is Charles Ives. He is different from
the others. His music has a 'saveur' peculiarly his own . . . "

## The Boston Herald

How many of those now throwing overboard sane rules, traditions of proved worth, the adventurous and daring souls, have contributed to the glory of the art . . . ?

## The Danbury News

Boris de Schloezer, in *La Nouvelle Revue Française*, says: "Ives beyond dispute is a master and has something to say. He is self-made, self-developed, a forerunner of many contemporary ideas in the domain of rhythm and harmony; he possesses genuine originality and the courage of an artist who is hampered neither by school or traditions, doing his work without looking at the others . . ."

## The Boston Herald

They may say they are writing for posterity . . .

&c, &c, &c.

## Abstract

Quote.        wild eyed anarchists
              restless   experimenters
              followers  of  Europeans
       whose  position  in  the  musical  world
                    IS          NOT         YET          DETERMINED
                    .           MEN         WHO          NEGLECT
       the sensuous charm of stringed instruments    &
                    PUT          THEIR      TRUST
                         for  startling  effects      IN
              c o m b i n a t i o n s   o f           WIND
              a n d   p e r c u s s i o n
              c h o i r s            .

Unquote.

It is a conspiracy; a communist plot. Massed choirs of percussion on the Place de la Concorde, 71 furtive trombones in seditious communion below the Arc de Triomphe. Paris must be warned; tovarich Slonimsky, prime culprit, brought to heel, taught a lesson.

((( The Boston Chamber Orchestra had single winds—1 flute, 1 oboe, 1 clarinet, 1 bassoon, 1 horn, 1 trumpet, 1 trombone— timpanist, and 10 strings. 18 players in all. For his Paris concerts, Slonimsky engaged local players in like numbers. The Weiss, Ives, Ruggles, Cowell, Roldan, Sanjuan, and Varèse pieces had been scored—or rescored—for this combination. The Caturla called for 14 instruments, the Chavez 9, the Salzedo for solo harp and 9 instruments, the Riegger for wind quartet. With these forces, *The Boston Herald* implied, the Bastille had been in danger of storm . . . )))

### WIND IN TRUST & NEGLECT DETERMINED

" . . . the enclosed editorial, headed *Mr Slonimsky in Paris,* written by Philip Hale himself, will undoubtedly be of interest to you . . . "

### MEN WHO NEGLECT SENSUOUS CHARM PUT THEIR TRUST IN COMBINATIONS

" . . . thank you for the enclosed pretty lines from a nice old lady. Mr Hale has quite the philosophy of Aunt Maria—'when you don't understand some'm, scold some'n . . . '

### FOR STARTLING EFFECTS . . . . .

" . . . Where does he get all the facts underneath his 'pronunciamento'—where does he find the authority for all his sweeping statements ? Does he actually know all the music he knows so much about—and do 'the conductors of our great orchestras,' in whose mouths Mr Hale puts his own opinions, know it ? I can say for one, they do not. Not enough conductors have seen enough of my music to get even a good impression of how bad it is . . .

*Aunty Philip Nathan Hale,*
*90 if a day;*
*Bright of eye & bushy tail,*
*Slonimsky in his way.*

*O, Rollo for our President,*
*Our President is nice . . .*

" . . . It is interesting (and perhaps funny) to know that I (since I am included in his sweeping statement) have been influenced by one Hindemith (a nice German boy) who didn't really start composing until 1920, and several years after I had completed all my (good or bad) music which Aunt Hale says is influenced by Hindemith. It happens that *3 New England Places* was completed and scored (for full orchestra) almost a decade before Hindemith started to become active as a composer . . .

> *Little Mr Philip Hale,*
> *Busy little bee;*
> *Rattling pans to no avail,*
> *Virgil on his knee.*
>
> *O, Rollo for our President,*
> *Our President's a dear . . .*

" . . . In other words, the gist of Aunt Hale's remarks is that the music of one man was influenced by another man ten years after the music so influenced was composed by the man who was influenced by the other man. It's funny how most men, when they see another man put the breechin' under a horse's tail, wrong or right, think that he must be influenced by someone in Siberia or Neurasthenia. No one man invented the barber's itch . . . "

> *Mr Philip Nathan Hale,*
> *Boston's OK Kid;*
> *Writing diatribes for sale,*
> *Without the "quo pro quid . . ."*

. . . because Philip Hale, fine legal mind that he had, 42 years' experience as a Boston music critic that he had, trained under Rheinberger and Guilmant as he had, hadn't done his homework. He knew the Paris concerts were going to take place because he'd been sent the advance notices. Two programs of American music in Europe—and in Paris/France. Such a thing had never happened before. It was an American "first." If nothing else, he could have congratulated the Pan American Association of Composers on their initiative. But no. Two piddling little concerts of American music in Europe, composers no one had ever heard of, conducted by someone who wasn't one of "the con-

ductors of our great orchestras," not worth the attention of a leading music critic. Then, when the concerts were enthusiastically
received, he couldn't afford to say he'd known about them all
along. Questions might be asked, touching his infallibility—why he
hadn't taken the trouble to acquaint himself with these composers'
music, hadn't heard any of it, hadn't seen any of their scores. So
he damned the concerts out of hand, implied they had been clandes-
tine affairs the French authorities would do well to look into, drew
a smoke screen over his own lentitude by launching a petulant and
meretricious attack on "modern music" in general and 35-yr-old
Nicolas Slonimsky in particular. Bear in mind these two Paris programs—11 composers in all—included the names

> CHARLES IVES
> CARL RUGGLES
> HENRY COWELL
> CARLOS CHAVEZ
> WALLINGFORD RIEGGER
> EDGAR VARÈSE

Against these 6 names—then unknown to the musical world at
large—Hale placed his own choice of 4 "more likely to succeed"

> LOEFFLER
> EDWARD BURLINGAME HILL
> DEEMS TAYLOR
> ARTHUR FOOTE

Now, a critic may be forgiven for not spotting six winners and
backing four losers if he has the grace to keep his mouth shut and
the sense to realize that racing form is not sonata form. But it takes
a special quality of 35-yr-old genius that can compile a program of
eleven dark horses, six of whom would be winners, and two at
least, "whose position in the musical world" would later be determined in the most positive way. Ives showed restraint when he
wrote, in August 1931, "all one can say is that she, Aunty Philip
Nathan Hale, is either musically unintelligent or deliberately unfair; to say it quickly, he is either a fool or a crook." He could,
as he wrote somewhere else, have said something far worse, which he
occasionally knew how to do . . .

15 years on, Yaddo Music Festival again, Sunday September

15 1946—and the Walden Quartet playing Ives's 2nd String Quartet.
Noel Straus, for *The New York Times*, Sunday September 22:

> At long last, Mr Ives is coming into his own as a creative artist,
> and his outstanding importance in American music begins to be
> widely recognized. If it has taken several decades for this to hap-
> pen, the reason is simply that he wrote compositions that were
> half a century before their time, and it has taken all these years
> to catch up with him . . .
>
>                         . . . the only reason ?) ) ) ) )
>
> His Second String Quartet, though of extreme rhythmical
> and technical difficulty for all four players, has a lovable naivety
> of feeling in its initial two movements, the first a friendly discus-
> sion, the second an argument filled with humorous touches, but
> finally ending with blows.
>     This argument, concerned with the relative merits of the North
> and South, judging by the Civil War tunes from both parts of
> the country that are introduced, quiets down in the introductory
> measures of the superb finale, a movement which in its exalted mood
> and depth of expressiveness must rank as one of the masterpieces
> of chamber music. It depicts the religious sentiment of the men
> of the argument as they walk up the mountainside and view the
> firmament, expressed in an Adagio of almost unequalled poig-
> nance . . .

*The Herald-Tribune:*

> . . . It is difficult to convey in words what everyone present felt
> at this moment. Music of this kind happens only once every fifty
> years or a century, so rich in faith and so filled with a sense of
> completion . . .

This—33 years after its completion—was the Quartet's first per-
formance. It might not have been performed even then, if the name
of Charles Ives had not been brought to the attention of the great
Mrs Ames, of Yaddo, by the National Institute of Arts & Letters.
In their abundant wisdom, they had elected Ives to their number in
March 1946. It was the only public honor he ever acknowledged.
When, the following year, his 3rd Symphony was awarded the

Pulitzer Prize without his prior sanction, he rejected it, with the terse admonishment: "Prizes are the badges of mediocrity."

Ives was nearly 72 when the 2nd String Quartet was first played. It had not been published—none of his chamber music had been published. In fact, apart from *3 New England Places* and a few pieces in Cowell's *New Music*—all in "study score" form, with no instrumental parts available—his only published music of any description was the *Concord* Sonata and *114 Songs*, both published at his own expense in 1921/22.

The real difficulty about playing Ives's music or anyone's else is not the music itself, but simply getting hold of the material—the music. The pieces of paper with notes written on them that musicians play from. I spell it out because there is a whole mystique to this that musicians take quite for granted. In the case of established composers of the 18th & 19th centuries, from Mozart to Mahler, there is no great difficulty—the real difficulties start when the music is there, sitting on the musicians' desks. The material exists in printed form, on sale to any musical organization that wants to buy it. Most of them—schools of music, orchestra libraries, &c—have it already. Anyone who wants to put on a performance of music by an established composer, from a symphony to a string quartet, has simply to ask the music librarian for it, and they can get it. If the music librarian doesn't have it, he can get it. It is "available"—on sale.

This music wasn't always in printed form. Its earliest performances, until the composer established a reputation for himself, were invariably from hand-copied manuscript. The clearer the manuscript, the easier it was to read, the better the music got played, and the quicker a composer established a reputation for himself.

But, at some point in the life of this music, if it had any value (commercial or aesthetic), a publisher would publish it—which entailed editing it, engraving it, printing it, and putting it out on sale to the public. The initial, editorial, stage was the heaviest responsibility—and remains so. So long as music remained in manuscript form—either the composer's or a copyist's—all decisions about wrong notes, doubtful notes, miscopying, general illegibility, devolved on the performer. The moment a publisher undertook to publish, he tacitly assumed this responsibility.

Perhaps we take it too much for granted, when we handle a nice printed score of Beethoven's music—and the nice printed set of orchestra parts that goes with it—the unstinting patience, unremitting loyalty to the composer's text, enormous musical scholarship that went into deciphering and editing Beethoven's barely legible MSS. They could do this, not only because Beethoven was a serious composer, but because they were serious publishers. Even then, even when Beethoven himself was available to read the proofs, the first editions often contained errors that no one, not even the composer, had spotted. It is the inevitable hazard of taking music publishing seriously. You have to take decisions—even the composer has to take decisions, where the original MS has been ambivalent—and you may be wrong.

At the time of his death, only three of Ives's orchestral works existed in published form: *3 New England Places,* by Birchard in 1935; the 3rd Symphony, by Arrow Music Press in 1947; and the spurious first edition of the 2nd Symphony, by Peer/Southern in 1951. Today, nearly 20 years after Ives's death, only two more orchestral works are properly published, a third republished: the 1st Symphony, the *Robert Browning* Overture, and the restored original text of the second edition of the 2nd Symphony—all three by the same publisher, Peer/Southern. The material of the 4th Symphony, the *4 New England Holidays (Washington's Birthday/ Decoration Day/4th Of July/Thanksgiving)*, the 2nd Orchestral Set, all the works for chorus and orchestra, and most of the smaller orchestral works, exists only in manuscript form, copied by Ives's copyists 40, 50, and 60 years ago, recopied from those copies by other copyists and the copying errors compounded, or photocopied in the cheapest possible way. The material has become so defaced with age, heavy pencilings, corrections, private messages from players in one orchestra to players in another, private comments about the music, general wear and tear, that it is now unusable. Yet it still goes on being sent out.

This problem is not confined to Ives—it afflicts all music that exists in rental form only. Rental material commonly carries the strenuous injunction:

## WARNING

This material must not be marked in any way. If markings, in light pencil, are made, they must be erased before the material is returned, otherwise a charge will be made . . .

But the material is never inspected when it comes back, the charge never levied. Rental departments commonly plead shortage of staff or, when pressed, admit that it is more trouble to them than it is worth. Conductors who don't want to waste their players' time trying to decipher the composer's original text, who haven't rehearsal time to waste in any case, have long adopted the policy of sending the material straight back, unplayed, if it arrives in a mutilated state. And usually it does.

*4th Of July* was one case in point. In 1968, the BBC programmed the work in one of their summer Promenade Concerts at the Royal Albert Hall—a first London, first British performance. There had been no lack of eagerness to perform the work, either in Europe or America, but the material was never, hardly ever, "available." The BBC tried the usual channels, then more devious ones, was met at every turn by excuses and prevarications. They were about to cancel the performance when the material suddenly showed up, looking like a contingent of redcoat stragglers from Bunker Hill—incomplete set of string parts, no contrabassoon part, no tuba part, no bells part, two pages missing from the full-score, the whole, score and parts, totally illegible from the accumulated heavy pencilings of other conductors, other players, other orchestras. One marking was in Slonimsky's hand, showing conclusively that the material was the same used for the first performance, 36 years before, in Berlin. It was the only set in existence. It took the BBC music staff five days to clean up the material into playable condition and get the missing parts copied, and the conductor, Frederick Prausnitz, had to make do with half an hour's rehearsal—for a work that properly requires six hours.

Such laxity breeds other mischief. One heavily marked score that once passed through my hands—*Decoration Day*—had been used by the recording engineer of a major recording session. At one point in the score where there is a second's complete silence, a cross had been marked in to remind him to edit out an extraneous sound. Underneath the X was written: "Leave it. Good for laughs . . ." Now there may be some works by Ives where the "leaving in" of an extraneous sound—a carelessly dropped violin mute, for example, where Ives has allowed too little time for the player to take it off silently—might, arguably, be considered "good for laughs." As I see it, *Decoration Day* is not one of those works. Is it then justifiable to leave such a sound in the master tape, simply to register someone's protest that Ives was making unfair demands ?   Most composers do, in the opinion of most orchestral players. But that isn't the point. If you leave a sound like that in the master tape, the recorded impression left with posterity won't be of a hick composer, but a hick recording company. And a hick orchestra. And a hick publisher, for leaving the marking in the score for other conductors to see.

Another hazard, probably not unique to Ives, is where a publisher is presented with an MS which purports to be a faithful copy of the original and turns out to be a fake. That was the fate of the first edition of the 2nd Symphony, based, in all good faith, on an MS score that had been "reconstructed" from an existing set of parts—the original score, from which those parts were extracted, having mysteriously disappeared. 18 years later, the publishers were put to the labor and expense of getting out a second, "revised" edition. Evidence that the "reconstructed" score was bogus had become overwhelming, and in that bogus guise the symphony had been played all over the world, recorded a number of times, hundreds, perhaps thousands of copies of the score sold. And the guise ?   Dozens of minor, two major "improvements," the attempt of some cornball artist to jazz the whole score up, as though Ives were some homely old crank who needed a face lift.

Then you have the PERFORMANCE SCORE: FACSIMILE EDITION of the 4th Symphony. After the copyright owners finally acquired the copyright to the entire work—the copyright to the second and third movements originally held by other publishers—it lay idle in one of their filing cabinets for nearly 10 years. Finally, demands for its publication became so insistent, they realized they were going to have to do something. Having implicated every reputable musical organization, every reputable musical figure they could, indulged themselves in months of advance publicity about the "well-nigh insuperable" task that had been laid on their shoulders, they announced their PERFORMANCE SCORE: FACSIMILE EDITION to an MGM fanfare of trumpets and drums.

The original MS and the Reiss MS of the 4th Symphony are, admittedly, a little hair-raising to decipher, but no more so than some MSS I've seen. Compared to them, this "realization," as the copyright owners call it, looks as the House of Usher, after the Fall. The crude and clumsy copying in the first and third movements would matter less if both movements were not riddled with far more errors than the originals they were copied from. The second movement is basically Langinger's handsome work, taken from the *New Music* plates, but a number of Langinger's pages "found to contain so many errors and unnecessarily complex rhythmic notations" that newly copied pages and patches were inserted, in the same childish, arrogant, "error-free" hand that copied the Prelude. In the last movement, the words PERFORMANCE SCORE acquire an almost Ivesian sense of satire. Its pages are "landscaped," averaging 2 to 3 measures to each double page, the score turned sideways on. To "perform" from this PERFORMANCE SCORE, the conductor must turn the pages upwards, bottom to top, at such a speed he has less chance than a virgin at Gomorrah of taking in music written so small, it takes almost a magnifying glass to identify the individual notes. And, once again, riddled with errors, that don't leap to the eye because the eye can't see them.

In the Prelude, a point so trivial it seems barely worth mentioning: the copyist's misspelling, "ought" for "aught," in the line of choral text "Watchman, *aught* of joy or hope ?" A mere slip of the pen . . . If so, how many other slips ? The proofs were read, many times over. No one picked it up. If they could be so insensitive to the precise sense, and nonsense, of two simple words in a simple context, what was their sensitivity to the sense of not so simple notes in a not so simple context—e.g. all those "unnecessarily complex rhythmic notations" in the second movement ?

Compare this PERFORMANCE SCORE: FACSIMILE EDITION (only 3 pages of facsimile, by the way, one in Ives's hand, two in Reiss's) to the full-score of Alban Berg's WOZZECK, published 12 years earlier by Universal/Vienna, the publishers Langinger used to work for. Two works, so different in manner, so alike in substance. The Berg, in its way, far more complex than the Ives. I often used to go and watch the copyist who copied the pages of WOZZECK, sitting in the small cafeteria in the basement of the Vienna Konzerthaus because he liked to feel people around him while he worked. The artistry of that copyist, working with microstylus and magnifying glass ((the proper stage for a magnifying glass, in copying, not in performance)), surpassed even Langinger's work on copper, every page matching the blazing integrity of Berg's music. And the Ives 4th Symphony ? With three times as many pages in the Berg, both scores sell, in Europe, for the same retail price.

It all comes down, in the end, to price, and most music publishers are so shortsighted. I once ordered the Berg Violin Concerto and Ives's *General William Booth*—both handled by a publishing house in Pennsylvania—the one a 25-minute work for full orchestra, the other a $4\frac{1}{2}$-minute work for chamber orchestra (plus baritone solo & chorus). The rental on the Berg was $70, on the Ives $35. I telephoned the rental department to ask whether there wasn't something anomalous about charging $70 for a 25-minute work for full orchestra, and $35 for a $4\frac{1}{2}$-minute work for chamber orchestra ((plus baritone solo & chorus)). The man I spoke to said no, it wasn't worth their while renting material for less than $35, regardless of its brevity. So I said, couldn't they have the score and parts printed and put out on sale, make a small margin of profit and go on to better things, which is what music publishers used to do in the past, and they seemed to have done quite well out of it. He said no, it wasn't their policy to do that until a demand for rental material reflected in the figures they sent upstairs warranted it. And besides, it would involve a tremendous outlay and an awful lot of work, they were short-staffed enough as it was. Quite frankly, he'd be glad when this run on Ives was over, it was crippling the trade. So I said to send the material anyway, I'd already programmed the Berg and *General Booth*, and hung up. But the Ives material, when it came, looked dreadful—the Becker MS reproduced by a cheap hectograph process using a blueberry blue ink that smudged and ran all over, more thumb prints than notes. One 2nd Violin part was blue from top to toe, not rice in green soup—blueberries in blueberry soup. I had the librarian send the material straight back, and take out another $4\frac{1}{2}$-minute work for us to do.

Then again, miniatures like *The Pond* and *The Indians*, 12 and 22 measures long respectively, in their chamber orchestra versions. Scored for a handful of instruments, they are available FOR RENTAL ONLY at $25 a time, each, the material shabbily photocopied from the original copyists' MSS. On the other hand, a score like *Over The Pavements*, much longer and more complex, is available, properly printed, FOR SALE, at $12 the set. Other of Ives's music, like *Lincoln, The Great Commoner*, though assigned to publishers 10 and 15 and 20 years ago, is still not available, for rental or for sale, and the publishers in question take refuge behind the myth that the pieces are impossibly difficult to perform. The truth is, they can't be bothered.

Magnify all this a hundred-fold, two hundred-fold, to equal the normal, day-to-day experience of performers trying to put on performances of Ives's music—any composer's music, that hasn't been properly published, and most of it hasn't—and you get at the real reason why it's difficult to play. Publishers get blamed because that is where music starts to be made public—and ends, if they haven't done their job, as most of them haven't. They have made excuses for so long now, that musicians, concert promoters, recording companies, orchestra trustees, managements, the concert-going public at large, have started to believe them, and music, old music as well as new, has started to die of atrophy. Concert halls are empty, record sales falling off. Like *The Sorcerer's Apprentice*, the situation has got out of hand, and it is going to take a Grand Wizard to stop the flood of lies and prevarications. But it is sad to see one benign old conjur man, who once performed a celebrated sleight-of-hand with 4 Saints, taken in by all the music publishers' blah. He thinks Ives must have been a very arrogant man, to be so rude about the musical establishment when he left so little music in a fit condition to be played . . .

## Quodlibet

In his will, Charles Ives made a few small bequests to his immediate family, to his next-door neighbors, the Ryders, to his two god-daughters, and to the Danbury Home. The bulk of his estate, including all his MSS, was left to his widow. She directed that the MSS should go to Yale University, where they now form the substance of the Ives Collection, and at her own death, in April 1969, bequeathed the royalty income from performances of Ives's music to the American Academy of Arts & Letters, for setting up a fund for scholarships and special awards. ((These royalties derive, in the main, from performances outside the United States. Income from performances inside the country is still minimal, and any major Ives performance or recording must still seek substantial private subsidy.))

At a recent meeting of the American Academy it was decided that the time was already overdue for devoting all these funds to a 10-year project, in collaboration with the Ives Foundation, as yet amorphous, to republish all of Ives's music in a legible, properly engraved and printed, "definitive" edition. It is a consummation devoutly to be wished.

The project, if it materializes, will be not unlike the enterprise of the Bach Gesellschaft, which, in 1850, a century after Bach's death, issued the first of 46 volumes that form the Bach Gesellschaft edition. Other similarities between Bach and Ives have been commented on. Both were professional organists whose strange preludings bewildered the congregation and angered the clergy. Bach is regarded, by many, as the first great European composer, Ives, by many, as the first great American composer. Bach also, by some, as the last great European composer. Maybe Ives will come to be regarded as the last great American composer, the last great composer anywhere, of music as western civilization has understood the term.

# A Varied Air...

Compassion is very untenable ground. It must be expeditious. Its pleadings will not bear to be stereotyped.

HENRY DAVID THOREAU: *Walden*

Music criticism, good or bad, right or wrong, only comes after. Music publishing, good or bad, right or wrong, before. In between, the music itself, in performance—now, this instant, actual, willful music-making, good or bad, right or wrong. Here, Ives's ultimate protest, the winter of his discontent.

Ives himself wasn't much interested in psychological niceties; Harmony, his wife, even less so. Yet for all her native prudery, she was probably the more compassionate soul—he, by present-day standards, a square, a redneck almost, entangled in a web of conventional prejudice about conventional things that would have dismayed his father. When Ives's closest friend, Henry Cowell, was charged with a homosexual offense in 1936, it was to Harmony that he instinctively wrote, and it was a long time before she dared tell her husband. She was probably more shocked than he was, but more immediately forgiving. He was not so much shocked, as angered by a mode of behavior that he only understood as a threat to the heterosexual ego. And his other prejudices—conventional prejudices (there is no other kind)—were of a like order. Yale had most to do with that —his Danbury upbringing, Aunt Amelia and Uncle Lyman, something to do with it. His adulation of his father, the loss of his father and his lifelong search for someone/something to take his father's place, mirrors America's search for a father-figure that still goes on. Nothing very abnormal here, unless a national abnormality, a symptom of inexperience. The ancient Hebrews used to count a child's age from the year of its father's death.

Ives's "parapraxis," as paranormal psychology calls it: "wrok" for "work" at the age of 5 wasn't very unusual, "dosen't" for "doesn't" and similar infelicities all his life probably was—"wrong or right" for "right or wrong," "Piano & Violin" for "Violin & Piano," "Orchestra & Chorus" for "Chorus & Orchestra," "Meastoso" for "Maestoso," "80 = $\downarrow$" for "$\downarrow$ = 80," lists of "things to be done" arranged in reverse order of deadlines, last deadline first—commonly accepted, among psychiatrists today, as symptoms of genius. Well, Ives was a genius. Would his genius have been the less if he had followed conventional usages ? Perhaps it would. Perhaps he was born naturally left-handed—he got 100 for writing & spelling his first term at New Street School—but made to write with his right hand by someone like Aunt Amelia. If his handwriting had been better, he might have been able to dispense with professional copyists, learned at first hand the problems his music posed for performers, saved himself a lot of worry, trouble, and heartache. He might even have spared himself his 1918 heart attack. And the later diabetes mellitus. And his music might have been different. Even nice. Doctors nowadays are agreed that it is very dangerous to make a naturally left-handed child write with its right hand—probably as dangerous as making a right-handed child write with its left hand because fond parents or schoolteacher wants him to be a genius. If Wagner, who was left-handed, had been made to write with his right hand, perhaps Ives would have found him less of a "soft-bodied sensualist = pussy . . . " But who cares ?

Ives's physical infirmities. A family history of heart disease. Reason enough for his having a weak heart himself. But heart specialists today think a family history of heart disease can induce weakness, psychosomatically, in an otherwise healthy heart. Particularly in someone with a lively, even morbid imagination like Charles Ives. When his cousin Dr Granville White gave him an examination in 1906, he sent him on two weeks' leave with Julian Myrick. That was when they decided to set up in business on their own account. Sitting hunched over a desk all day long, hunched over his desk or piano all night writing music, smoking strong cigars, not enough exercise, was debilitating. He was probably suffering from chronic indigestion—indistinguishable, 70 years ago, from a heart condition. But Ives probably assumed he had a heart condition—doctors never told you anything—and worrying about it only made it worse. Or induced it.

Again, his very real heart attack in 1918: first diagnosis, Spanish influenza. Harmony, a trained nurse, was probably relieved to learn it was actually a heart attack—there was no treatment for influenza in those days, aside from taking aspirin, and severe cases were terminal. Yet, earlier in the year, Ives had had a medical examination for the Volunteer Ambulance Corps, and failed it. He can't have told Harmony about the examination at the time or she would have wanted to know why he failed it, wouldn't have let him do 3 weeks' strenuous work on Frank Ryder's farm during the summer. The medical examiner probably diagnosed arteriosclerosis—hardening of the arteries—perhaps Ives's long fingers made him suspicious from the start. But the medical profession was clothed in secrecy and Ives never found out what was wrong with him. Maybe the doctor didn't know himself. Medical examinations were pretty much routine formalities then—especially just then—X-rays, cardiography, blood tests unknown. Still, a stethoscope in skillful hands could find out a lot.

So Ives probably had a heart condition in 1918 but didn't know it. It may have been congenital, but there were contributing factors. Like his marriage. Before that, at Poverty Flat, even at Yale, his life had been mildly Bohemian: *Over The Pavements, Central Park In The Dark*, his remark to Ned Park when he went up to Yale for an alumni reunion—"I shall be out all night and daytimes sleep under a tree." Then came marriage and all that went out the window. But marriage, physically speaking, went wrong. 10 months later Harmony had to have an emergency operation. Whether or not the loss of a child was involved, or a hysterectomy, it seems likely that Charles Ives wasn't allowed to sleep with her again. The native prudery evident in Harmony's earlier journals may have helped her meet this contingency, but it wasn't much help to someone as full-blooded as Ives, and he was too hidebound by convention, intellectually speaking, to bring himself to look for physical gratification elsewhere. Result: enforced celibacy made him irritable and foul-mouthed, Harmony had to admonish him for his bad language by letter (like Mark Twain's wife before her), "emasculated" became his favorite word, and his sexual appetite was sublimated into some of the most riotously sensual music written this century.

None of which helped his heart. Nor the decision to adopt Edith in 1915/16. Nor the God/Mammon bit in 1916/17, when Ives began to play the market. In December 1916, he wrote the New York *Evening Post:*

> The tragic results of traditional political expediency which the world is witnessing today—that kind of expediency which is reflected throughout the history of academic economics—suggest the following questions:
>
> Has there been a war, during, say, the last two or three hundred years, where the primal cause has not been the desire of a small number of men to conserve and increase their property, and where most of the fighting has not been done by a large number of men of little or no property ?
>
> Would a limited property right be a natural or unnatural, efficient or inefficient, means of increasing the unit of energy and the resulting economic goods, and the power of man to utilize and enjoy them in such a way that, as his material benefits increase, his mental, moral, and spiritual life can develop proportionately ?
>
> Further, can a man of average social consciousness feel that he has a moral right to all the property he can acquire legally and honestly ?

Man of average social consciousness or not, less than two years later Ives was worth nearly $2 million. His conscience, heart of the matter, paid the price.

Then again, Ives's gullibility. In music and business alike, he tended to accept anyone's opinion as being more valid than his own. In 1918 Julian Myrick, secretary of the newly formed Mutual Life Managers' Association, and Charles Posey, its president, went to present their views on "company growth" and "enlargement of business" to Charles Peabody, the President of Mutual Life. Peabody was unimpressed, and Myrick told Ives that Peabody was a conservative reactionary. Ives believed him, went on believing him for 10 years. Peabody's policy on limiting property was identical with Ives's own, but it wasn't till Peabody retired in 1928 that Ives realized, and retired himself the following year. It was Myrick, in his conventional greed for power and wealth, who was the conservative reactionary.

Ives's gullibility over musical matters was more marked, and cost him much anguish. Whatever Harmony may have written to Nicolas Slonimsky in 1936, it was the universal rejection of his music during the fertile years that affected him most. He could never tell her this because the worst of the criticism came from friends and acquaintances of hers. Had he been more of an egotist he might have been able to brush it off; as it was, he accepted it, even acted on it, and it was only, 10 or 15 years later, when his music began to be recognized and acclaimed that he felt justified in exploding in a Wagnerian contempt for the establishment musician. The only record of something more abiding than passing animosity before 1916 is his marginalia about Franz Milcke, scrawled over all three movements of the 3rd Violin Sonata. And Milcke had come to West Redding in October 1914 at Harmony's behest.

Ives's isolation during the creative years was both normal and necessary for him. Every artist lives, must live, in isolation, voluntary or enforced, and society the world over has never been able to comprehend it. Ives's boyhood and college experiences were no different from, say, Hans von Bülow's in Germany, or Bach's or Handel's or Haydn's or Schubert's or Dvorak's or Elgar's—being taken away from the piano to run errands for his mother, music regarded, even today, by middle-class Germany and middle-class France and middle-class Italy and middle-class England, as something for girls, not boys, and quite unacceptable as a vocation or profession. American artists have generally been a little spoiled because they could always earn a living, inside or outside their art, whereas the European artist had to make a living inside his art or starve—no one outside would give him a job. In fact, Ives's musical upbringing showed greater enlightenment, family and national, than was usual in late 19th century Europe. Just read some of the childhood experiences of Ives's European contemporaries. The real tragedy, the real isolation, in Ives's case, started after 1916, when his creative powers deserted him—or did he desert them?—and his other faculties began to leave him one by one. The heart attack in 1918, diabetes in 1930, cataracts over the visionary eyes in 1936, a second, massive heart attack in 1938. His hands grew arthritic and he couldn't write or play the piano. No more baseball in the back yard, or Sunday-afternoon tennis. His only contact with the outside world was through Harmony. As a final torture, his hearing was left unimpaired, but with little music he wanted to hear. And he could make none himself. No wonder his final dictations of the Memos reveal all the pent-up frustrations of an emasculated artist.

The last recorded outburst was in September 1934, 20 years before his death, 20 years largely wasted. It is a ridiculous account of a concert in London, Henry Wood conducting a marathon first half devoted to Sibelius—*Karelia Suite* Overture, 7th Symphony, *Luonnatar, Pohjohla's Daughter,* and the 1st Symphony:

> Last evening Harmony, Edie, singer Holmes, and Daddy went to a Queen's Hall Promenade Concert—a Sibelius program. The music on the boat and in Green Park didn't bring it home to me more strongly or hopelessly surely, than sitting there for an hour or so and hearing those groove-made chewed-cuds (those sound sequences tied to the same old nice apron-strings, which have become greasy in the process), that music (and all art, like all life) must be part of the great organic flow, onwards and upwards, or become soft in muscles and spirit, and die! I was never more conscious of the vapidity of the human minds that accept anything, round, soft, fat, or bazoota, which somebody else with a nicer silk hat than theirs hands them—commercial silk hatters—music conservatories (the better known the worse)—the paid newspaper critics—the prima donna monopolists—and perhaps lowest of all, the publishing, broadcasting, and recording for profit . . .

(((NB   The BBC has never broadcast for profit. Perish the thought . . . )))

> . . . The *Valse Triste* (as brown-sugar-coddle as it is) is bigger than what we heard last night—for it is a nice lollypop and doesn't try to be something else—but these symphonies, overtures, &c are worse, because they give out the strut of little music making believe it's big. Every phrase, every line, and chord, and beat went over and over the way you'd exactly expect them to go—even when it didn't go as you expected, you didn't expect it would—trite, tiresome awnings of platitudes, all a nice mixture of Grieg, Wagner and Tschaikowsky (et al, ladies). But the worst part—a thing hinting that music might someday die, like an emasculated cherry,

dead but dishonored—was to see those young people standing downstairs, seriously eating that yellow sap flowing from a stomach that never had an idea. And some of them probably composing, and you can see them going home, copying down those slimy grooves and thinking they are creating something—helping music decline—dying—dying—dead . . .

All this sounds like a carbon copy of the groove-made clichés about Sibelius that used to come out of central Europe—from "nice German boys" like Paul Hindemith. Now Sibelius may not be everybody's cup of tea, but it's hardly what I would call "ladies' music," as Ives used the term. What did he mean by "ladies' music" anyway ? And "soft-ears," "lily-pads," "lady-boys," "pussies," &c ? Homosexual musicians tend to get uptight because some of them think Ives must have been referring to them. Perhaps he was, some of them, but that's not the whole story. Music, the arts in general, have been regarded as effeminate, the world over, by compulsively masculine male (and female) chauvinists because the practice of art implies not being able to earn a living, *ergo* being kept, and that, in the past, was a feminine prerogative. Men and women who have no doubts about their sex—heterosexual or homosexual or both—don't need to indulge in compulsive masculinity or femininity to prove themselves to the public at large. In fact, short of treading on other people's toes, they don't give a damn about the public at large. Neither does the public at large itself. To understand all is to forgive nothing. If you want to forgive, you do well not to try to understand too much. Understanding takes time. Compassion must be expeditious.

Ives was a pretty average male chauvinist for his generation, but if you read "full-blooded" for "masculine" and "anemic" for "feminine" you get nearer to what he was on about. Except that that doesn't fit in with his diatribe about Sibelius either—there's nothing much anemic about his music, whatever else you think of it. Maybe Ives was simply jealous. Sibelius was often mistaken for a successful businessman, some of his music sounds like Ives, he was awarded a life pension by the Finnish government when he was 32, didn't write much after the age of 45. Maybe Ives remembered one Fourth of July, 20 years ago, when Sibelius conducted his *Oceanides* at the Norfolk Festival and received an honorary doctorate from Horatio

Parker; the only thing Ives received was a rocket from his wife about his swearing. And maybe Ives was right about Sibelius. It doesn't really matter, because, right or wrong, it makes no difference to a composer's music what other people think of it. His music is still his music, "but it takes a conductor to break it into the existence of others . . ."

No fears here about Henry Wood, one of the most stalwart European champions of new music in the first half of this century, whose Promenade Concerts, each well over 3 hours long, ran uninterruptedly six nights a week during the summer months from 1895 to 1942, when Queen's Hall was destroyed by German bombs, then at the Albert Hall till 1944, when the concerts were stopped for the duration of the war. What Ives didn't know was that Eugene Goossens had written to Henry Wood saying Ives would be in London—he'd heard that from Slonimsky—and that Henry Wood, always on the lookout for new music, had spent an hour on the telephone one afternoon early in September 1934 trying to locate him. He made one call to the American Embassy, who were sorry, but they'd never heard of an American composer called Charles Ives. Now the City of London is putting a blue and white plaque on the house where Ives lived—18 Half Moon Street, Mayfair—which will read:

CHARLES IVES—AMERICAN COMPOSER
Stayed here September/October 1934

One artist's views about another artist are often interesting, but they don't often throw very much light on either one, viewer or viewed. An artist's life may be interesting, but it throws no light on the caliber of his or her work. A work of art can only be assessed in isolation, because it must, to be a work of art, be created in isolation —irrespective of the number of collaborators, the artist, creative or recreative, composer or performer, is always alone. A work of art is its own sole vindication.

# VARIATION I
# 114 Songs

... In fact, gentle borrower, I have not written
a book at all—I have merely cleaned house. All that
is left is out on the clothes line.

CHARLES IVES: *Postface to 114 Songs*

The first issue of *114 Songs*, 500 copies bound in dark blue buckram,
was made in June 1922. In having them engraved and printed at his
own expense, it was Ives's primary concern that there should be "a
few clear copies that could be sent to friends who, from time to time,
have been kind enough to ask for copies of some of the songs." Obviously his few friends didn't amount to 500, and the bulk of them
were intended as complimentary copies—one, since he had used one
or two poems published in the paper, went to the New York *Sun*. On
August 29 some moron on the paper wrote a column headed "Here's
a Chance to Get a Nice Song Book for Free," and encouraged its
readers to take full advantage of the opportunity. They did, Ives was
deluged with requests, and though angered, felt morally obligated
to make a supplementary issue of 1,000 copies, bound in light green
paper. Almost all were sent out.

It was a supreme act of faith. He had few close friends—no
close musical friends at the time. He had lost touch with Max Smith,
with David Stanley Smith since he became Dean of Yale School of
Music, John Griggs had left Vassar College and gone to China as a
missionary. Ives had no missionary instincts, no interest in converting
any of the people the songbook was sent to, no interest in the public at

large; only an all-embracing warmth, like Beethoven's, for mankind. Somewhere, if he scattered copies wide enough, some might fall on fertile ground and break his music into the existence of other, congenial spirits. Some did, and the act of faith was justified. But it took a long, long time, and in the meantime his name became a figure of fun. Ives must have expected that, may even have been prepared for it, but he didn't enjoy it. Even 10 years later—July 1932—Paul Rosenfeld, for *The New Republic,* wrote à propos the Postface of *114 Songs:*

> The tone bears witness to life driven back on itself. It is half-apologetic, half-defiant, and altogether self-conscious, like that of a man who had found no support and anticipates an unsympathetic reception, and feels continually forced to explain and to justify an occupation which under normal conditions requires no explanation or justification . . .

That may be. But back in 1922, Ives had no wise editor to guide him. Conditions weren't normal—the only movement artists showed any interest in was Dada, and look what happened to that. A year earlier, Schirmer had agreed to let Ives use their engraver and printing press for the *Concord* Sonata, on condition that their name didn't appear anywhere on the printed copies. Ives had gone to Schirmer because he knew someone there who had played in one of his ragtime pieces at the Globe Theater, back in 1905—someone who recalled it as "the craziest collection of sounds I ever heard." Maybe Ives hadn't gone out of his way to find a sympathetic publisher to advise him—advice, even good advice, doesn't cost much—but he was almost justified in thinking there weren't any, in 1922. By 1932, part of the 4th Symphony had been played at Town Hall and warmly received by the press, *3 New England Places* had been played in New York and Paris, *4th Of July* in Paris and Berlin. If Ives had written the Postface to *114 Songs* in 1932, when Rosenfeld reviewed it, its tone might have been less apologetic, more defiant. Instead, Ives wrote his Memos in 1932.

In May, at the first Yaddo Festival, Copland accompanied Hubert Linscott in seven of the *114 Songs*—the 7 Songs published by Cowell's Cos Cob Press, all photographed unchanged from the original pages of *114 Songs,* even the page numbers unaltered—sung in the order: *The Indians, Walking, Serenity, Maple Leaves, The Se'er, Evening,* & *Charlie Rutlage* . . .

((This ordering, decided on by Linscott and Copland, shows a phase of intelligent music editing—the 7 songs acquire a unity not present in the original order, which simply followed the order they appeared in the original 114. The copyright to 7 Songs has now been assigned to the copyright owners of the 4th Symphony, *4th Of July,* &c, but the songs have not yet been issued because of the cost and editorial work involved in renumbering the pages . . . ))

. . . In 1934, Copland reviewed *114 Songs,* with great compassion but small perception, for *Modern Music:*

> It is self evident that this publication was not designed to give the musical public a clear conception of Ives's gifts as a composer. In fact—and this seems to me to be crucial—Ives apparently not only had no public in mind when printing this book, but he hardly had even the "few friends" of whom he speaks in mind. The truth is he had only himself in mind. For after gathering together the fruits of thirty years' work (which, in effect, literally was a kind of "house-cleaning") Ives found himself alone with his songs . . .

"  . . . all that is left is out on the clothes line"— Ives wrote that himself. But Copland must have known, by 1934, that this wasn't true—or ought to have known. The day after he was soloist with the Boston Symphony Orchestra in the first performance of his own Piano Concerto, part of Ives's 4th Symphony, under the title "Symphony for Orchestra & Pianos," was given at Town Hall, New York. It would be churlish to suggest that Copland might have learned more about the effective use of ragtime if he'd studied Ives's score before writing his own. He couldn't have done, because, like the American Embassy in London, he'd never heard of Ives then. But Copland does say, somewhere else, that composers of his generation were all looking, in the '20s, for an American father-figure to guide them. If Copland and most American composers of his generation—and earlier generations—hadn't been running off to Paris and Berlin and Leipzig and Munich, had stayed home, they might have found out a little more about what was going on. And not going on. Ives wasn't wholly to blame for his continuing obscurity.

The same month as Copland's review—February 1934—the
following reprint appeared in the *Danbury News:*

"FATHER OF MODERNS"
*Charles Ives Called "Most
American" Composer.*

Charles Ives, of Redding, formerly of this city, and a pioneer
in America of the ultra-modern school of musical expression, is
discussed as follows in the February issue of the "Music Lovers'
Guide":

Ives, Charles: To my mind (and in the opinion of many
others) the most original and most characteristically "American"
composer the United States has yet produced. Largely self-taught,
a business man rather than a professional musician, tied to no
schools and refusing to propagandize his own music, he has been
an almost unknown name until the last few years when the younger
school of radical composers has suddenly awakened to the fact that
Ives is its spiritual father. He was—and still is—years ahead of
his time, anticipating many of the "discoveries" of Schoenberg,
Stravinski, and their followers. We are just beginning to catch up
with Ives, but his will be a powerful voice in the future. It is to
professional musicians' lasting disgrace that they have consistently
ignored his work. Few of his major works have even been performed; none of course has been recorded, but the NMQR ((*New
Music Quarterly*)) promises to make a beginning. One of his songs,
probably "General Booth," will be included in the first batch of
NMQR releases (1934), and it is devoutly to be hoped that this
society will get the backing it needs to record some of his works
in the larger forms. The future generation is going to have sardonic
contempt of us for ignoring Ives and his music for so long . . .

That was nearly 40 years ago, and there are still many Americans—
musicians among them, God help them—who have never heard of
Ives.

The reason for *114 Songs* is surely plain and straightforward.
Ives realized, with the *Concord* Sonata if not before, with the Violin
Sonatas and other instrumental pieces, that his music went beyond
the technical capacities of most musicians, regardless of their attitudes towards it. The orchestral and chamber orchestral works were

still an unknown quantity in 1921/22—the reading of *Decoration Day*, one of his most accessible pieces, technically speaking, had been a catastrophe, and Ives felt no confidence about trying to have anything else of his orchestral music performed. Most of his songs, on the other hand, posed modest technical demands for singer and pianist, and the song literature was a favorite and accessible medium of performance. The mistake Ives made was in trying to include almost everything he had written. In 1923 he made a careful anthology of 50 of the original *114 Songs,* and these gave a much fairer perspective of his "gifts as a composer." Old hand though he was, Ives was no psychologist, but he was learning to adjust. 500 copies of the anthology were printed and sent out, and it is an irretrievable disaster that none of them found their way into the hands of musicians like Rosenfeld and Copland. A lot of poppycock about Ives might have been averted.

To begin with, all the songs containing embarrassed and self-deprecatory footnotes were dropped. Ives might have left them in and cut out the footnotes, but he decided the footnotes were pretty accurate, and "association's sake" insufficient grounds for retaining them.

The Postface was dropped.

So were the political songs—*The Masses, An Election: "Nov 2 1920,"* even *Lincoln, The Great Commoner.* This could have been for political expediency—Harding's administration had plunged America back into the dark ages, red hysteria, &c, even Lincoln no longer an unassailable political figure. Or perhaps Ives was bored with politics—he didn't get out his political hobby-horse again till 1938, and his letter to President Roosevelt. But he realized too, that these transcriptions for voice & piano—*Lincoln* especially—failed to make the terrific point, as he saw it, of the original chorus & orchestra versions. Not that he had heard any of them in their original versions, but a composer doesn't need to hear an original version to know when a makeshift version is inadequate. ((50 and 60 years after the composition of the original chorus & orchestra versions, all three, to the best of my knowledge, still remain unperformed. I know of several people who would like to perform them, but haven't been able to get hold of the material from the copyright owners . . . ))

Also dropped, the "3 Songs of the War"—*In Flanders Fields, He Is There!* and *Tom Sails Away* (( . . . this was the song that started life as a violin sonata movement, shown to Franz Milcke in 1914, two years later had "W W elected!" scribbled on it . . . )). Like politics, patriotism is dangerous ground for a composer—unless it is distilled into a mythology, like the American Revolution or the Civil War. Curiously, Ives never set any Civil War poems.

Also dropped, three of the "5 Street Songs"—*In The Alley* ((memories of George Felsburg and Poli's)), *Son Of A Gambolier* ((memories of Yale)), *Down East* ((memories of regional New England)). The two best—*The Circus Band* and *Old Home Day* (("Ducite ab urbe domum, mea carmina, ducite Daphnin . . .")) —were retained.

Also dropped, *Thoreau*, a setting of lines from *Walden* to music drawn from the Thoreau movement/*Concord* Sonata. No use gilding the lily.

Next, all but three of the songs based on orchestral scores were dropped—*The Housatonic At Stockbridge* ((third movement/1st Orchestral Set)), *The Camp Meeting* ((third movement/3rd Symphony)), *The Cage* ((first movement/Theater Orchestra Set)), *Rough Wind* ((first movement/1st Symphony)), and *Tolerance* ((orchestral source untraced)). This is getting close to the nub of one of Ives's most important compositional procedures.

In *Rough Wind*, for example, Shelley's text was superimposed on the music—very astutely, but not, in Ives's final view, astutely enough; or rather, the first movement of his 1st Symphony had not been written with Shelley's text already in mind. Therefore the song setting, though excellently fine, lacked ultimate integrity and must go.

*The Cage* is less problematic. These were Ives's own words, probably conceived simultaneously with the music that Sunday afternoon in Central Park, standing outside the leopard's cage with Bartlett Yung. The words are even inserted in the orchestral score —a common procedure with Ives, meant to invoke an extra-musical response in the players. But, once again, the orchestral movement was written first, and the song must go.

*The Camp Meeting*, drawn from the Communion movement of his 3rd Symphony, is something else again. The last movement of the symphony already contains the melody of Bradbury's hymn *Woodworth*—"Just as I am . . ." What more natural than to include the text and turn it into a song setting ? For Ives, it was too obvious. Either the hymn tune or the hymn text, not both together. I know that *Watchman,* used in the prelude of the 4th Symphony—less successfully, as no 44 of *114 Songs,* and retained in *50 Songs*—is a glorious exception. But, apart from'this one instance, Ives never used the same tune and text together, because they canceled one another out. So *The Camp Meeting* had to go. ((Elgar's setting of "Praise to the Holiest" in *The Dream Of Gerontius* is analogous—people were dreadfully disappointed he hadn't used the old familiar hymn tune they all knew—the audience might have joined in—such a pity . . . ))

With *The Housatonic At Stockbridge* you get to the core. Ives had the idea of the piece some little time before Robert Underwood Johnson's poem appeared, but it didn't start to take definite shape until his honeymoon with Harmony, and was one of the last orchestral works to be finished. It is clear from the vocal line of the song setting that he had Johnson's text engraved on his mind while he was writing the orchestral.score—aside from a few minor variants to accommodate the voice, the two pieces are identical. The song setting was not made till 1921, for express inclusion in *114 Songs.* And, though exacting to sing, it is one of his greatest songs—far greater than *Paracelsus,* for example, which is retained in *50 Songs.* Why did he exclude *The Housatonic* ? I can only suggest, because it already existed, like all the other exclusions I have mentioned, in another, more expressive state, and that spelling out a text that had become so familiar to him was burdensome, supererogatory, ultimately intolerable.

*Tolerance* is an enigma. In his notes at the end of *114 Songs,* Ives mentions it as one of four songs "adapted from orchestral scores"—the other three being *The Housatonic At Stockbridge, The Camp Meeting,* and *Rough Wind.* The footnote to *Tolerance* itself— no 59 of *114 Songs*—reads: "Adapted, from a piece for orchestra, to the above words, 1921." There is no doubt about the "piece for orchestra," which is *A Lecture,* second movement/1st Chamber Orchestra Set, written at Gramercy Park in 1907 or 8:

II A Lecture (by Arthur Twining Hadley—approved of
by Bart & M Yung, George Lewis    34 Gramercy Pk . . .

The enigma is that *Tolerance* is only 12 measures long, *A Lecture* only 24, whereas the other three songs "adapted from orchestral scores" are all from extended symphonic movements. It is true there are other short songs in the collection that are drawn from more extended orchestral movements—*Walt Whitman, West London,* perhaps *The Se'er* and *Serenity*—but Ives doesn't mention them in his notes. Why does he pick out *Tolerance* ? Was he simply making a mistake ? Or is *Tolerance* what he says it is, an adaptation, to Hadley's words, of part of an extended orchestral movement that has been lost ? On balance, I would think that it is.

Another song that is excluded from *50 Songs, Incantation,* originally formed the last movement of the 1st Chamber Orchestra Set. Here the reason for the exclusion is a technical one. The chamber orchestra version is for trumpet, flute, 3 violins, and piano, and a masterpiece of rhythmic subtlety—time signature 13/16, with a maze of inner syncopations. It is based on Byron's "When the moon is on the wave," and the slight 1/16th-note prolongation of an otherwise fluid 12/16, coming at different points of the measure in the different parts, gives a fragile hesitancy to the effect of gently lapping waves. But the effect evaporates like moonshine in the voice & piano arrangement, for there is no rhythmic counterpoint to avert a seemingly untidy rhythmic sense on the singer's and pianist's part. So *Incantation* had to go too.

The 1st Chamber Orchestral Set is really one of the main keys to *114 Songs,* and a further key to another of Ives's compositional procedures. One that shows his enormous patience, too, and tidier compositional habits than he has been given credit for. His later Chamber Orchestra Sets—nearly all derived from pieces that later became elements of *114 Songs*—follow the 3-movement, Slow-Fast-Slow format of all Ives's Sets. But the 1st Chamber Orchestra Set, compiled in 1913, contains six pieces written between 1907 and 1911 —four years apart, that is to say—*but all written on 9 consecutive pages of MS, and so numbered.* The main point is, whether Ives originally intended them to be sung at all.

No 1 is *Scherzo: "The Se'er,"* for cornet, clarinet, alto horn, drums, and piano. At the end, page 3 of the MS:

Mr Price Please copy but leave words out

The words were Ives's own, the adaptation for voice & piano done early 1913.

Page 3 also has the start of "II A Lecture"—mentioned above—

for cornet, wind, brass, and strings, 25 measures long, the 1921 adaptation for voice & piano only 12. No copying instructions.

Page 4 contains the end of *A Lecture* and the title and first six measures of *The Ruined River,* for 2 clarinets, 2 cornets, trombone, drums, piano, and strings. On page 5, the last 14 measures and the copying instructions:

Mr Greinert    Please copy without words & call me when ready

Ives's own words again. The adaptation for voice & piano is marked: "arranged 1913 . . . "

The bottom half of page 5 has the title:

IV    Keats "Like A Sick Eagle"

and the first six measures, scored for English horn (later bassethorn), flute, piano, and strings.

Page 6 has the last 4 measures of *Like A Sick Eagle,* and the title and first 17 measures of *Calcium Light Night*—originally for piccolo, clarinet, cornet, trombone, drums, piano 4-hands; rearranged by Henry Cowell in 1936 for piccolo, oboe, clarinet, bassoon, trumpet, trombone, drums, piano 4-hands:

approved by Yale Club of Gramercy Park . . .

That could have been 1907/08, but Bartlett and Morrison Yung and George Lewis were frequent guests at 70 West 11th Street during 1908/09. More likely there.

Page 7 has the rest of *Calcium Light Night* and the title and first 4 measures of the Byron piece:

VI    Byron's "When the moon is on the wave"    Just copy notes— leave out words    Ink sheet starts 5th measure (page 8)

So you have I written no later than fall 1908, II written no later than May 1908 ((that is, before CI's marriage)), III written no earlier than June 1911 ((visit to Zoar Bridge)), IV written in April 1909, V written between 1907 and 1909, VI written no later than fall 1908—all on consecutive pages of MS, the individual pieces overlapping on pages 3, 4, 5, 6 and 7. One hypothesis—the only possible one, as I see it—that Ives had all six pieces in mind, knowing pretty exactly how much room they would take up, give or take a

1/16th-note, right from the start, sometime in 1907 or 8. *Calcium Light Night* has no text—Ives never intended it should—and in these original versions of the five other pieces later adapted as songs, the texts are incidental and not substantive. Which leaves us where Ives finished the Postface to *114 Songs:*

> —In short, must a song
> always be a song!

In my view the greatest of Ives's songs—*The Pond, The Indians, Like A Sick Eagle*—are not in the voice & piano arrangements of *114 Songs,* but in their original settings for chamber orchestra, "with or without voice." Plus four others that are not in *114 Songs* at all—*Soliloquy* (1904), *On The Antipodes* (1904 and 1915), *General Booth* (in the original version for baritone solo, chorus, and brass band, 1914), and *Aeschylus & Sophocles* (1905 and 1922):

> ". . . We also have our pest of them which buzz around us,
> and sting . . ."

# In Re Browning Et Al

> . . . If I stoop
> Into a dark tremendous sea of cloud,
> It is but for a time; I press God's lamp
> Close to my breast; its splendour, soon or late,
> Will pierce the gloom: I shall emerge one day.
> You understand me? I have said enough?
>                 ROBERT BROWNING: *Paracelsus*

Between 1908 and 1913, Ives planned a series of overtures on "Men Of Literature"—Emerson, Browning, Matthew Arnold, Hawthorne, Walt Whitman, John Greenleaf Whittier, and Henry Ward Beecher. The Browning piece, designed as second of the series, was the only one that became an overture as such. The Emerson and Hawthorne pieces were transfigured into other things. The Arnold, though finished, at least in sketch, has disappeared.

The three overtures that never got written, the one that is lost, point another aspect of Ives's creative personality, of transcendentalism as a whole: a preoccupation with questions of social reform, of social/political injustice, inequity, ineptitude. In the case of Whitman, Whittier, and Beecher, the preoccupation was bound up with Abolition and Civil War issues. In the case of Arnold, it concerned social reform in general.

Ives designed the *Arnold* Overture as third of the series, completing the sketch, for chorus & orchestra, within the single week of December 9/15 1912:

1 week job done—Good or Bad ?  But not all done . . .

By 1932, the score had been mislaid, and Ives wrote that it "probably has been lost." It remains lost. Only other evidence of Arnold in Ives's music is the Sonnet "West London," set in 1921 as no 105 of *114 Songs*. Sometime in 1922/23, Ives made a note to arrange the song setting for "wood, strings, piano, perhaps a little brass occasionally—1st part a London Street Band." The arrangement was never done.

((NB   Nor is there any evidence, in the song setting, of "a London Street Band" in the first part. This would have had to have been newly composed—or taken from the *Arnold* Overture . . . ))

Ives had a copy of *Arnold's Poetical Works*, bound in red buckram, copyright 1897 by T Y Crowell & Co, NY. One of the poems has some underscoring—*The Scholar-Gipsy*, conjuring the image of Thoreau. Or what Thoreau might have been, in Emerson's estimation:

> Had his genius been only contemplative, he had been fitted for his life, but with his energy and practical ability he seemed born for great enterprise and for command; and I so much regret the loss of his rare powers of action, that I cannot help counting it a fault in him that he had no ambition . . .

Ambition was the Scholar-Gipsy's aspiration, though this is not inferred from the passages Ives underlined. If Arnold's poem brought Thoreau to his mind, Ives was interested in other traits in Thoreau's/Arnold's character. Yet the Sonnet "West London," which Ives used for a song setting, has no markings at all. Its message, however obese with Victorian condescension, was clear-cut: Arnold's concern, after his fashion, with an aspect of social inequity—

> "It's the rich wot 'as the pleasure,
>     It's the poor wot gets the blame . . . "

John Greenleaf Whittier, another champion of social reform. Active in the Abolitionist cause from 1833, when he "left the Muses' haunt to turn the crank of an opinion mill"; active in the Transcendental Club from 1838, the year of *Poems Written During The Progress Of The Abolition Question; Voices Of Freedom* in 1846; *Songs Of Labor* and *Ichabod* in 1850; in 1865, *Laus Deo!*, inspired by the "clang of bell and roar of gun" that proclaimed the passage of the 14th Amendment—the one that outlawed discrimination against color. "O Sabbath rest of Galilee, O calm of hills above"—Whittier's

lines that Ives set for unison chorus, strings, harp, and timpani
((later arranged as no 42 of *114 Songs*))—could not be in stronger
contrast. The mood of both the poem and the music reflects the consummation of the final line in Arnold's "West London"—"points us
to a better time than ours"—a line that Ives makes a point of repeating three times over. He excludes the Whittier setting from *50
Songs*, hadn't much good to say for it in later years: it was too
"namby-pamby," "nice." Yet the muffled off-beat drum strokes of the
original setting, done sometime between 1908 and 1911 when Ives
was reading a lot of Whittier, suggest a sublimation of the poet's
experience during the years of crucial conflict—"emotion recollected
in tranquillity," &c. Their continuing ostinato from out the im-
penetrable darkness, far below the celestial fabric of unison voices,
upper strings, and harp, give some idea of Ives's intentions for a
*Whittier* Overture.

Henry Ward Beecher is a problem. Not even an outline sketch
for his Overture survives—only Ives's recollection that he intended
writing one. And an extraneous note that seems to identify Beecher
with "an old man with a straw in his mouth"—Ives's opening words
for *The Se'er*—surely a false portrait of Beecher. Nor was Beecher
a "man of literature" even in the sense that Whittier was—and
Whittier pales beside giants like Emerson, Hawthorne, Whitman, and
Browning. But Beecher had a background that appealed to Ives. His
sister was Harriet Beecher Stowe, author of *Uncle Tom's Cabin*.
His father, Dr Lyman Beecher, Presbyterian minister noted for his
fiery denunciations of liquor and the Church of Rome; Lowell
Mason 10 years his organist & choirmaster at Hanover Street Church,
Boston. Beecher himself, native of New Haven, in his own right a
celebrated Congregationalist minister, moral crusader, ardent champion of antislavery, gifted in rhetoric. During the Civil War he lec-
tured in England for the Union cause; in New England the same.
On July 10 1862, Emily Dickinson noted the account by the Springfield *Daily Republican* of Beecher's appearance in Amherst:

> The address before the united literary societies of the college was
> delivered at three o'clock this afternoon by Henry Ward Beecher.
> It was the exact counterpart of the forenoon's performance in every
> particular. Lord was hunkerish, unmagnetic, unpopular; Beecher
> was eloquent, earnest and right, and carried away the sympathies
> of the audience with him by storm . . .

Judge Lord had spoken out against Abolition—this, shortly after
the Seven Days' Battles, when the Union armies had suffered further
setbacks. The North was sensitive, his criticisms untimely, unwel-
come. In 1874—Ives's birthdate—Lord was judge in the Tilton-
Beecher case, where Beecher stood charged of adultery with Tilton's
wife. In his lengthy summing up, Lord attempted to prejudice the
jury against Beecher and outraged the judiciary authorities. Notwithstanding, the following year Lord was elected to the Supreme
Court. The *Daily Republican:*

> . . . He will strengthen the court by introducing a vigorous dis-
> senting element, now and then . . .

All in all, man of literature or not, Beecher was a crystal that threw
off colors enough for Ives's radical palette. Except that no music was
written.

Walt Whitman poses a lesser problem, a greater complexity.
Though less than 20 measures long, the 1913 chamber orchestra
sketch gives a clearer indication of Ives's intentions for a *Whitman*
Overture. The text—"Who goes there ?  Hankering, gross, mystical
and nude . . ."—was added later, after Ives's habit. His habit too,
to have the text by heart, ingrained mind & soul, before setting an
imagined vocal line for a solo instrument—in this case the cornet,
his father's instrument, his Civil War band instrument. ((And all
those chamber orchestra settings, that later became songs—most of
them are for solo cornet.))

The poem that includes Ives's 5-line extract was part of the
untitled preface to *Leaves Of Grass*, a collection of 12 poems published in 1855. Though they went unnoticed—except for a few seers
like Emerson—they were the direct outcome of Whitman's mystical
conversion. Earlier he had denounced "the mad fanaticism" of the
Abolitionists; now his writing had abandoned faction, emerged as
frankly transcendental, acknowledged its debt to Emerson. ((Acknowledged too frankly, perhaps—Emerson's famous "but . . ."
when the 2nd edition appeared.)) Reason enough to invite Ives's
interest—though, even in 1913, Whitman still was regarded as "dis-
graceful" in some otherwise enlightened circles. The volumes in the
New York Public Library that Ives probably consulted were kept on
reserve; there were no circulating copies.

It was unlike Ives not to include full details of a title and its source if they were known to him at the time of his initial interest— if they became known later, he was too deeply engrossed in any one of a hundred other projects to be bothered. The 1913 orchestra version was transcribed for voice & piano in 1921 ((no 31 of *114 Songs*)) with the simple title *Walt Whitman*—the source of the text: "(from 20th stanza), Walt Whitman, *Leaves Of Grass*." The 20th stanza of *Song Of Myself* begins "Who goes there ?"—but the prefatory poem was not titled *Song Of Myself* till the 1881 edition. Therefore Ives must have had access to an earlier edition, else the full source would have been given. Since the first three editions sold few copies, it is likely that the one Ives used was the 1867 edition, in two volumes—*Leaves Of Grass* now grown from 12 to 236 poems, including *Drum-Taps, Sequel To Drum-Taps, When Lilacs Last At The Door Yard Bloom'd*, "O Captain! My Captain!" More than likely, since the Civil War poems had a direct reference for him through his father's involvement.

On the evidence of the three song settings Ives made—Whittier, Whitman, and Arnold—their respective overtures were to have made little use of parody. There is no parody in the Whittier and Whitman settings, only one at the very end of the Arnold. But there is no telling. Ives uses the phrase "Captain, my Captain . . . Captain, oh my Captain!" right at the end of the late, politically oriented song *An Election: "Nov 2 1920,"* against a parody of his own music from *Lincoln, The Great Commoner*, written in 1912. He undoubtedly knew Whitman's "O Captain! My Captain!" when he chose part of a then obscure stanza from *Song Of Myself* in 1913. He might well have used his own Lincoln material in the projected—or lost—*Whitman* Overture. The ingenuity of his mind was inexhaustible.

The seemingly irrelevant parody at the end of *West London* is a fair example of this ingenuity. His note about arranging the song for chamber orchestra mentions "a London Street Band." The only bands likely to have played in the open street in Arnold's day, in that very exclusive area of London's West End—"close by Belgrave Square"—were the bands of the Salvation Army, founded in London's impoverished East End in 1865, by William and Cather Booth.

Now look at Arnold's sonnet—like all his sonnets, it follows the Petrarchan format, the octave containing the observation, the sestet the moral:

Crouch'd on the pavement, close by Belgrave Square,
A tramp I saw, ill, moody, and tongue-tied.
A babe was in her arms, and at her side a girl;
Their clothes were rags, their feet were bare.
Some labouring men, whose work lay somewhere there,
Passed opposite; she touched her girl,
Who hied across, and begg'd and came back satisfied.
The rich she had let pass with frozen stares.

Thought I: "Above her state this spirit towers;
She will not ask of aliens, but of friends,
Of sharers in a common fate.
She turns from that cold succour, which attends
The unknown little from the unknowing great,
And points us to a better time than ours."

The song setting is *quasi* d minor/F major, the music accompanying
the final line matching its platitude, ending with a half-close ( (i.e.
"feminine" ending—C major in the key of F))—a favorite device
of Ives's, that leaves a question mark hanging in the air wherever
a worthy sentiment is not backed up by native conviction. The ending
is all *fortissimo*, in every other respect, radiant with expectation of "a
better time than ours." Then follows the brief parody—a semitone
lower, *pianissimo*—of the first notes from "Fountain," Lowell
Mason's setting of William Cowper's gory hymn:

There is a fountain fill'd with blood
Drawn from Emanuel's veins;
And sinners drench'd beneath its flood
Lose all their guilty stains . . .

Now Ives used the parody of "Fountain" on four occasions:
here, at the end of *West London;* in the second movement/3rd Symphony, c 1904; in the second movement/Piano Trio, also c 1904;
and as the entire basis of his 1914 setting of Vachel Lindsay's poem
"General William Booth Enters Into Heaven." The poem has the
recurrent refrain "Are you washed in the Blood of the Lamb ?"—
and Lindsay intended the poem sung to "The Blood Of The Lamb,"
the Salvation Army battle hymn. As I've said, Ives didn't generally
like to set a text to the obvious music—especially not when there
was other music, originally written for another text that would

throw off fresh overtones. The choice of "Fountain" for the *General Booth* setting seems obvious now. In fact it was a masterstroke, for the ramifications of the choice are endless—Mason as organist at Lyman Beecher's church, Beecher's fulminations against liquor, Prohibition, Abolition, revivalist zeal, militant evangelism, sinners drench'd in the Blood of the Lamb, &c, &c—*cf* Lindsay's text, *passim.*

Now go back to Ives's setting of Arnold's sonnet, and the lost *Matthew Arnold* Overture. "1st part a London Street Band." Inevitably, a Salvation Army band. The British Salvation Army, in Victorian times, the epitome of condescension towards the waifs, strays, and derelicts of society—"cold as charity." In the soft, 2-measure echo of "Fountain" at the end of *West London,* Ives was surely pointing a moral to Arnold himself. Heaven knows what may have happened in the *Arnold* Overture.

There should be a central figure that embodies this spirit of transcendentalism-in-action, concern with inner social/political questions. It would have been convenient to the pattern of these projected overtures if Amos Bronson Alcott were among them. But Ives did not include the *Orchard House* Overture—his portrait of the Alcott family in their second Concord home—in his "Men Of Literature" series. The Alcotts movement of the *Concord* Sonata, derived from the *Orchard House* Overture, is generally quiet, orderly, nostalgic with Auld Lang Syne and Scottish lochs, has, except once, no overt social/political MESSAGE. Alcott himself, New England's Mr. Micawber, very much the gentleman-about-town, fastidious in dress with silver-knobbed cane, voluble champion of lost and present and presently lost causes, never quite making ends meet. Thomas Carlyle spoke of him as a Don Quixote, Thoreau as "the sanest man I know," Emerson as "a great man—his conversation sublime—yet when I see how he is underestimated by cultivated people, I fancy that none but I have heard him talk . . . " Emerson was a far abler champion of justice and equity, his attacks on social and political malpractice withering. So, too, Thoreau's. Orestes Brownson, stormy petrel of the Transcendental Club, Theodore Parker, "our Savonarola," Whittier, Beecher, Matthew Arnold—all more eloquent, more articulate, in the cause of social/political reform, than Alcott.

Yet these were men whose command of rhetoric enabled them to achieve reform through the media of speech and the pen. Though not lacking physical courage, they were not called upon to display it in support of their ideals. In his piece on Alcott, from *Essays Before A Sonata*, Ives quotes the anecdote given by E W Emerson, Ralph Waldo's son:

> . . . It has been recorded of Alcott, the benign idealist, that when the Reverend Thomas Wentworth Higginson (later, a Colonel in the Northern Army), leading the rush on the United States Court House in Boston to rescue a fugitive slave, looked back for his following at the court-room door, only the apostolic philosopher was there, cane in hand . . .

((("Jesus came from the Court House door,
         Stretched his hands above the passing poor.
         Booth saw not, but led his queer ones
         Round and round the mighty Court House square . . .")))

A few lines back in the Alcott essay, Ives says that the Boston Court House incident "helps confirm the theory—not a popular one —that men accustomed to wander around in the visionary unknown are the quickest and strongest when occasion requires ready action of the lower virtues . . . " The Alcotts movement—presumably the lost *Orchard House* Overture too—is the only one in the *Concord* Sonata that gives out, as an isolated, unequivocal event, the elemental Beethoven figure from the opening of the 5th Symphony in its naked, aboriginal, ready-for-action state. Ives uses the figure again in *The Anti-Abolitionist Riots*. And he also mentions that piano piece as one of the sources of the *Browning* Overture . . .

Apart from the *Browning* Overture, so little of the music for his projected "Men Of Literature" series survives—not much more seems to have been written, in any case. Did he lose interest in social/political questions ? Did they become so absorbed into his nature that a direct expression of interest became irrelevant ? Did he come to realize that too close a social/political involvement must inevitably wound his creative processes ?

The *Browning* Overture gives a different slant on the ultimate defeat of Ives's creative powers, diving back into darker transcendental sources, metaphysics, astrology, alchemy.

The 16th century was their heyday—heyday, too, of a lot of related ideas: Humanist enthusiasm, Metaphysical Poetry, the Parody Mass. The Metaphysical Poets used the symbols of metaphysics, but the image, often as not, was an alchemical one. Their language: the translation—transmutation, metamorphosis—of ideas. Their rhetoric: the elaborate use of metaphor—substance *as* essence/essence *as* substance, bypassing simile, "likening to." As Christopher Marlowe, *Tamburlaine:*

> The essentiall Fourme of marble stone,
> Tempered by science Metaphisicall,
> And Spels of magicke from the mouthes of spirites . . .

Essential form/substantial stone coextant as elements; *science Metaphisicall* their tempering agent; *Spels of magicke* the supranatural factor. The image is of medieval chemistry.

The image was known to Hawthorne. He introduces it in its haunted, hag-ridden aspect where Roger Chillingworth, ultimate victim of *The Scarlet Letter*, speaks of:

> . . . my old studies in alchemy . . . I have learned many new secrets in the wilderness, in requital of some lessons of my own, that were old as Paracelsus . . .

It was known to Melville. He introduces it in a still darker aspect where Ahab baptizes his newly forged harpoon—the harpoon that is to have supranatural powers—in his sailors' blood:

> *Ego non baptizo te in nomine patris, sed in nomine diaboli* . . .

The image is of Faust. But Faust, true to the Christian/romantic ideal, redeemed at length. After *Moby Dick:*

> I have written a wicked book, and feel spotless as the Lamb . . .

And it was known to Charles Ives. The *Robert Browning* Overture is based on Browning's dramatic portrait of Aureolus Paracelsus, the 16th century alchemist, humanist, and metaphysicist. 10 years later, Ives incorporated the salient features of the Browning music in the song setting *Paracelsus* ((no 30 of *114 Songs*)), the text drawn from three brief extracts from Paracelsus' dying peroration:

> . . . for God is glorified in man,
> And to man's glory vowed I soul and limb.
> Yet, constituted thus, and thus endowed,
> I failed: I gazed on power till I grew blind . . .

39 lines later:

> What wonder if I saw no way to shun
> Despair ?   The power I sought for man seemed God's . . .

7 lines later still:

> I learned my own deep error; love's undoing
> Taught me the worth of love in man's estate,
> And what proportion love should hold with power
> In his right constitution; love preceding
> Power, and with much power, always much more love . . .

On page 1 of the pencil sketch of the song setting:

> from Paracelsus ( see score . . .
> p 120/121   Works of R Browning   Redding Shelves

The score is the *Browning* Overture—pages 120/121 the pages Ives's extracts were drawn from, near the end of an epic, in 5 parts, nearly 5,000 lines long, 122 pages long in the edition Ives used, copyright 1889 by Smith, Elder & Co, 15 Waterloo Place, London. On the flyleaf, the inscription: "to Charlie, with love, Oct 20 1908"—his 34th birthday, spent, out of work, at Saranac Lake with Harmony, and David and Ella Twichell. Nine weeks later, the letter from George Dexter appointing him senior partner of Ives & Myrick, and the jubilant, spontaneous outpouring of a substantial portion of the *Browning* Overture:

> . . . chromatic leap around the block—steppin' nice,
> backwoods &c—but now to serious purpose . . .

Eighteen weeks later still, Harmony in hospital, Sally singing, "the spirit too weak, mortality weighing heavily like unwilling sleep, each imagined pinnacle and steep of Godlike hardship telling . . . " But Ives must have known already, by April 29 1909, that his marital relationship with Harmony must now undergo a radical change. "Love's undoing taught me the worth of love in man's estate . . . " The line, from Browning's original text, is left out in Ives's song setting. Why ?   Why else than that, still 12 years later, Ives felt the sense of having been cheated. After a spectacular first two pages that are note for note identical with crucial passages from the

*Browning* Overture score, the music suddenly falls off, deteriorates almost to incoherence with the words—either side the missing line—

> I learned my own deep error......
>
> ...........................
>
> And what proportion love should hold with power

—the words, incidentally, to new music—if it can be called that—not contained in the Overture. And the Overture, completed in 1911, contains so much music that might have served his purpose here. He surely knew the whole of Browning's text for this closing passage, perhaps wanted to set it all, or at least more than he did. But even with the lines he chose, 10 of them, the last 5 are a pale echo of former powers, a bitter recognition of creative impotence. Yet *Paracelsus* clearly meant something special to him. It was retained in *50 Songs*, while *The Housatonic At Stockbridge* was discarded. It was republished, with slight revisions but no structural strengthening, in *New Music*, vol 9/no 1, October 1935—shortly before *3 New England Places* appeared in print. It was not mentioned, in the notes to *114 Songs*, as one of the four songs "adapted from orchestral scores," though it had a clear precedence over *Tolerance*. It *was* mentioned, in the notes, as one of 21 songs that "may be found suitable for religious services." Paracelsus ?  Alchemy ?  Alchemy is still regarded, by most churchmen, as one of the black arts.

But whatever is lacking, in the way of potency, in *Paracelsus*, it is there in sevenfold abundance in the *Browning* Overture. It is an overwhelming work, saturated with alchemical implications, astrological implications, erotic implications—and, in a sense that constantly evaded Ives, MEDIEVAL implications. The sensuality of the music derives more than from a superficial resemblance—as in the insistent trumpet writing, for instance—to Skryabin's *Poem Of Ecstasy*, because its ecstasy goes deeper, to the core. It is a medieval ecstasy, the ecstasy of Mahler's 8th Symphony, and his setting of Goethe's *Faust*—Marlowe's *Faust*, come to that. Ives wasn't too sure about the *Browning* Overture, in later years—"too much of a classroom piece, augmentations, diminutions, inversions, &c"—and maybe he found the recollection of its birth-pangs too painful, the kind of ecstasy Hesse's Goldmund sensed. Certainly all the standard serial devices are there—years before they became standard: the riotous 12-tone chord that ends the exposition, the famous 12-tone trombone passage in the coda and the serial canon that follows it. And the great moment where "the Forest ends its Communion with men, the Elms & Cedars end their songs." And the fragment of *Adeste fidelis* at the passing of Paracelsus' Catholic/Humanist soul: "If I stoop into a dark tremendous sea of cloud, it is but for a time . . . " Almost greater are the passages of sheerest innocence —the very opening, for instance, that has a cosmic power. And the middle section, with its Bruckner simplicity—had Ives belonged to another culture, he would have used Wagner tubas here.

And there are ecological implications too, if you look for them —the Golden Sections, Fibonacci numbers that you find in nature, leaves, pine-cones, any organic life. It is not likely that Ives was familiar with these terms. But he understood the proportions of irrational numbers, just as the builders of the Parthenon did. The middle section of the Overture is a perfect Golden Section, and the vertical constellations follow the Fibonacci numbers—like Bartok. Most of Ives's harmonic structures are identical with Bartok's— though years ahead of him, of course.

The serial sections of the Overture—the Allegros, broadly speaking, and especially the Coda—are rational, inorganic, like nature's crystals. Ives showed an interest in serialism many times during his creative life: the early Psalms, in *Soliloquy* and the piece that became *On The Antipodes*, here in the *Browning* Overture, in *The Masses*, in *Tone Roads* No 3, in the "Universe" Symphony. His marginalia in *The Masses* MSS show that he didn't think much of serial devices—and he implied later, in response to the French critic who thought he must have been influenced by Schoenberg, that he didn't think much of Schoenberg either. Yet he continually felt drawn. "The Devil tempted me . . . "—Faust's problem. Perhaps that is another reason why Ives stopped composing, because he saw serial writing as the only musical avenue left, and his few expeditions into that territory had frightened him. Thomas Mann's *Doktor Faustus* was a 12-tone composer. Maybe Ives saw himself like Faust—like Ahab—having to make a compact with the Devil, signed in his own blood . . .

" . . . You understand me ?   I have said enough ?"

# The Celestial RR & Other Stories

There is in all Hawthorne's writings something cold
and light and thin, something belonging to the
imagination alone, which indicates a man but little
disposed to multiply his relations, his points of contact with society . . .

HENRY JAMES: *Hawthorne*

The Emerson and Hawthorne pieces from the Men Of Literature
series started out as one-movement piano concertos. The *Emerson*
Concerto became the first movement/*Concord* Sonata, its four intro-
ductory cadenzas four of the 21 Piano Studies. The *Hawthorne*
Concerto became three things: the second movement/*Concord*
Sonata, the second movement/4th Symphony, and the Piano Phantasy, named, around 1919, *The Celestial Railroad.*

Ives's notes for the second movement/4th Symphony, quoted
by Henry Bellamann in his program book for the 1927 performance,
refer to the music as "comedy, in the sense that Hawthorne's Celestial Railroad is comedy . . . " The Hawthorne essay, in *Essays
Before A Sonata*, records "The Celestial Railroad" as one of several
other incidental sources—"wilder, fantastical adventures into the
half-childlike, half-fairylike phantasmal realms"—for the Hawthorne movement of the Sonata. The Piano Phantasy—*The Celestial
Railroad*—seems to be based directly on the original (now lost)
*Hawthorne* Concerto. An extraneous patch for page 1 of the MS has:

from Piano Concerto   Aug 20 1913   see copy in safe   I & M
38 Nassau Street

By August 1913 Ives had finished the first draft of the *Concord* Sonata and played it over to Max Smith at Hartsdale. During his convalescence from the 1918 heart attack, he was still revising the Hawthorne movement for publication. By August 1913, too, the Hawthorne movement of the 4th Symphony was well under way. It was not finished and sent to the copyists till late 1916. And by August 1913, the original *Hawthorne* Concerto sketch seems to have been finished and being used as the basis for the Piano Phantasy. It was still incomplete, 12 years later, when Robert Schmitz wrote to Ives about it. In short, there was an elusive quality in Hawthorne that was giving him more than a little trouble.

In the Hawthorne essay, finished in 1919, Ives has:

> The substance of Hawthorne is so dripping wet with the super-natural, the phantasmal, the mystical, so surcharged with adventures, from the deeper picturesque to the illusive fantastic, that one unconsciously finds oneself thinking of him as a poet of greater imaginative impulse than Emerson and Thoreau. He was not a greater poet, possibly, than they—but a greater artist . . .

again:

> Like Poe, he quite naturally and unconsciously reaches out over his subject to his reader. His mesmerism seeks to mesmerize us—beyond Zenobia's sister. But he is too great an artist to show his hand in "getting his audience," as Poe and Tschaikowsky occasionally do . . .

again:

> Emerson's substance, and even his manner, has little to do with designed effect; his thunderbolts or delicate fragments are flashed out, regardless. They may knock us down, or just spatter us—it matters little to him. But Hawthorne is more considerate—that is, he is more artistic (as men say) . . .

This preoccupation with Hawthorne as "the greater artist" was crucial to Ives's conception ((misconception ?)) of the role of the artist in society. From his own writing, it is clear that Ives could not reconcile himself to the artist who (1) used his art "primarily to make a living," or (2) accepted the old system of patronage. He regarded both as "un-American," both as forms of prostitution

—the second direct, the first more insidious because, in a capitalist society, there were no clearly defined boundaries between making a bare living and making a substantial one. Or rather, there *were* clearly defined boundaries, but Ives never saw that they were artificial. His inherited work-ethic equated success with substance, not manner, demanded that anyone who made a living must make a substantial one. Anything less than substantial success was failure, second-rate, NG. The arbiters of success or failure, not his musical peers, for he accepted none, but the majority mind. Or ultimate suburbia, "keeping up with the Joneses."

Yet Hawthorne, in his ability to support himself and his family by his writing, was more immediately successful than his American contemporaries. It is true that he worked as "weigher & gauger" at the Boston and Salem customs houses (George Bancroft's patronage, here), later, at President Pierce's behest, as American consul in Liverpool, spent less than eight of his sixty years in Concord. The fact remained that, during Hawthorne's lifetime, the royalties from his published works were more substantial than Emerson's or Melville's or Thoreau's or even—till the last years—Whitman's. And yet there was no spirit of compromise about Hawthorne. Ives made no attempt to rationalize this, but it did make it the harder for him to capture Hawthorne's musical likeness.

Of Hawthorne's materials, Ives wrote:

> Hawthorne may be more noticeably indigenous or may have more local color, perhaps more national color, than his Concord contemporaries. But the work of anyone who is somewhat more interested in psychology than in transcendental philosophy will weave itself around individuals and their personalities. If the same anyone happens to live in Salem, his work is likely to be colored by the Salem wharves and Salem witches. If the same anyone happens to live in the Old Manse by Concord Battle Bridge, he is likely "of a rainy day to betake himself to the huge garret," the secrets of which he wonders at, "but is too reverent of their dust and cobwebs to disturb . . . "

again:

> Hawthorne would try to spiritualize a guilty conscience. He would sing of the relentlessness of guilt, the inheritance of guilt, the shadow

of guilt darkening an innocent posterity. All of its sins and morbid horrors, its specters, its phantasmas, and even its hellish hopelessness, play around his pages . . .

and in the final paragraph:

This fundamental part of Hawthorne is not attempted in our music . . .

Not in the Hawthorne movement of the Sonata, certainly; and this is what Ives was writing about. Here there is only the faery wickedness of "the less guilty elves of the Concord Elms, which Thoreau and Old Man Alcott may have felt, but knew not as intimately as Hawthorne . . ." But in the Hawthorne movement of the 4th Symphony there is an all-pervasive sense of irredeemable guilt, a nightmare phantasmagoria, "all of its sins and morbid horrors, its specters, its phantasmas . . ." Yet music self-shriven at the last, "without posture, without noise, but penetrating." The penetration of silence, open-ending. Arguments unresolved, unredeemed. Melville's "madness & right reason, seeking converse with the Intelligence, Power, the Angel." All this, in a movement that declares itself to be "comedy, in the sense that Hawthorne's Celestial Railroad is comedy." In a tale that most Hawthorne scholars dismiss as lightweight allegory, Ives had found a key to Hawthorne's darker personality, a lens that reflected, as in a distorting mirror, the fires of Gehenna itself.

"The Celestial Railroad," in *Mosses From An Old Manse,* is an obvious instance of Hawthorne's use of satire. But then, as I see it, very much of Hawthorne's writing is tinged with satire. His Latinized 18th century vocabulary, sparse in qualifiers, plays the impartial witness, innocent bystander. Or seems to. Always the moral left to inference, never importuned; underscoring, lightly but firmly, exposing entire, for those that had the wit to see, the pain and hubris of his society. At its most poignant in *The Scarlet Letter,* its most pungent in "Endicott & the Red Cross"; at its most stringent, but still discernible, "vanishing between the lines," in Hawthorne's last completed novel, *The Marble Faun.*

The word "satire" has been devalued in 20th century currency: archery and sword-play, its standard metaphors, are lost arts, forgotten skills. Because its role, historically, has chiefly been social/

political, it smacks to the literal-minded of burlesque—or sedition. The "human"—i.e. "compassionate"—satire goes unrecognized.

I don't know what else to call it, in Hawthorne's case. "Socratic irony" won't do. "Irony" by itself is no good—its action is slow-moving, like poison, not like a shaft. It is not the sardonic quality of Daumier; more like Goya, perhaps—or Picasso. D H Lawrence called it "duplicity"; Henry James, too well-bred to use the single word "satire," speaks of "nothing too trivial to be suggestive." Of *The Scarlet Letter*, he wrote:

> It was a necessary condition for a man of Hawthorne's stock that if his imagination should take licence to amuse itself, it should seek this grim precinct of Puritan morality for its playground . . . But how much more darkly would they ((the characters in the Custom House preface)) have frowned could they have understood that he had converted the very principle of their own being into one of his toys!

But whatever this elusive quality in Hawthorne, the manner of Ives's music, very much of it, has it. And, being discovered by the 20th century, is accounted burlesque.

## 1, Fact

The first American rail was laid in 1828 by the Baltimore & Ohio Railway Company. New York & Harlem followed in 1829 with $1\frac{1}{2}$ miles of track—extended, in 1845, to Morrisania, Hartsdale, and White Plains . . . By 1830, B & O had 23 miles in operation—by 1843, the year "The Celestial Railroad" was published, a partial network reaching to the Midwest, the South, and up through much of New England. Hawthorne may have taken the Boston/Pittsfield line from West Roxbury when he left Brook Farm for Concord the year before.

By 1843, then, rail travel was fast becoming the "in" thing, hailed by an innocent society as the ultimate panacea. But not hailed by all. The early railroads had as many opponents as, say, supersonic air travel today. And for much the same reasons: social/political, economic/ecological. Perhaps Hawthorne understood, even then, the far-ranging implications the American railroads were to have for "an innocent posterity." Certainly, 70 years later, by

August 1913, Charles Ives understood. Most of the stock market crashes during the last 20 years involved, one way or another, the railroad tycoons.

By 1843, too, an innocent society in its perennial quest for a comfortable ride to heaven, each traveling in the religious compartment of his choice:

> The Christian reader, if he have no accounts of the city since Bunyan's time, will be surprised to hear that almost every street has its church, and that the reverend clergy are nowhere held in higher respect than at Vanity Fair . . .

No writer of his generation perceived the broad spectrum of Protestant sectarianism—at its height by 1843—more acutely than Hawthorne. This, to a large extent, was part & parcel of his Salem heritage: his ancestors were among the first Puritan settlers of Salem, more than one of them darkly involved in the Salem witch-hunts. Part & parcel, too, of his literary heritage: Bunyan's *Pilgrim's Progress* was his staple reading—almost his only reading—during childhood and early adolescence. He absorbed both concepts—largely parallel, largely coeval products of 17th century empiricism—digested them entire, observed their inevitable disintegration into sectarianism with clinical satisfaction.

Hawthorne and Ives shared a common interest in four aspects of the religious experience:

(1) the original Puritan/Calvinist stem;
(2) Jonathan Edwards and the New Lights, as the core of re-
    vivalism, "The Great Awakening";
(3) the Half-Way Covenant, centered around Boston, that
    drifted in time towards Unitarianism; and
(4) Transcendentalism, Unitarianism's foster-child, which ul-
    timately rejected its foster-parent.

Hawthorne was more preoccupied with the Puritan/Calvinist stem—Ives, underneath it all, the more rigidly Puritan in his attitudes. But it was a Puritanism fired with revivalist zeal: long after his direct childhood experience of the Camp Meetings near Redding, his remembrances of them invade his music, "with advantages." There is no evidence that he read Jonathan Edwards—as Hawthorne and Mark Twain had done—but reason assumes he must have. His music is too much infected with Edwards's exalted, nigh ecstatic enthusiasm and rhetoric.

The Half-Way Covenant was a compromise that Jonathan Edwards despised—a compromise that permitted the children of church members to become communicants without undergoing a demonstrable experience of conversion. Unitarianism, had he lived to see its ascendancy, Edwards would have viewed with even greater distaste: a labyrinth of compromise, rejecting the Trinity on the one hand, clinging with the other to a last stronghold of Calvinist orthodoxy, the literal interpretation of the Miracles—the transcendent miracle of transubstantiation conveniently excluded. Theodore Parker, a prominent Unitarian, found himself in hot water in 1836, when he said:

> The doctrine of the Trinity, the very Achilles heel of theological dogmas, belongs to philosophy not religion. Its subtleties cannot be expressed in our tongue . . .

That its subtleties could be expressed in another tongue—the heathen tongue of Latin, with its Papist trappings, no less—did not suit the Calvinist conscience of the Unitarians at all. Andrews Norton, leader of the Unitarian church, was prevailed upon to "excommunicate" Parker, who found refuge for his beliefs among the transcendentalists. Then, on July 15 1838, Emerson, the white hope of the Unitarians, exploded their faith in him with his address to the Harvard Divinity School:

> There is no doctrine of the Reason which will bear to be taught by the Understanding. The understanding caught this high chant from the poet's lips, and said, in the next age, "This was Jehovah come down from heaven. I will kill you, if you say he was a man." But the idioms of his language and the figures of his rhetoric have usurped the place of truth; and churches are not built on his principles, but on his tropes. Christianity became a Mythus, as the poetic teaching of Greece and Egypt before. He spoke of miracles; for he felt that man's life was a miracle, and all that man doth, and he knew that this daily miracle shines as the character ascends. But the word MIRACLE, as pronounced by the Christian churches, gives a false impression; it is a MONSTER. It is not one with the blowing clover and the falling rain . . .

This left Andrews Norton rattling sabers from his Brattle Street pulpit, and discoursing on "this latest form of infidelity." But vital transcendentalism, shorn of formal Unitarianism, went forward by going back over an ocean and three centuries, back to its ancestral roots, back to 16th century humanism and the Metaphysical Poets. Yet retaining its New England speech, a Yankee gumption. By 1843 it had become an eminently practical philosophy. The pages of Emerson and Thoreau are alive with practical wisdom—those of Melville and Hawthorne are become socially aware, inhabited with living human beings, interwoven with a consuming interest in the progress of their personalities.

"The Celestial Railroad" is Hawthorne's only work to make explicit mention of the word "Transcendentalist"—and then, at a casual reading, none too generously. But he knew that transcendentalism could fend for itself by now. He was part of it, after all.

So Hawthorne is passenger in this new-fangled train, bound for the Celestial City. As they approach the Slough of Despond, his traveling companion assures him to have no fear—

> "You observe this convenient bridge ?" cried Mr Smooth-it-away. "We obtained a sufficient foundation for it by throwing into the slough some editions of books on morality; volumes of French philosophy and German rationalism, tracts, sermons, and essays of modern clergymen; extracts from Plato, Confucius, and various Hindoo sages, together with a few ingenious commentaries on the texts of the Scriptures . . . "

—the literature, in fine, of transcendental philosophy.

Passing the cave, Hawthorne observes that Bunyan's two giants are no longer there, their place taken by one—

> German by birth, who is called Giant Transcendentalist; but as to his form, his features, his substance, and his nature generally, it is the chief peculiarity of this huge miscreant that neither he for himself, nor anyone for him, has ever been able to describe him. As we rushed by the cavern's mouth we caught a hasty glimpse of him, looking somewhat like an ill-proportioned figure, but considerably more like a heap of fog and duskiness. He shouted after us, but in so strange a phraseology that we knew not what he meant, nor whether to be encouraged or affrighted . . .

By the time they reach Vanity Fair, the caviling reader is comfortably reassured that the ministers of the city's churches—"the Rev Mr Shallow-deep, the Rev Mr Stumble-at-truth, that fine old character the Rev Mr This-today-that-tomorrow"—are intended as caricature of certain Concord clerics of transcendental persuasion.

All these allusions must have warmed the gray cockles of Andrews Norton's heart, along with the orthodox Unitarians' and the orthodox Calvinists' and the heart of an as yet undeclared third party, non-conformist Horace Bushnell, off writing smoldering anti-Calvinist sermons at Hartford Congregational Church. He finally came out strong against transcendentalism—after all the fuss was over—and wound up supporting Joseph Twichell's candidacy for the Asylum Hill pulpit in 1865. 43 yrs more to the day and Twichell married his third daughter to Charles Edward Ives. But that was another story.

Back at Brook Farm, Hawthorne's story caused grave twitterings among the newly migrated Fourierists. But not at the Transcendental Club in Concord. Emerson surely got the point at once, and gave license to one of his rare high chuckles. When Henry Hedge next arrived from Bangor, he was shaking with mirth; he had introduced the Club's members to the writings of Immanuel Kant and other German transcendental writers, and saw at once what Hawthorne was at. This pathologically shy Hawthorne, who would go under cover like a partridge if he caught sight of a stranger in the road, who habitually took flight at the appearance of a stranger in the room! The joke was not on transcendentalism at all, but on its most virulent critics—formal Unitarianism in general and Andrews Norton in particular.

You probably needed to be alive 130 years ago and living in New England to get the full savor of it. What you would have got is this:

(1) Bunyan's two giants were Pope & Pagan—Hawthorne is careful to mention them both by name, for the benefit of, say, the 5% of his readers who didn't know *Pilgrim's Progress* by heart.

(2) The fusion of Papal & Pagan doctrines—occurring pre Bunyan—was 16th century theological humanism. Most 19th century New England clergymen knew that, even if they didn't care to acknowledge it. Humanism, first cen-

tered in Italy—"that Holy Land of humanist enthusiasm"—Rhodiginus, Bruno, Bonifacii, Carducci, Galileo,
Monteverdi, all "learned humanists," all, except Monteverdi, excommunicated . . .

(3)  Humanism spread next to England—the Metaphysical
Poets were all humanists, William Byrd was a humanist, John Milton, the madrigalist, father of the
poet, a humanist; Matthew Arnold wrote that Milton
himself "was born a humanist, but the Puritan temper
mastered him . . ."

(4)  Next, in the late 18th century, to Germany, and via
German lineage—Kant had coined the word "transcendental"—to GIANT TRANSCENDENTALIST: "He shouted
after us, but in so strange a phraseology, that we knew
not what he meant, nor whether to be encouraged or affrighted . . ."

The Unitarians were affrighted all right, those that realized, because
humanism they could not abide. Though they shared with it one
vital doctrine—denial of the Trinity: Christ as Human, not "Jehovah
come down from heaven"—humanists were heathen Catholic who
subscribed to every other phase of the Catholic ritual. Unitarianism
could share none of their enthusiasm: it was too literal, "corpse-
cold," had neither the faculty of wonder nor Jung's "precious gift
of doubt."

And the Slough of Despond ?  Vast repository for all that
transcendental philosophy, so Hawthorne's informant had said ?
He turned out to be Satan himself in the end, breathing fire and
smoke, an unlikely advocate of transcendental ideas. Hawthorne
was not unacquainted with him, having met his disciples at first
hand . . .

This may be extracting more from "The Celestial Railroad"
than Hawthorne intended putting into it. But come back to the Hawthorne movement of the 4th Symphony—"comedy, in the sense
that Hawthorne's Celestial Railroad is comedy"—with its opening,
as John Kirkpatrick says, "like the awakening of a great city,"
with its prodigious tumult of sound, its glistening strands of fire
hurling like meteors across a gulf of chaotic darkness, its ending,
"vanishing like an hallucination . . . " This is *urban* comedy, the

comedy of Dante's Inferno, his *Comedia*. It was a fitting close to
Ives's creativity.

## 2, Fantasy

Ives of course had read Hawthorne's last novel, *The Marble
Faun*. In the copy that I like to think he used, there is a penciled
line down the margin of a passage in the chapter "On the Edge
of the Precipice." The passage reads:

> They again moved forward. And still, from the Forum and the
> Via Sacra, from beneath the arches of the Temple of Peace on
> the one side, and the acclivity of the Palace of the Caesars on the
> other, there arose singing voices of parties that were strolling through
> the moonlight. Thus the air was full of kindred melodies that en-
> countered one another, and twined themselves into a broad vague
> music, out of which no single strain could be disentangled. These
> good examples, as well as the harmonious influences of the hour,
> invited our artist-friends to make proof of their own vocal powers.
> With what skill and breath they had, they set up a choral strain—
> "Hail Columbia!" we believe—which those old Roman echoes must
> have found it exceeding difficult to repeat aright. Even Hilda poured
> the slender sweetness of her note into her country's song. Miriam
> was at first silent, being perhaps unfamiliar with the air and
> burden . . .

Ives knew that Hawthorne—like Ulysses Grant, like Keyes Winter
—had the reputation of being tone deaf, "couldn't tell one note from
another." Beside the words

"Hail Columbia!" we believe

is scrawled, in a hand that might be anybody's

"we believe" WRONG! 'Twas the Red, White & the Blue . . .

# 2 Sets / 3 Places / 4 Holidays

... several things dovetailed in my mind, & at once struck me, what quality went to form a Man of Achievement especially in Literature & which Shakespeare possessed so enormously—I mean NEGATIVE CAPABILITY, that is, when man is capable of being in uncertainties, Mysteries, doubts, without any irritable reaching after fact and reason— Coleridge, for instance, would let go a fine isolated verisimilitude, caught from the Penetralium of mystery, from being incapable of remaining content with half knowledge.

KEATS: *Letter to his brothers, Dec 25 1818*

The "regional" Ives. Boyhood nostalgia, quaint, provincial, parochial even—one view. A sense of PAST—America's past—the marriage of transcendental spirit to vernacular source; a tense of mythology that is not PAST, but PRESENT & FUTURE: 2nd view. Fact and reason suggest that Ives himself was largely unaware of this other dimension. Does that make it invalid ? Bach—so he said—wrote the "48," the 2- and 3-Part Inventions as studies for students. Does that mean they are fit only for students, that only students may play them ? I say that part of an artist's work—perhaps the major part—remains concealed from him. His actions—many of them— are like the expert interpreter's, who can realize the "exact" translation of a passage given him by God knows whom, without understanding the half of it. Once he stops to try and understand, he runs the risk of losing the thread of what he is translating, of what he is acting the vehicle for. Ask most artists what motivates their work and they won't be able to tell you. Ask them what it means, what it is all about, and they won't be able to tell you either. Though they may invent something—as Bach did.

Leaving aside *Thanksgiving*, which came before, and *Hanover Square North*, which came afterwards, there are three main threads, ideas, that run through the Orchestral Sets and the *New England Holidays*—all finished, at least in advanced sketch form, at Hartsdale. Aside from *Hanover Square North,* all are concerned with New England—"regional" New England, ritual New England. Including *Hanover Square North,* all are concerned with "independence"—personal, national, universal: PEOPLE. And, starting with *The Black March, An Elegy To Our Forefathers, Decoration Day,* and infecting the other movements in all three works, all are concerned with the musical catharsis of the Abolitionist/Civil War idea, but transcending the social/political issues and creating of them a personal/national/universal mythology.

Or you can go at it like this:

(1) *Black March = Elegy To Our Forefathers =* the minor-3rd figure from Foster's *Old Black Joe;*

(2) *Black March = Decoration Day =* Abolition/Civil War;

(3) *Black March = Decoration Day = Elegy To Our Forefathers = Thanksgiving, or Forefathers Day;*

(4) *Washington's Birthday = Putnam's Camp = 4th Of July;*

(5) *4th Of July = The General Slocum =* Pine Mountain *= Thanksgiving ((= Elegy To Our Forefathers = Black March = Decoration Day;* &c, &c . . .

This leaves *The Housatonic At Stockbridge* and *Hanover Square North,* the one based on Zeuner's *Missionary Chant,* the other on Webster's *In The Sweet Bye & Bye*—the one suggesting the sophistication of the organ bench, the other the innocence of the Camp Meeting. Both last movements—1st and 2nd Orchestral Sets—both suggesting Evangelical Christianity. As in the final hymn of *Thanksgiving,* last movement/*4 New England Holidays..*

It also leaves out *The Rockstrewn Hills*—second movement/2nd Orchestral Set—based in part on revivalist hymns, part on earlier ragtime pieces. The association between revivalist hymns and ragtime wasn't new, of course—the one grew out of the other—and Ives maintained that it wasn't something that was a monopoly of the South: it was practiced, he said, in the North before the South. He may have been right, but that doesn't affect the validity of what he does with the material; or the difference of effect the same material will have on someone from South Carolina or Georgia or Alabama and someone from New England. Or Old England.

(Though Old England's associations with Virginia and the Carolinas went back farther than with New England, remember.)

*The Black March*—first movement/1st Orchestral Set—is a direct allusion to the Civil War: Augustus St Gaudens' statue, on Boston Common, of the 54th Massachusetts Regiment of Black Contrabands, commanded by Col Robert Gould Shaw. Ives wrote—"to be placed, in small print, at the end of the music, so as not to over-influence the hearer"—the words:

> Moving—Marching—Faces of Souls!
> Marked with generations of pain,
> Part freers of a Destiny,
> Slowly, restlessly swaying us on with you
> Towards other Freedom!
> The man on horseback, carved from a native quarry
> Of the world's Liberty Rock your country was made from—
> You—Images of a Divine Law—
> Carved in the shadow of a saddened heart—
> Never light-abandoned—
> Of an Age and of a Nation!
> Above and beyond that compelling mass
> Rises the drum-beat of a common heart
> In the silence of a strange and sounding afterglow—
> Moving—Marching—Faces of Souls!

((St Gaudens' statue was the subject of the later title-poem in Robert Lowell's "For The Union Dead." It was also the earlier object of a prime instance of Boston municipal graft when a garage had to be dug to house it, prior to its unveiling in 1897 . . . Augustus St Gaudens was the sculptor who did the statue of General Sherman, also on horseback, on 5th Avenue—who also did the controversial statue of Diana, on the roof of the original Madison Square Garden in 1891.))

I explained earlier how Ives, as I see it, came to regard Stephen Foster as the minstrel of Abolition. The minor-3rd figure that permeates the fabric of this movement is common enough to all folk music—all art music, for that matter—yet it seems to typify something essential to the American slave-culture. You find it again in Delius, in the music written on the orange plantation near Jacksonville—especially in the *Florida* Suite—emerging in unmistakable contour above his chromatic harmonies. There is, too, more than a suggestion of Delian chromatic harmony in *The Black March,* almost as though this—a chromatic exoticism—were also part & parcel of the musical flavor of the South. (((Curiously, Delius was also organist for a while, back in the 1880s, at Central Presbyterian Church/N Y . . . ))) But Foster as the minstrel of Abolition only came to Ives later. There is no evidence that it was in his mind in the early *American Woods* Overture—still less in the 2nd Symphony, although it contains an extended parody of *Old Black Joe.*

The same minor-3rd figure finds its apotheosis in *An Elegy To Our Forefathers*—originally *An Elegy To Stephen Foster*—a title that, as I also said earlier, placed Foster, in Ives's mind, among the Forefathers of America's music. The original title has more obvious logic, the later title no other logic than the germination of an idea, a seed, *qui transtulit sustinet,* symbolic of the struggle for survival of New England's forefathers. The piece has none of the "stern, outdoors strength" of *Forefathers Day,* alias *Thanksgiving,* the first orchestral piece that Ives felt, later, was "much or any good." *An Elegy* shows infinite care of cultivation.

*Decoration Day*—second movement/*4 New England Holidays* —is the other work that makes direct allusion to the Civil War. Or its aftermath. "We are the dead." It contains no Foster parodies. It is just possible that Foster as minstrel of Abolition had not occurred to Ives, even as late as 1911, when he started working on *Decoration Day.* More likely, that Foster had no place there: he was *legomena,* the things uttered, the pre-echo, the warning; the Civil War *dromenon,* the things done, the acting out as ritual, the purging.

(((By the by, and to clear up a point of contention about Ives's grasp of the grammar of composition: *Decoration Day* and *The Black March* share one other characteristic that suggests he wasn't 100% master of his craft. In the last measure of *The Black March* there is an unplayable harmonic in the viola part. At letter B in *Decoration Day* the second violins have to take off their mutes within a split second—any competent composer must know it takes longer than that to take a violin mute off. And in the march there is a written middle C for piccolo—a note that simply isn't on the instrument.

One can try and excuse Ives by saying he was anticipating slide mutes—now out of fashion, but all the rage in the '40s and '50s— that he wrote middle C for piccolo in the hope that an extra key would some day be added to the instrument. But the viola harmonic— natural or artificial—in *The Black March* is acoustically impossible. So what does that prove ? That Ives wasn't 100% master of his craft ? These are flaws a publisher does well to edit out. That is his legitimate job. But I suppose none of them has noticed. Only the players. And players talk.) ) )

Next, *Putnam's Camp, Washington's Birthday,* and *4th Of July* —all interrelated through the Independence War. Musically speaking, *The 4th Of July* towers above the other two—it was the last of the three to be completed, later, much later, extensively revised and a lot of the original patina rubbed off. *Washington's Birthday* as a musical record of New England pastoral practice—the barn dance at Brookfield Centre—is only related to the Independence War by inference, as one reason why America celebrates the birthday as a national holiday. Then why all Ives's marginalia about Columbus and Independence and Election Day 1908 on the score of *Washington's Birthday* ? Whatever Ives himself says about the piece, whatever the music itself seems to say, there is in the bleak portrayal of a New England midwinter a spiritual bleakness as well—a reminder, maybe, of the bleak midwinters spent by Washington's armies, when a jew's harp was the only music there was to keep their spirits up. And "Good night, Ladies"—a traditional British air, sung by British officers to the ladies of Boston back in Colonial days, to the ladies of Spain before them.

*The British Grenadiers* is another British air that Ives used, in *Putnam's Camp* and, fleetingly, as the first fragment of melody that emerges from the smoke-shrouded woods and valleys near the beginning of *4th Of July*. In his *Memos*, Ives wrote that a captain in one of General Putnam's regiments put the tune to words, "which were sung for the first time in 1779 at a patriotic meeting in the Congregational Church in Redding Center . . ." And *The Red, White & Blue*, which comes as the mounting climax of *4th Of July*, just before the rocket over the steeple blasts off like something out of *Space Odyssey 2001*—"O, Columbia the Gem of the Ocean . . ." Originally, "O, Britannia the Gem of the Ocean," in the days when

Britannia ruled the waves and Britons never, never, never would
be slaves. The concept of freedom was known to the world before
1776. Before Christ even.

All of which, Ives of course knew. The conspiracy that puts
him into a regional, provincial, Yankee/Americana straitjacket
was not his idea, though what he has to say about his own music
hasn't helped his image. What I am trying to say is that Ives's
music transcends the regional, national image he tends to place on
it—whether out of diffidence, or an unawareness that it has other,
universal qualities. By concentrating on a regional, national expression, his music becomes—can become, becomes for me—at once
more personal and more universal, a personal testament translated,
allegorically, into universal mythic terms. As Thoreau said, myth
as the fiction of liberty. As Olson said, the myth, at once com-
memorative, magical, and prospective. As Aristotle said, "by myth
I mean the arrangement of the incidents." Myth as allegory, collage.
A collage of vernacular images arranged in significant order, telling
a story.

Thus, whatever Ives may say about it, *The 4th Of July* isn't
"a boy's 4th" at all, at least, not what "a boy's 4th" signifies to the
average unfantastical adult—"a babbling of children's voices," as
D H Lawrence put it. It's a boy's 4th, as I've said, as Ives said,
"that only children are old enough to understand": in the most
tremendous sense of the word, a SATIRE that commemorates the futility of war—ALL war, Independence War included—the futility of
freedom even, in that damned "regional," "patriotic" sense. It commemorates equally—celebrates, in childlike magic ritual—1776 as
"the overflowing of natural right in every clear and active mind of
the period." And it is prospective. It contains Ives's own personal
& private brand of superlative optimism. People. Not just the American people. Mankind. Mankind as a concept of all that July 4 1776
signified for Americans. Ives's personal & private brand of Americans.

*Thanksgiving* was the genesis of all this, *The Housatonic At
Stockbridge* its consummation. *Thanksgiving* goes back to the roots
of New England, the Plymouth Brethren giving thanks for their first
fruitful harvest. Compared with the other works—with *An Elegy To
Our Forefathers* especially—its structure is gauche, rough-hewn,
primitive. Which is as it should be, perhaps, though the orchestral

writing is clumsy, near inarticulate at times. It was scored, from
the 1897 organ pieces at Centre Church, on Pine Mountain in 1904.
Nearly twelve years later, Ives finished *The Housatonic At Stockbridge*, the piece that first took conscious shape in his mind on his
honeymoon in 1908. The progress in the mastery of his craft is
extraordinary. And, beside and beyond *The Housatonic At Stockbridge*, the last movement/4th Symphony, using the same identical
progressions drawn from the Memorial Slow March of 1901. "Vex
not his ghost. O, let him pass! . . ."

Between had come, suddenly, the two pieces that complete the
2nd Orchestral Set—to give their titles in full, *The Rockstrewn
Hills Join In The People's Outdoor Meeting* and *From Hanover
Square North, At The End Of A Tragic Day, The Voice Of The
People Again Arose*. Both times, again, this reference of Ives's to
THE PEOPLE—ultimately expressed, in the subtitle of *An Election:
"Nov 2 1920,"* as "Down With Politicians And Up With The People!" This last expression was political—social/political, i.e. "national." In *The Rockstrewn Hills* it is personal—a people's personal
expression of faith heard through a revivalist/ragtime framework.
In *Hanover Square North*, universal—the Voice of the People rising
AGAIN in commemoration, celebration, condemnation of a "national"
act that held personal and universal overtones for them: the sinking of the *Lusitania* was the act commemorated, personally, condemned, universally, "celebrated" nationally—"celebrated," in the
sense that an apocalyptic event must be celebrated AS RITUAL. As
catharsis. None of this—commemoration, celebration, condemnation, personal, national, or universal—in the tabloid/banner-head-
line/SHOCKING TRAGEDY sense. It was that, at the time, for most
people, of course. The supreme alchemy was that Ives, within the
space of a few months, was able to translate the incident into a
totally other dimension, elevate it from a sordid little "national"
aggression into a towering musical monument of faith in mankind.

The experience that Charles Ives underwent, at the age of 42,
that Friday evening on the station at Hanover Square North was,
above all else, an URBAN experience. Among all his major works,
this and the Hawthorne movement/4th Symphony are the only two
that wear an unequivocal URBAN aspect. *The Housatonic At Stockbridge* has a rural melancholy, the fourth movement/4th Symphony,
its counterpart, a sense of Olympian tragedy. The other pieces from

the 1st and 2nd Orchestral Sets, the *New England Holidays*, the 3rd Symphony, the other movements from the 4th Symphony, all speak from the Lakes and Steeples and Mountains—especially the Mountains: Pine Mountain, the Adirondacks, Olympus. *Hanover Square North* and the Hawthorne movement/4th Symphony speak, not with a New England, but a New York, a Manhattan toughness—a Manhattan sentimentality, too, at times. They are the music of the City, Faust, Caesar, reflecting both sides—the light and dark, humility and arrogance, hope and desperation. It was marvelously right that, preparatory to finishing them, Ives should embark on the final draft of the last movement/*Concord* Sonata—Thoreau.

# VARIATION V
# Concord Revisited

*Salem, Sept 1629*

Right worthy Sir: It is a thing not usuall, that
servants of one Master and of the same household
should be strangers; I assure you, I desire it not,
nay, to speake more plainely, I cannot be so with
you. Gods people are all marked with one & the
same marke, & sealed with one & the same seale,
one & the same harte, guided by one & the same
spirit of truth; & where this is, there can be no
discorde, nay, here trust must needs be sweete
harmonie. And the same request (with you) I make
to the Lord, that we may, as Christian brethren,
be united by a heavenly & unfained love; bending
all our hartes & forces in furthering a work beyond
our strength, with reverence & fear, fastening our
eyes allways on him that only is able to prosper
all our ways. I acknowledge my selfe much bound
to you for your kind love & care in sending Mr
Fuller amoung us, & rejoyce that I am by him
satisfied touching your judgement of the outward
forme of Gods worshippe . . .

JOHN ENDECOTT: *Letter to Governor William
Bradford of Plymouth Plantation*

I come down again on the social/political Ives, that part of him which
showed a deepening social/political awareness even as his creative
powers began to desert him. Not, goodness knows, all that social/
political nonsense he wrote about THE MAJORITY, &c. He was impotent by then, creatively speaking, and thrashing about like a soul
dispossessed. No, before then, before his 1918 heart attack; between
1916 and 1918, when a growing perception of all the social/political
influences that had been distilled in his music—a sudden focusing of
historical perspective, really—brought him up short, made him take
desperate issue with current social/political events. And lose out.
Lose out so completely.

No artist, composer least of all, can afford too close identification with current affairs. The first newspaper Ives saw after his heart

attack—many months after, and he seldom read the paper in any case—he said the world seemed to have gone on just about how he expected it would. And he was right. The ending of a World War, the signing of the Armistice, Wilson's 14 Points, these could be of no concern to a composer—any artist. They were too immediate, too ephemeral. Art, philosophy, religion—*culture*, in its organic, anthropological sense—moves in another dimension of time. Only when current events cease to be current (and especially the world-shaking ones), when they acquire that historical perspective, that property of the mythus, can an artist have anything valid to say about them. A composer, at least. Like Berlioz with the Trojan Wars. Or Liszt with the Battle of the Huns. But not Beethoven with his "Battle" Symphony. Close identification with a current social/political event— the Battle of Waterloo, in that case—may not be fatal for a composer, but it won't have any artistic validity. *Hanover Square North* was as close to a current social/political event as Ives—as any composer—could come without compromising his art. Even so, its wound was mortal.

I say "composer least of all." Drama, poetry, painting, sculpture, dance, these all have an advantage over music. All are visual, invoking a visual image, perceived, one way or other, with the sense of sight so far as reader or audience are concerned. A current social/political event can have an artistic validity for them if it is thrust out of focus, distorted, stylized, removed from the topical—Arthur Miller's *The Crucible*, for instance, that put Senator McCarthy and his henchmen in their proper historical perspective, back among the Salem witch-hunters. Even opera—Berg's *Wozzeck*, Menotti's *The Consul*, Verdi's *Don Carlos*—where current social/political injustices are seen through the lens of another place, another time, where words are there in any case to interpret the musical argument. Again, painting. "Guernica," with its stylized, universal symbolism will always be more immediate than, say, "Custer's Last Stand," because it is so much more than a pictorial record of a current social/political event. Record a current event too literally and you forfeit its currency. Like money, as dangerous as hard coin to a banker. Allegory, mythology are the only solvents.

But music, outside vocal music, has no mythology. Unless by extramusical association of ideas, it is incapable of allegory. What sound, unless with the aid of a massed chorus, expresses the idea

GOD ? What chord the concept SATAN ? What sequence of notes explains A SOCIAL/POLITICAL EVENT ? Who would know, without a program note to tell them, that Liszt's *The Battle Of The Huns* was based on a specific painting ? Where words or pictures are there to convey the verbal/visual message, music can support and transcend them. But only there, only then. In all else, the composer does well to stay away from social/political images, lest they betray him.

This isn't to say that a composer can be oblivious of current affairs. Ives didn't need a newspaper to know what was going on in World War I. Still less composers in Europe. And see what became of them. I think that Europe has never recovered from the cultural devastation of the 1914/18 war. Richard Strauss, after writing *Elektra, Salome, Der Rosenkavalier* in a blaze of pre-war creativity, lapsed into nearly a quarter century's perfunctory operatic writing before the final masterpieces, *Metamorphosen, The 4 Last Songs,* the opera *Capriccio,* and compromised himself irretrievably with the social/political events of the '30s. Edward Elgar, already conscious he was writing for an order that was passing when he composed *Falstaff,* in 1913, wrote only one more major work, the 'Cello Concerto of 1917, then nothing except *Pomp & Circumstance* No 6 till his death, 17 years later, in 1934. Sibelius, after *Oceanides* in 1914 and the 5th Symphony in 1915, wrote nothing of consequence for the next eight years; then the 6th and 7th Symphonies, *Tapiola,* the incidental music to *The Tempest* followed one another in quick succession, and thereafter silence till his death, at the age of 92, in 1957. Debussy wrote his last orchestral piece, *Berceuse héroïque,* in 1914 and followed it with only one other composition, the Violin Sonata of 1917. Schoenberg, so near the solution of the 12-tone riddle in 1914, the problem was shelved till 1923. Ravel joined the French Army. Stravinsky, after *Renard* in 1915, wrote nothing else during the war years except an orchestration of *The Volga Boatmen.* And so on.

Charles Ives, though quite unknown at the time, was the only notable American composer writing during the war years. Carl Ruggles, his near contemporary, did not start composing till 1920. Copland, Piston, Sessions, Thomson, were all of them youngsters. Daniel Gregory Mason, Frederick Shepherd Converse, David Stanley Smith, Edward Burlingame Hill, if they were writing during

World War I, their music has been quite forgotten. Ives was fortunate that America did not become directly involved in the war till April 1917. Between 1914 and 1916 most of his greatest music was written, and by the end of 1916 *Essays Before A Sonata* was well under way. That was where the sudden focusing of historical awareness took place. He never stood a chance after that.

The 2nd Piano Sonata—"Concord: 1840/1860"—is a major distillation of the social/political forces that were at work in America at the middle of the 19th century. Not that there is anything overtly social/political about the music. On the contrary, it is one of Ives's most esoteric works. Even his use of vernacular parody is esoteric —and sparse: *The Red, White & Blue* in the Hawthorne movement, Foster's *Massa's In De Cold, Cold Ground* in the Thoreau movement; plus Zeuner's *Missionary Chant* in The Alcotts, as tragic/lyric trans-figuration of the Beethoven figure that serves as a motto for the whole Sonata—the figure Ives used earlier in the *Emerson* Concerto, then as the basis of Piano Study No 9, *The Anti-Abolitionist Riots*. The association in his mind became inseparable: Beethoven's 5th = "Fate knocking at the door" = The Clenched Fist = Abolition. And Anti-Abolition. Except that Ives had no doubt which side Beethoven would have been on. "You—Images of a Divine Law," "Part freers of a Destiny." "*Alle Menschen werden Brüder . . .* "

(((In the Emerson movement, the Beethoven figure is used as an "intellectual force"; it is the only parody material, apart from the four ascending whole tones in the right hand at the outset of the movement, which recur in various guises at crucial moments in the musical discourse—which may or may not be consciously derived from the opening phrase of the Bach chorale *Es ist genug:* it would be wholly appropriate if they were, and it is not too early to decide that Ives, after all, was nobody's fool. In The Alcotts, the Beethoven figure is used as an "emotional force," appearing in its naked, ready-for-action state, for reasons that have been given. In the Thoreau movement it undergoes one of the most sublime metamorphoses in all music—kin to, though overreaching, Strauss's use of the Funeral March figure from the *Eroica* Symphony in his *Metamorphosen.* Only in the Hawthorne movement is the use of the Beethoven figure incidental. This was the movement Ives had most trouble with—to-gether with the Hawthorne movement of the 4th Symphony. And

Hawthorne himself, as a creative writer—the only creative writer among the four transcendentalists under discussion—was the most removed from current social/political issues, from Abolition in particular. As "the greater artist," this was imperative to him. Like Arthur Miller in *The Crucible*, the lesson of those days was inferred through the lens of Salem—*The Scarlet Letter*, "Young Goodman Brown," "Endecott & the Red Cross"—and "the hymn tune that sings only to those in the churchyard, to protect them from secular noises . . .")))

So, in this sense, then, ABOLITION as the prevailing undercurrent, the emotional/structural underpinning of the *Concord* Sonata, a thing as much ingrained in Ives's national heritage as a Lutheran chorale to Bach—a Lutheran chorale that Bach, mind you, somewhere in his own national heritage, knew had been written by the hand that wrote the 95 Theses and nailed them to a church door in Württemberg. That had been another "Fake knocking at the door," nearly 300 years before Beethoven's 5th.

(((( . . . Trafficking in slaves—running slave ships out of Africa—was declared illegal by Britain in the 1790s, by America in 1801. It still went on, while chattel slavery—the ownership of slaves—was taken almost universally for granted. 30 years later, William Garrison's was one of the first voices that actively demanded its abolition, in the weekly newspaper *The Liberator*, published in Boston, which first appeared on January 1 1831, went on appearing for the next 34 years, till slavery was abolished: "Our country is the world—our countrymen all mankind . . ." *"Alle Menschen werden Brüder."* Garrison was outlawed in the South, a price placed on his head, a U S Post Office in South Carolina broken into and copies of *The Liberator* seized and ritually burned alongside Garrison's effigy, Garrison himself dragged through the streets of Boston in 1835 and his printing press smashed. That was the year Emerson wrote:

> Let Christianity speak for the poor and the low. Though the voice of society should demand a defense of slavery, from all its organs, that service can never be expected from me. My opinion is of no worth, but I have not a syllable of all the language I have learned, to utter for the planter. If by opposing slavery I go

to undermine institutions, I confess I do not wish to live in a country where slavery exists . . .

( ( ( ( ("America/Love it or Leave . . ." ) ) ) )

10 years later, in 1845, Thoreau wrote, at Walden Pond:

How does it become a man to behave toward this American government today ? I answer, that he cannot without disgrace be associated with it. I cannot for an instant recognize that political organization as *my* government which is the *slave's* government also. When a sixth of the population of a nation which has undertaken to be the refuge of liberty are slaves, and a whole country ( (Mexico) ) is unjustly overrun by a foreign army, and subjected to military law, I think that it is not too early for honest men to rebel and revolutionize. What makes this duty the more urgent is the fact that the country so overrun is not our own, but ours is the invading army . . .

( ( ( ( ("America/Love it or Leave it/I fought for it . . ." ) ) ) )

. . . If a thousand men were not to pay their tax bills this year, that would not be a violent or bloody measure, as it would be to pay them, and enable the State to commit violence and shed innocent blood . . .

( ( ( ( ("America/Love it or Leave it/I fought for it . . ."

   *NB 1:* Fought where ?
   *NB 2:* Charles Ives, in 1938—"Patriotism is but an inflated
      form of personal vanity . . ."                ) ) ) )

. . . Why is not the government more apt to anticipate and provide for reform ? Why does it not cherish its wise minority ? Why does it cry and resist before it is hurt ? Why does it always crucify Christ, and excommunicate Copernicus and Luther, and pronounce Washington and Franklin rebels ?

After the enactment of the Fugitive Slave Law in 1851—the law that required the North to send back fugitive slaves fled from the South—Emerson again:

I go for those who have received a retaining fee to this party of Freedom before they came into the world. I would trust Garrison,

I would trust Henry Thoreau, that they would make no compromises. The Union is at an end so soon as an immoral law is enacted, and he who writes a crime into the statute-book digs under the foundations of the Capitol to plant there a powder magazine, and lays a train . . .

Among the transcendentalists, Melville and Hawthorne remained cautious. As creative writers, neither could risk compromising themselves by getting involved in current social/political issues. Hawthorne took that risk, fractionally, by writing the campaign biography of his former classmate, President Franklin Pierce, and compromised himself, not by undertaking the commission, but by having to reflect establishment platitudes— "the little band of Northern abolitionists, as unfashionable as they were indiscreet . . ." Again, in 1859, after the hanging of John Brown:

> He himself, I am persuaded (such was his natural integrity), would have acknowledged that Virginia had a right to take the life which he had staked and lost; although it would have been better for her, in the hour that is fast coming, if she could have generously forgotten the criminality of his attempt in its own enormous folly . . .

Hawthorne's, perhaps, the more balanced view. To Thoreau and Emerson, to Bronson Alcott, John Brown was a saint and martyr. And so he became, to the Union armies, when the hour had come. His body is buried in North Elba, in the Adirondack Mountains, between Keene Valley and Saranac Lake. His soul ?   Still marching on, would you say ?                          ))))

I want to quote one more writer because I believe it relevant to this whole business—Abolition, the Civil War, Civil Rights, Human Rights, Freedom, Independence, Charles Ives. I believe that Ives saw the period 1840/60 as a turning point in America's history, when the forces of culture, as an active, organic process, accomplished substantial social/political reform, that he saw one of these forces as emanating from Concord, and that this is what motivated the *Concord* Sonata. In 1922, around the time *114 Songs* was coming off the press, D H Lawrence wrote:

> . . . England had more freedom of worship in 1700 than America had. Won by Englishmen who wanted freedom, and so stopped at home and fought for it. And got it. Freedom of worship ?   Read

the history of New England during the first century of its existence. Freedom anyhow ? The land of the free! This the land of the free! Why, if I say anything that displeases them, the free mob will lynch me, and that's my freedom. Free ? Why, I have never been in any country where the individual has such an abject fear of his fellow-countrymen. Because, as I say, they are free to lynch him the moment he shows he is not one of them . . .

That letter of John Endecott's to Governor Bradford in 1629 was a giveaway. The Salem community had suffered a severe epidemic of smallpox at its inception, and Endecott was writing to thank Bradford for sending the Plymouth community's physician, Samuel Fuller. But his letter has a sharp odor of sanctimonious distaste. The Plymouth Brethren were Separatists, separated from the main stem of Puritan/Calvinist orthodoxy because they could not go along with its arrogance, their Pilgrim church in Scrooby/Yorkshire persecuted by the Puritans in 1608 and relocated in Leyden/Holland. In 1620 the Separatists got the Merchant Adventurers to sponsor the voyage of the *Mayflower*—not because they, the Merchants, were interested in founding a church, but because they wanted to further trade that had been opened up 12 years earlier in Virginia. " . . . I rejoyce that I am . . . satisfied touching your judgement of the outward forme of Gods worshippe . . . " Humbug. Endecott was seething with ill-concealed rage at the rebel Separatists, at their *inward* form of "Gods worshippe." ((And when Rhode Island Colony was settled, the Salem and Boston communities were given license to shoot its Antinomian settlers on sight.)) This is what Lawrence was on about, that "those who profess and call themselves Christians" could indulge such religious intolerance in the 17th century, still indulge all those other intolerances in the 20th.

The fact is, Europe has always been suspicious of certain snobbish and undemocratic behavior that Americans take for granted. The snobbery of the Calvinist work-ethic—class distinction by wealth, the only mark of distinction there is. For which you get a nice tin badge that becomes a status symbol. What kind of culture is that ? And the tyranny of THE MAJORITY—51% or 99%, it makes no matter, it still ignores the minority, Thoreau's "wise minority," perhaps, and the minority still is PEOPLE. What kind of Democracy is that ? Henry James wrote of Americans being "the most addicted to the

belief that the other nations of the earth are in a conspiracy to undervalue them." He was wrong. It is not a world conspiracy, but a national one. Americans undervalue themselves. The 51% majority
undervalues the 49% minority, the $20,000-a-year man the $15,000,
the established commercial product its newest identical rival. Like
the March Hare, "No room! No room!," they say. And it is all such
a waste.

In February 1923, around the time Ives was writing the song
*The One Way*, Lawrence wrote to Gilbert Seldes, music critic of the
Philadelphia *Evening Ledger*:

> No, I am not disappointed in America . . . But I feel about U S A,
> as I vaguely felt a long time ago: that there is a vast unreal inter-
> mediary thing intervening between the real thing which was Eu-
> rope, and the next real thing, which will probably be America,
> but which isn't yet, at all. Seems to me a vast death-happening
> must come first. But probably it is here, in America, that the quick
> will stay alive and come through . . .

50 years later the death-happening hasn't happened yet. The quick
have not come through. Most of them are alive and well and living
in Europe. Or would like to be.

## Postscriptum

The year Charles Ives graduated from Yale—1898—Gertrude
Stein, his exact contemporary, graduated from Harvard Annexe,
now Radcliffe College, with a paper on Motor Automatism, a study
of elementary behavior patterns. It showed the influence of William
James, brother of Henry James and a leading American behaviorist,
and she spent the next four years studying behaviorist psychology
at Johns Hopkins. In 1903 she abandoned medicine for creative
writing, and made Paris her "home town."

Ives, the only time he mentioned Gertrude Stein ((August
1934, en route for England, and shortly before his diatribe about
Sibelius)), could only be rude about her, call her "Victorian without the brains," and lampoon her style in a way that exposed him
as never having read her writing. Like Arnold Schoenberg and Paul
Hindemith 3 years earlier: he was rude about them, by inference,
while boasting he had never heard or seen a note of their music.

I don't know whether Gertrude Stein ever expressed an opinion about Ives's music, though one of her chief disciples, Virgil Thomson, has been fairly waspish from time to time. And from the same uninformed position as Ives about Gertrude Stein. What matters, both Ives and Stein were interested in one & the same thing—BEHAVIOR: Stein in the behavior of words as sounds, Ives in the behavior of notes as sounds. And their findings, as expressed in what they wrote —words & music—are amazingly parallel.

Gertrude Stein was incidentally in on one of the first phases of American behaviorist psychology and adapted the science to her literary use. Charles Ives, through the social/political involvement that came with the loss of his creative powers, was compelled more and more to examine the motives behind human behavior. Totally unequipped, professionally speaking, totally unsuited, temperamentally speaking, he floundered. And, except that he now had nowhere else to direct his intellectual energies, he needn't have troubled. All the answers—wrong and right, but mostly right—were already present in his music.

## Subscriptum 1

Benjamin Lee Whorf was born in Winthrop/Mass, April 24 1897, studied chemical engineering at MIT, and in 1919 was apprenticed as a fire prevention engineer to Hartford Fire Insurance Company, becoming a Special Agent in 1928 and Assistant Secretary in 1940. He is known today for his pioneer work in linguistics, his study of the languages of the Aztecs and the Hopis, and the lost writing system of the Mayas. His essays and articles, published in 1966 under the collective title *Language, Thought & Reality*, include "The Relation of Habitual Thought & Behavior to Language," "An American Indian Model of the Universe," "The Punctual & Segmentative Verbs in Hopi," "Science & Linguistics," "Linguistics as an Exact Science," "Languages & Logic," "Language, Mind & Reality." His unpublished novel, *The Ruler Of The Universe*, written in 1924, is an attack on the complacency of secular modern man, and closes with a vision of the universe which God created and man perverted, returning in judgment to its preformed state of chaos:

> . . . The earth would spout lava from 10,000 volcanoes; the earth's green coat of vegetation would char, smoke, and blaze; the earth

would become red hot, orange hot, golden hot, white hot, *blue* hot; liquify, gasifying, expanding with the rush of broth boiling over; now an enlarging sun bigger and hotter than the old sun, now enveloping that sun and the planets. The nebula explodes; all its energy becomes rectilinear; it flashes into pure light. When this huge blast of energy reaches the nearest stars they likewise expand and explode; the disturbance is propagated from star to star to the farthest outposts of the universe; and *bodiless* light is all that remains . . .

(((and "The Silences," heard beyond in undisturbed solitude . . . )))

Whorf died in 1941, at the age of 44, following a heart attack . . .

## *Subscriptum 2*

Ezra Pound was born in Idaho, October 30 1885, and died in Brunnenburg, Italy, in 1972, at the age of 86. He is linked incidentally with Benjamin Whorf in his close study of esoteric languages and their linguistic quantities, more directly with Gertrude Stein in their application to the creative use of language, which progressed from VORTICISM (*c* 1912) through IMAGISM and *vers libre* (*c* 1918) to the PROJECTIVE VERSE of the Cantos. Pound shared 4 things in common with Charles Ives:

(1) A sensitivity to inner metrical structure that went far beyond current musical intelligence: e.g. Pound's operas— one, based on the verse of Cavalcanti, a contemporary of Dante, unfinished, the other, *Le Testament*, a 1-act opera based on the poetry of François Villon, first performed in Paris in 1926. In later revivals—by the BBC in 1962, for the Spoleto Festival in 1966—its "unnecessarily complex metrical notations" (5/8, 11/16) were "ironed out" (into 4/4 ?) because it was thought, by musicians, that Pound didn't really understand what he was doing . . .

(2) A concern with "duration," i.e. the time span involved before two or more metrical designs overlapped. Pound

was an early champion of George Antheil (b New Jersey, 1902) and, in 1927, compared him with Stravinsky thus:

> . . . The *Sacre* stands, but its cubes, solid as they are, are in proportion to the *Ballet mécanique* as the proportions of architecture are to town-planning. Technically, the fact is, that Mr Antheil has used longer durations than any other musician has attempted to use—much longer . . .

(((Charles Ives, unknown to Pound, had been using even longer durations back in 1904, and more especially in 1915, with the "Universe" Symphony and its vision of cosmic durations . . . )))

> According to Pound, Antheil, as early as 1923, proposed the "tuning in" of whole cities, and "silences 20 minutes long *in the form*"—anticipating the inspired whimsies of Claes Oldenburg in the '60s, with monster windshield wipers sweeping the Chicago sky, a baseball half a block wide rolling ceaselessly from one end of Madison Avenue to the other. And always John Cage, of course, bringing up the rear . . .

(((Ives's "Universe" Symphony was to have had "from 6 to 10 different orchestras placed on separate mountain tops, each moving in its own independent time orbit, and only meeting one another when their time cycles eclipsed . . .")))

(3) As an extension of 2, a mastery of medieval, renaissance, and oriental styles—highly cultivated in the case of Pound, largely intuitive in the case of Ives, whose concern with oriental music extended to a serious interest in quarter tones and an implicit understanding of the function of Indian *raga* and *tala*. Writing of Arabic music, Pound says:

> In especial, one notes the "extraordinary" length of the rhythmic pattern units, comparable to the medieval rhyme schemes of Provençal canzos, where, for example, one finds a rhyme pattern which begins its 6-ply repeat after the seventeenth terminal sound. In this Arabian music, as in the Provençal metrical schemes, the effect of the

subtler repetitions only becomes apparent in the third or fourth strophe, and then culminates in the fifth or sixth, as a sort of horizontal instead of perpendicular chord. One might call it a "sort of" counterpoint, if one can conceive a counterpoint which plays not against a sound newly struck, but against the residuum and residua of sounds which hang in the auditory memory . . .

(4) A command of PROJECTIVE style, "open" as opposed to "closed" verse, using both poetry and music as a 3-dimensional form, as sculpture not painting. In the mature music by Ives, the small as well as the large works, one is aware, as with Pound, of SHAPE rather than SIZE, of FORM that has grown out of the substance of the materials. This had happened before, of course. In the case of music, it has not, conspicuously, happened since. All the ideas are there, but the materials are generally substandard.

Ezra Pound, 11 years younger than Charles Ives, became progressively more involved in social/political issues in the '20s, as had Ives in the teens. Pound suffered stigma in his native country during and after World War II, as Ives, during and after World War I, had not. But Pound, though compromising himself in the United States, found in Italy a *modus vivendi* which did not compromise his work. Ives, forced by a sense of patriotism to no social/political compromises, yet compromised his work irretrievably.

In 1934, Pound wrote a Postscript to his Memoir of the Polish sculptor Henri Gaudier-Brzeska, killed in action on the Western Front in 1915, at the age of 23:

> For eighteen years the death of Henri Gaudier has been unremedied. The work of two or three years remains, but the uncreated went with him.

> I dare say there never was a man better fitted to serve in trench warfare, and his contempt for war is a message. A contempt for war is by no means a contempt for physical courage.

> With a hundred fat rich men working overtime to start another war or another six wars for the sake of their personal profit, it is very hard for me to write of Gaudier with the lavender tones of

dispassionate reminiscence. The real trouble with war (modern war) is that it gives no one a chance to kill the right people.

Good sculpture does not occur in a decadence. Literature may come out of a decadence, painting may come out of a decadence, but in a decadence men do not cut stone . . .

.  .  .  .  .  and MUSIC ?    ) ) ) )

# The Breechin'
# Under the Horse's Tail

Or, as Charles Olson put it, sarcastically, "There is nothing which happens to us which we don't have the right to know what the —— goes on."

Mister Jones: modern infallibility personified. Can't stand mystery. Every fact and fetish neatly labeled and tidied away in a nice new pigeon hole. But there's a lot of people now can't stand Mister Jones any longer. NO MORE BULLSHIT, they say to him. And quite right. The curious thing is, a late Victorian square, name of Charles Edward Ives, born a century ago, was saying the same thing all along. In his music.

You can discount most of what Ives wrote, about his music or not about it. If you don't know the music it is misleading. If you do know it, it can be even more misleading, especially to the literal-minded Mister Jones = ROLLO.

You can discount most of what Ives was—insurance man, armchair politician, &c—aside from his being a composer and a performer. And the man, the example of him.

But you can't discount the music, for the music contains every stance of youngminded rebellion: ardor, anger, satire, high comedy, low comedy, deep tragedy, the suffering and expectation of youth, above all, its optimism, its confirmation of FUTURE. Some of it staidly conventional, old-fashioned; much of it ill-fashioned, poorly made, awkward, self-conscious. This also is a stance of youth. Human nature does not change. Old men still dream dreams, young men still have visions.

Except, today, there is abroad in the world a spirit of complacency that would like to put a stop to all this. It would like to see change the only thing about human nature that can never change, its will to change. In its overweening impudence it would stop the world if it could, halt its motion, its changing seasons, enjoy high summer all year round, careless that the other half the world endure perpetual winter for its benefit. This spirit of complacency has always had music for one of its creatures. And music, too much of it, has been a willing creature.

Ives once told Carl Ruggles that he became middle-aged "long before the Kaiser hog-marched into Belgium"—August 1914, when Ives was 39. That was the first summer spent in his own home in West Redding, and West Redding, really, was the undoing of him. Strange irony, that there is a dimension of genius that is destined to be homeless, like Emerson's American Scholar, destined to be poor. Home & hearth, family, prosperity, happiness even, are the especial confounders of genius.

For these, all of them, are the appurtenances of THE SYSTEM, the "fringe benefits," what the Protestant work-ethic is all about. It cannot produce genius, except in despite of itself, because genius, greater or lesser, is an absolute; THE SYSTEM a compromise, a *modus vivendi*. Genius has no use for a *modus vivendi* because it can survive only in isolation; THE SYSTEM only as a community, a corporate enterprise, team sports, competitive, conformist. Genius is an active: it makes things happen; THE SYSTEM a mediocrity that prevents things from happening. It is bad taste to talk about genius, THE SYSTEM says; genius is elitist, exclusive, undemocratic, "not like us." But if we can't talk about genius what shall we talk about ? Trade schools ?

Go back to Thoreau, to his apperception of a freshness, a wildness "which no Augustan nor Elizabethan age, which no CULTURE, in short, can give." This was Ives's enchantment. "Mythology comes nearer to it than anything . . ." Liberty as a fiction of the past. Plus Melville's quest for honesty: ". . . I hold it a verity, that not even Shakespeare was a frank man to the uttermost. And, indeed, who in this intolerant universe is, or can be ? But the Declaration of Independence makes a difference . . ." George Bancroft, Hawthorne's sometime sponsor, caught the flavor of it fourteen years earlier, in 1835:

> If with us the arts are destined to a brilliant career, the inspiration must come from the vigor of the people. Genius will not create, to flatter patrons or decorate salons . . .

Compare then with Melville again, in 1851:

> In Shakespeare's tomb lies infinitely more than Shakespeare ever wrote. And if I magnify Shakespeare, it is not so much for what he did as what he did not do, or refrained from doing. For in this world of lies, Truth is forced to fly like a scared white doe in the woodlands, and only by cunning will she reveal herself, as in Shakespeare and other masters of the great Art of Telling the Truth,— even though it be covertly and by snatches . . .

A mere moment of emphasis separates this from what Charles Ives tries desperately to say, in 1934:

> Even those considered the greatest (Bach, Beethoven, Brahms, &c) have too much of it, though less than the other rubber stamp great men. They couldn't exactly help it—life with them was such that they had to live at least part of the time by the ladies' smiles —they had to live by the ladies or die. And this is the reason— through their influence—that no one can prove (not even the ladies) that there has been any great music ever composed—that is, in this world. And this is not criticizing or running down or underappreciating Beethoven, Bach, et al, as it is a respect and wonder that they didn't do a lot worse under the circumstances.

The specter, stigma, of artistic compromise. The struggle with the material apparatus, acting hustler for THE SYSTEM, "working for the Yankee doll*aaaar* . . . " Entertainer, jokester, monkey on a stick. No one wants the job except the most isolate/desolate souls, but every original mind must go through the struggle, come through it one way or other, compromised or not, emasculated or not, *wanted* or not—alive or dead. The establishment, THE SYSTEM, at bottom wants only to be amused, play games. It has no use for men of originality, unless originality be prostituted as "entertainment."

Ives chose to cut the Gordian knot by going into business, using business to subsidize his music-making: He had this paranoia about artists—composers—who used their art "primarily to make a living." It was so much moonshine, because an artist who was open to corruption by the establishment, by patrons and flatterers, started out with something less than artistic integrity in the first place. But Ives occupied a strange position in American music *c* 1900/1916. A writer like Herman Melville at least enjoyed the fugitive love of fellow genius, Hawthorne, the more enduring friendship of fellow writers like Richard Henry Dana, publishers like Evert Duyckinck. Ives enjoyed the friendship or even the passing interest of NO PUB-LISHER during his creative life, no fellow musicians except David Stanley Smith and Max Smith. And they, truly, were the best the musical establishment had to offer. It hardly seems credible, the musical waste-land that prevailed in America at the time. All those American composers who went to Europe, instead of staying home and building something indigenous. Consider that the authors of *Moby Dick*, *The Scarlet Letter* found at least the wherewithal for material survival in 1852. Who, in American music, could survive, 50 and 60 and 70 years later, with works of equivalent originality ?

The 3 PROPOSITIONS, then:

(1) Genius can survive only in isolation;
(2) Genius will not create, "to flatter patrons or decorate salons";
(3) Genius is an active: it makes things happen.

Ives had no problem over (1). Like Hawthorne, his native shyness was a defense against the outside world. His Danbury upbringing was provincial/suburban: apart from his father, none spotted the seeds of genius awakening in him, and that was well. His mother, interrupting his work to have him run errands for her, Aunt Amelia, fussing about him not getting enough fresh air, "shut up all day in that stuffy room," even Moss, parading his new piccolo in front of him for him to look at: all these were commonplace—Melville fared no better. At Yale, Ives earned the blessed neglect of Horatio W Parker and found musical anonymity in extramusical popularity, being "a nice guy," with a string of nicknames long as your arm. At Poverty Flat the same: Edwards Park was astonished to learn, in later years, that Ives had been "a musical genius"—he had no idea, he said, and was none the wiser, for having learned it, what "being a musical genius" entailed. Even in marriage, Ives instinctively sought a mate who would not intrude herself on his music, who favored isolation in their daily lives. He had no need to avoid his musical peers because he sensed there were none, in America, at the time. And he was right. He was not masochistic. He showed some of his music to a few friends and acquaintances who didn't like it; he wasn't going to risk showing it to strangers—"some of them famous, so-called." Except Damrosch. Damrosch was the brother of Clara Mannes who had been at Farmington School with Harmony, so he showed him one "safe" score—the 1st Symphony—and sent him another—the 2nd Symphony. But it was never Ives who was on trial. It was Walter Damrosch. And he was weighed in the balance and found wanting, so far as Ives was concerned.

And so the continuing obscurity. No one recognized Ives's genius because no one was qualified to recognize it. Yet who, during his lifetime, had recognized Bach's genius, *as a composer* ? Who Schubert's ? Who Mozart's, even ? Precious few. Genius is not concerned with recognition; it creates because it must. Maybe Mahler recognized Ives's genius. Certainly Goossens and Slonimsky did, later. All three had the advantage of a European cultural heritage, where the phenomenon of "being a musical genius" was not unknown. But for Ives himself, during the creative years, isolation and obscurity were welcome—more, essential.

Except that, even then, they were not quite complete enough. His letters to his future father-in-law in 1907, to John Griggs in China in 1922, are their own tell-tale: his search for a paternal blessing, for paternal absolution, continues even there. Most of this other paranoia of his, about Mozart, was because Mozart had been taught largely by his father; so had Ives, by his father, and he never forgave himself, in those later years, that he failed to live up to his father's expectations for him, to elect poverty, to "live as simply as Thoreau." So he took it out on Mozart. But unlike Mozart, Ives did not die penniless. So he took it out on Sibelius, who used to enjoy being mistaken for a successful businessman . . .

No apparent problem, either, with Proposition No 2. Ives had

no instinct for flattery or decoration. Fair of face/full of grace—
that, yes, perhaps. But that asked pedigree, the pedigree of a cultural
heritage, something that didn't come out of a bottle or a test-tube.
The pedigree of a Mozart—and how close to corruption Mozart himself came. Only think, if the Viennese musical establishment had
continued to bestow its favors on him, instead of turning to Salieri.
Mozart chose poverty, had poverty thrust upon him, and survived—
the spirit of him. Ives chose wealth, had wealth thrust upon him, and
ultimately did not survive. But not because he ever became a flat-
terer or decorator.

He could afford not to have to become one, of course. So could
Gertrude Stein, Jan Sibelius, George Gordon Byron. Wealth really
has nothing to do with it. There have been those of independent means
whose whole life was flattery and decoration, those of meager means
whose sole ambition. If Ives did not ultimately survive, as an artist,
it had nothing to do with his being a man of wealth. But if Horatio
Parker had "recognized" him, back at Yale ? Or Elizabeth Sprague
Coolidge ? Only look at David Stanley Smith, Daniel Gregory
Mason.

PROPOSITION NO 3. "Genius is an active: it makes things happen." This is the reverse image to (1), Genius in isolation. It took
nearly 100 years for the genius of J S Bach to be acknowledged,
longer to get his MSS into some articulate order, and new readings
still are coming to light. That is the price society must pay for its
neglect of an artist, the bankruptcy of its soul. In Ives's case, all his
MSS—all that had not been lost—went into the barn on Umpawaug
Road after his retirement, and lay there virtually untouched till his
death, 25 years later. Untouched, that is, except by Ives himself. His
closest friends—the Ryders, Nicolas Slonimsky, Carl and Charlotte
Ruggles, the Cowells—all are/were agreed that Ives, in his later
years, diabetic, arthritic, palsied, diseased heart and failing eyesight,
still retained his youthful vigor, animation, enthusiasm, that there
was nothing "tragic" about him. This was the face he chose to show
them, and it was a precious face. But there was another Charles Ives,
restlessly brooding over his forgotten MSS, pulling out sheaves at
random to live for a while with some incident of the past, add a few
notes or marginalia, shove them back haphazard into one of the
drawers—anywhere but where they had come from. Was this evidence of any faith that they would some day be considered valuable

to others ?   Behavior you would expect from someone who once
had been a successful businessman, had the orderly mind and self-
discipline that characterize a successful businessman ?   And this
went on for 25 years. Is it any wonder the MSS were found in dis-
order ?   What can have been the innermost thoughts of this man,
once so fertile, now, his last 37 years, creatively impotent ?   What
can they have been after rave reviews for the 4th Symphony in 1927,
major performances in Paris and Berlin in 1931 and 2, and then
nothing, or so little, till shortly before his death, when everyone was
climbing on the bandwagon ?   And nothing accepted for publication as a commercial venture till his 74th year. Small wonder he was
so scathing about "commercialism" in music. Melville, Hawthorne,
Whitman had not to suffer such indignity.

For, although he somehow forfeited his creative powers in early
middle age, Ives knew that he had done right by American music.
But American music had not done right by him. By 1930, by 1935,
there could be no excuse for his genius not being recognized. Not
that he gave a solitary cuss for recognition—only flatterers and dec-
orators sought flattery and decoration. *But nothing had happened.*
There was still no authentic mainstream of American composition.

There could not be. Full, even adequate recognition of this obscure New England source would have meant the sweeping aside of
the musical establishment, of a host of middle-generation composers
who, one way or other, had paid homage to that establishment, the
uncloaking and exposure of its huge incompetence. It would have
been like Germany after the first recognition of Bach in the 1830s
and '40s: every intermediate German musical figure before Mendelssohn, Wagner, and Schumann ((Mozart and Haydn were Austrian/
Hungarian, Beethoven went early to Vienna)) has been passed over,
and posterity has forgotten them.

And what price posterity anyway ?   It is an establishment sop
we use to salve our consciences in, 99% lip-service, remembering
genius for a day, in a year's time, in fifty years, a hundred. More
than that is not possible, we live now and have all the problems, and
what do we care about those who had them before ?   Genius is
meaningful only if we see it happening, now, as it is supposed to
happen, living, vital, vivid—not paid homage to, written about, stuck
in a museum to atrophy and brought out once in a while for show.

What homage can vindicate the actual anguish of genius unless we are exposed to that anguish, capable of sharing it ?   If as musicians, then constantly ?

American posterity, it seems to me, is acutely embarrassed about Charles Edward Ives. He fits no convenient notion, no ready-made pigeon hole as to what genius and artistry are supposed to be like. He was not eccentric, except as posterity has chosen to portray him as eccentric. He was not Bohemian. He was not avant-garde— though years ahead of the avant-garde. He did not die young, or go deaf, blind, or insane. He did not go on composing till his dying breath. In every way except one, he was the stereotype of a gentle, genial, generous upper-middle-class American. But Ives the composer . . . . .

"Great geniuses," wrote Melville in 1850, "are part of the times, they themselves are the times, and possess a corresponding colouring . . ." 1850, if a single date can be apportioned, was the year in which J S Bach was first discovered to a wider audience, the first German composer of a Germany grown articulate, a Germany grown articulate in part by reason of him, his genius acknowledged in the moment of articulation and straightway transcending national limitations.

. . . . . Ives the composer remains, still in largely silent reproach of a nation's music-making, its way of life, the way of life of music-making as a whole. Still largely silent, because few have ventured his music to be properly heard, or, being properly heard, accorded proper attention. But the world cannot wait while America gets it together, and now the sound, impatient, is gone out into other lands. Charles Ives is FERMATA. Full stop/half circle. End and beginning.

Ishmael the son of Abraham was made outcast by his step-mother and became the founder of a new race.

The goddess Pallas Athene, according to another legend, in-

vented the flute, but, taunted by Eros for the grimaces she made playing it, cast it away. It fell to earth where it was found by the mortal,
Marsyas, who wrought upon it such strange and marvelous music, he
was flayed alive in punishment by Apollo.

# APPENDIXES
# AND
# INDEX

# APPENDIX I

## FROM THE STEEPLES AND MOUNTAINS

The source material for this book has been chiefly primary: the Ives MSS themselves, with their copious marginalia, now in the Ives Collection, Sprague Hall, Yale University, made available to me through the courtesy of Dean Luther Noss and the Curator, Mr John Kirkpatrick, and a number of discrepancies with the existing catalogue of Ives's MSS noted; the Public Records Office, London, for the will of Thomas Ives, of Swatham, Norfolk, and the passenger list of *Truelove;* Norwich Town Hall, for information concerning Capt William Ives and a letter addressed to "John Ives, Esquire, of Swatham"; the Town Halls and church records in New Haven, Wallingford, Meriden, Danbury, and Brookfield, for details of nine generations of the Ives family; the Danbury churches, the Public Library, and the Scott-Fanton Museum, for information about Ives's boyhood; Trinity Church, Boston, for information about Horatio Parker; St Thomas's Church and Centre Church, New Haven, for information about Ives's organ posts there; Mr Charles Stebbins, present owner of "Wood's Cottage," Keene Valley, where Ives stayed in 1896 as a guest of the Twichell family, and first met Harmony Twichell; the archives of the Mutual Life Insurance Company of New York, on Nassau Street; *The Armstrong Report,* in 16 volumes, which is a verbatim transcript of the investigation in

1905; St Luke's Hospital, New York, and the Trudeau Institute, Saranac Lake, for information concerning Dr David Twichell; the Probate Courts of Redding, Danbury, and Ridgebury, for the property title to 10 acres of woodland on Pine Mountain; Mr Peter Sanders, proprietor of Elk Lake Lodge, formerly owned by Mr Pell Jones; White Plains Town Hall, for the property titles to houses owned by Mr Edward Hamilton Whitman, of New York; Mr J LeViness, for information about Charles Ives, Thomas Healey, Commander Evangeline Booth, and the history of Hartsdale; the Keene Valley Historical Society and Mrs Anna Brode, of Keene Valley, for information about Ives's visit to Keene Valley Plateau in October 1915; the late Mr Thomas Matthews, of Scarsdale, New York, who was present at the convention of Life Underwriters at the Waldorf-Astoria in April 1917; the Danbury General Hospital, to examine medical records in connection with Ives's 1918 heart attack; the files of the Pro Musica Society and the International Composers Guild; unpublished letters to Mr Nicolas Slonimsky, which he kindly made available to me, and have since been published in the second edition of *Music Since 1900*, Charles Scribner's Sons, 1972; the Roosevelt Hospital, New York, for details of Ives's last illness; and Redding Probate Court, once again, for a sight of Ives's will.

Secondary sources—compared, wherever possible, with the primary source—have been a transcript of family correspondence from 1880 to 1894, made available to me through the kindness of Mr John Kirkpatrick; *Essays Before A Sonata* (Knickerbocker Press, 1921; W W Norton, 1972). Source material for the epigrams that appear at the head of most chapters, and for extracts from published material in the body of the book, is self-explanatory. The extract from Horatio Parker's diary is drawn from the biography by his daughter, Mrs Elizabeth Parker Semler. The topographical information in Ricercar II is drawn from Verplanck Colvin, *The Adirondack Wilderness*, and from Mrs Van Wyck Brooks, *Gramercy Park*. The copies of Stephen Crane's *The Red Badge Of Courage*, Arnold's *Poetical Works*, Browning's *Paracelsus*, and Hawthorne's *The Marble Faun*, referred to in the text, are all of them in the library of West House at Yaddo, and were discovered for me by Miss Pauline Hanson. The talk with Mr Eugene Goossens, which is at such variance with some of the views expressed in his earlier autobiography, took place at his home in Maida Vale, London, on July 4 1961, and is my own best recollection of the conversation. The diaries of Harry Ellis Wooldridge, and a number of letters to him, are in my possession. The note in Gustav Mahler's hand-writing is in the music librarian's ledger for 1910, in the archives of the Deutsches Museum, Munich. The anecdote about the late Sir Henry Wood was told me by his daughter, Miss Avril Wood, of the British Council. The anecdote about the American Embassy in Berlin was told to me by Dr Klemperer himself.

# APPENDIX II

## SELECT DISCOGRAPHY

Readers familiar with my idiosyncrasies will know that I am no champion of phonograph recordings. At best—the old electric 78s of the early 'thirties, even some of the early monaural LPs—they were like black & white photographs of sculpture: not to compare with the actual multidimensional experience, of course, but better than nothing, for black & white at least could convey the illusion of the original contour, and leave other dimensions of experience to the imagination. At worst—and this takes in most recording since the advent of Hi-fi Stereo, "Living Presence," &c—they are like color photography, obscuring the one dimension that black & white at least can suggest, perverting the imagination with their artificial "realism," and pandering to the unimaginative with a mishmash of mechanically induced sensations. Recording engineers, many of them, are become our latter-day prima donnas, holding court on their recording stages, demanding constant flattery, sabotaging many a fine performance because the recording artist is "difficult to work with," performing obscene miracles of face-lifting on mediocre interpretations that would never be allowed inside the concert hall. It is no longer possible to judge, without access to the recording history, whether an actual recorded performance was good or bad—though a very good performance will always transcend recording's limitations. It is only possible to say whether the level of engineering was good or bad. And much of it, for all the elaborate recording gear that is used nowadays, remains very inadequate. As the man said, we forget our roots.

However, one of the purposes of this book has been to stimulate interest in Ives's music, and it would be perverse of me not to include some sort of list and let readers judge for themselves. Most of Ives's music has been recorded now, and those who would like a comprehensive discography are referred to the excellent supplement by David Hall in the paperback reprint of the Cowell book, *Charles Ives & His Music* (Oxford University Press, 1968), and to the recent *Charles E Ives: Discography*, compiled by Richard Warren, published in April 1973 by Yale University Library. My own list excludes all those recordings which I have not heard—and there are many of them—and those recordings which do not measure up to what I would consider adequate professional standards, whether of performance, recording, or both. Where no satisfactory recording exists at all, or is out of print, I have said so. My list falls into the usual five major sections, viz: CHORAL MUSIC (Sacred & Secular), VOCAL MUSIC (including solo voice with chamber orchestra), CHAMBER MUSIC (including music for chamber orchestra), KEYBOARD MUSIC, and ORCHESTRAL MUSIC (for full orchestra).

## 1. CHORAL MUSIC

There are two albums that cover almost the entire gamut of Ives's mature choral writing, from *Psalm 67* (c 1893) to *On The Antipodes* (completed, from the 1904 sketches, between 1915 and 1923). Both albums are by the Gregg Smith Singers and the Columbia Chamber Orchestra, with the occasional addition of the Ithaca College Concert Choir and the Texas Boys Choir of Fort Worth. The first album, recorded in Hollywood during two recording sessions—July 1965 and May 1966—was released in 1966 (Columbia ML–6321/MS–6921) and has *Psalm 100, Psalm 67, Psalm 24, Psalm 90* (with Esther Martinez, soprano, and Melvin Brown, tenor), *Psalm 150, General William Booth Enters Into Heaven* (chamber orchestra version by John Becker; with Archie Drake, bass), *Serenity* (reconstruction of the original version by Gregg Smith), *The Circus Band* (orchestration, from the original MS fragments for band, by George Roberts; with

Archie Drake, bass), *December, The Ruined River,* and Three Harvest
Home Chorales. I have not heard the Gregg Smith Singers in the flesh,
and the poor sound quality and indistinguishable diction seems due,
either to capricious balancing, or to the acoustics of the Columbia
recording stage itself. There is a world of difference in the quality and
articulation on the first side of the second album, which was recorded
in New York City at the 30th Street studios in April 1965, and contains
the *Processional:* "Let There Be Light," and the four other extant
*Psalms—14, 54, 25,* and *135.* Back in Hollywood for the September
1967 recording session, the quality of the second side deteriorates
sharply for the original versions of *Walt Whitman, Duty, Vita,* and
*On The Antipodes,* and eight solo songs with chamber orchestra—*The
Last Reader, Luck & Work, Like A Sick Eagle, Tolerance, When The
Moon Is On The Wave, The Pond, At Sea,* and *The Rainbow.* The
soloists are William Feuerstein, baritone, and Adrienne Albert, mezzo-
soprano, who also sings *The Children's Hour,* from *114 Songs.* (Columbia MS–7321).

> There is a better version of *Psalm 67,* recorded by the Robert
> Shaw Chorale for WNBC/New York in September 1948.
> This is not commercially available. And there are two better
> recordings of the Harvest Home Chorales: one, again by the
> Robert Shaw Chorale, recorded in January 1962 and re-
> leased the following year (RCA Victor LM–2676/LSC–
> 2676), the other by the Indiana University Singers under
> Fiora Contino, recorded at a public performance in Recital
> Hall, Indiana University School of Music, in December
> 1968. This is the finest performance of an Ives choral work
> I have ever heard.

Of the other choral works, the *Hymn-Anthem:* "Abide With Me," for
male chorus, piano, harp, and organ, remains unrecorded by anyone.
So does the Cantata *The Celestial Country*—apart from the movement
for vocal octet a cappella, which was recorded for WNYC by the
Greater New York Chorus under Edgar Varèse in February 1945. ·

> According to Richard Warren, Columbia Records recorded
> *The Celestial Country* with the Gregg Smith Singers in 1972,
> but the record has not yet been released.

The four remaining major choral works—*Lincoln, The Masses, An Election: "Nov 2 1920,"* and the 1942 War Song March, *"They Are There!"*—were recorded for Columbia Records, all of them for the first time, by the Gregg Smith Singers and the American Symphony Orchestra under Leopold Stokowski, on October 17 1967 in New York City. At the time of writing, nearly six years later, they have not been released. In view of their explosively political texts, as it must seem today, it might be thought that Columbia Records were waiting for a more liberal political climate to prevail. But no. The Musicians Union has forbidden the release of this album, because they want to make an example of Stokowski, who had committed the unpardonable crime, as an American citizen, of making records in other countries. And this is a man who has been championing the cause of new American music since long before any of them were born . . . ((Subject to the payment of an enormous fine, the record was to be released in 1973. Meanwhile Stokowski has returned to his native England, and, at the age of 94, is still contentedly making music over there.))

## 2. VOCAL MUSIC

The bulk of Ives's song literature has been recorded, some of it many times over, much of it by assuredly very fine artists. And yet, though I have heard very few of these recordings, I find myself feeling unreasonably—unpardonably—skeptical about those I haven't heard. I feel that the whole approach to singing Ives's songs is fundamentally wrong. I remember hearing, many years ago, a BBC broadcast, by a fine English tenor, of the little song *"1, 2, 3,"* which was made to sound absolutely ridiculous because the singer's diction remained immutably, impeccably, inimitably "BBC English." On the other hand, I have heard many incontestably fine American singers who feel no compunction about reducing Ives's songs to the level of vaudeville. There is a deal of humor in these songs, many of them, of course, which speaks best if it is allowed to speak for itself, and is not undermined by a lot of burlesque grimacing. This is bad enough, in all conscience, where the singer's behavior is willful. It is intolerable where it is unintentional. There is a dry, sentimental frailty to *Down East,* for example, if the song is overlaid with a tinge of Maine dialect. But this vanishes utterly where the song is sung with a brash Hoosier vulgarity, like something out of a tenth-rate musical comedy. There is humor in *Charlie Rutlage*—but there is also pathos, poignance, a touch, even, of stark tragedy, all concentrated into a song which is one of the greatest songs written this century because it is so difficult to maintain a fine balance between all these conflicting elements. It calls for consummate mastery, and that is rare. The only masterful interpretations I have heard—in recording—are by Hubert Linscott and Aaron Copland, recorded in 1932 at the first Yaddo Music Festival, and by Mordecai Bauman and Albert Hirsh, recorded in 1938 for New Music Recordings (NMQR–1412: out of print).

This 78 disc also contains *Ann Street, Evening, The Greatest Man, Resolution,* and *Two Little Flowers.*

Then again, not many of the songs are equally suited to the male and the female voice. There are three recorded versions of *Soliloquy,* but I cannot bring myself to listen to any of them because all three are sung by sopranos. Very well, no doubt. But the widely spaced accompaniment, where 2 pianists are mandatory, calls for a male voice to fill out the middle register. And do masculine justice to the text. On the other hand, songs like *The Pond, The Indians, Like A Sick Eagle*—in their original chamber orchestra versions or the voice & piano arrangements—are eminently suited to a woman's voice, which can ride gloriously over the delicate complexities of the accompaniment. Not to mention the peculiarly feminine pathos of these songs. It takes a woman's voice to bring just expressive emphasis to words like "their children go to die," from *The Indians,* or the suppressed turmoil that was in Ives's mind when he wrote *Like A Sick Eagle.* Adrienne Albert is wonderful in the Columbia album (Columbia MS–7321).

Generally speaking, I believe that most of Ives's songs lend themselves more readily to black singers, because the black voice is more innately expressive than the white voice (English or American), has greater natural beauty, a wider dynamic range, is capable of taking awkward and unusual intervals with greater ease and flexibility, capable, in fine, of more "soul." Charles Ives was a WASP composer, to be sure, but in general his music goes beyond the WASP mentality, because it deals in a dimension of suffering that the average WASP may be able to empathize with, but has no direct experience of. Only imagine what a voice like Paul Robeson's might have done with *General Booth,* bringing to it a whole social/political/cultural identification. And I

marvel at what Cleo Laine does with the few Ives songs she so far
has in her vast repertoire, and wish to goodness her recording company
would allow her to record some of them. There is, for example, no
recording at all of *Aeschylus & Sophocles*—I suspect because it is
still waiting for a singer with something of Cleo Laine's vocal wizardry.

## 3. CHAMBER MUSIC

There are four main subdivisions: Chamber Orchestra, String
Quartet, Trio, and the four Violin & Piano Sonatas. I exclude the Pre-
1st Violin Sonata, which became other things, and also the pre-Pre-1st
Violin Sonata.

In the first category, there is the marvelous old 1951 monaural
recording by the Polymusic Chamber Orchestra under Vladimir Cher-
niavsky (Polymusic PRLP–1001), now sadly out of print, which includes *Over The Pavements, Hallowe'en, Central Park In The Dark,*
and *The Unanswered Question.*

> Another excellent performance of *Over The Pavements* was
> recorded by Denis DeCoteau and the Grinnell College Or-
> chestra in 1967. A fine performance of *Hallowe'en,* in its
> original piano quintet version, was recorded by Paul Zu-
> kofsky in 1970 (Columbia M–30230). There is no satis-
> factory version of *Central Park In The Dark,* but the re-
> cording of *The Unanswered Question* by Morton Gould and
> the Chicago Symphony Orchestra (RCA Victor LM–2893/
> LSC–2893) is superior even to the Polymusic version: it is
> really essential, in this work, to have a full string section
> playing off-stage, and the string section of the Chicago Sym-
> phony—not forgetting the wind and percussion sections—
> was second to none in this country by January 1966, when
> this recording was made.

Also in the first category, there are three pieces recorded in the summer
of 1968 by members of the American Brass Ensemble, and issued the
following year (Nonesuch H–71222): *From The Steeples And The
Mountains* (with the carillon of Riverside Church, New York, recorded
separately and dubbed in), *Song For Harvest Season* (with Jan De-
Gaetani, mezzo-soprano), and *Chromatimelodtune.*

*From The Steeples* is problematic in performance, because
the range employed by Ives for the four sets of tubular bells
exceeds, by a long way, the standard range of orchestra bells.
Since they are involved in a constant series of increasingly
rapid scale passages, it is neither feasible nor practicable
to transpose the missing notes in the octave. The only solution is to build extra tubes of the required length. This has
been done in the version by Lukas Foss and the Buffalo Philharmonic, recorded in April 1970 and released in 1971
(Turnabout TV–S–34398).

In the String Quartet category, there are three recordings that
should be mentioned: a sensitive performance of the 1st String Quartet,
by the Amici Quartet, recorded in Dagenham, England, in June 1967
(Pye GGC–4104/GSGC–14104), and the equally sensitive performance,
by the Walden Quartet, of the 2nd String Quartet, recorded in 1946
and released the following year on 78s, reissued in 1950 as an LP
(Period SPLP–501), now out of print. The Walden Quartet gave the
first performance of the work, at Yaddo in 1946, and that performance
is preserved in the recording still at Yaddo. A third recording, which
couples both Quartets on the same disc, is by the Juilliard String
Quartet, recorded in March 1967 and released that year (Columbia
ML–6427/MS–7027). These are both highly distinguished performances
by a very distinguished quartet, but the London *Times,* in a review of
the recording in May 1968, made the shrewd point that the playing was
"too well-bred to include Ives's marginalia . . . " ((Too well-bred to
include Bartok's marginalia, too, perhaps.))

In the Trio category—obviously the Piano Trio, first and fore-
most—there is a very good version by Paul Zukofsky, violin, Robert
Sylvester, 'cello, and Gilbert Kalisch, piano, recorded in May 1970
and released the same year (Columbia M–30230). This record also
contains *Hallowe'en* (mentioned above), *Largo Risoluto* Nos 1 & 2,
for Piano Trio, the Clarinet Trio (with Charles Russo, clarinet), and
the original version of *Hymn,* for violin, viola, solo 'cello, double bass,
and piano.

A major problem about the performance of the Piano Trio
has been that the published version, by Peer/Southern, is
riddled with mistakes. This was largely due to incompetent
editing, but in all fairness, the original MS had been lost,

the George Roberts copy was known to exist but could not be found, and the publishers had only three incomplete versions of poor photostat to work with. After the work had been published, the George Roberts MS came to light, and enabled John Kirkpatrick to discover a host of errors that had eluded him in the photostat MSS, and compile a 23-page, single-spaced typescript that in turn contains several errors —mainly of misjudgment, as in his misguided attempt to put the "Sunrise Cadenza" into a metrical straitjacket. But, alas, Kirkpatrick is a shy man, and kept all these "revisions" largely to himself, so that early performances—including the first recorded performance—were predestined to disaster. Peer/Southern, after nearly 20 years, are now considering a second, "revised" edition, restoring the original text.

Lastly, the Violin & Piano Sonatas. There are several versions of all four, but the recording which seems to me to outrank all the others is by Rafael Druian, violin, and John Simms, piano, recorded in August 1955 and released in Mono in 1956 (Mercury MG–50096/7), reissued in "electronic stereo" in 1966 (Philips PHC–9018/9).

Rafael Druian, subsequently concertmaster of the Cleveland Orchestra under George Szell and Pierre Boulez, is the violinist who has given such magnificent performances of the Berg Violin Concerto—which is the key to his equal understanding of Ives's violin writing. Another tremendous exponent of the Berg—David Abel, of the Francesco Trio—is the only other violinist I have heard give a convincing account of the 4th Violin Sonata, in a recorded recital at Grinnell College in January 1971.

## 4. KEYBOARD MUSIC

There are three versions that I know, of the *America* Variations, for organ: (1) by E Power Biggs, recorded the summer of 1960 in the First Universalist Church, Woodstock, Vermont, on an organ built in 1875—an organ such as Ives must have played in Danbury, where the piece was written—and released the same year (Columbia ML–5496/MS–6161); (2) by Christopher Dearnley, recorded October 1969 on the organ of St Paul's Cathedral, London (HMV CSD–3677); and (3) by Gerd Zacher, recorded November 1970 on the organ of the

Church of Imanuel, Wuppertal, Germany (Wergo 60058). In the chromium-plate orchestration by William Schuman, the only version I know is by Morton Gould and the Chicago Symphony, recorded in January 1966 (RCA Victor LM–2893/LSC–2893).

> William Schuman tells me that he conducted the Variations —the theme of which is identical with "God Save The Queen," the British National Anthem—with the London Symphony Orchestra in 1971. At the first rehearsal, one violinist in the orchestra was mortally offended, refused to play, and delivered a long admonishment about "this affront to Her Majesty." He was Hungarian.

### Three-Page Sonata

No satisfactory recording. The three available versions all have an Uncle Tom gentility about them that reminds me of Joplin's playing at its most sober.

### Piano Sonata No 1

The best recording by far is by William Masselos, who gave the first public performance of the work on February 17 1949. It was recorded on Mono in December 1950 and released in 1953 (Columbia ML–4490); reissued in 1967 by Odyssey (32–14–0059). In the meantime Masselos had rerecorded the work for RCA Victor, who released it in 1967 (LM–2941–LSC/2941) after all existing copies of the Odyssey issue had been bought up and—presumably—destroyed. When a second issue of the RCA Victor record was planned, it was found that the original master tape was substandard, and had disintegrated. The recording has now been withdrawn from the catalogue. The original Columbia Mono version is in any case much better, both as to performance and recording.

### Piano Sonata No 2   "Concord, Mass., 1840–1860"

Charles Ives himself gave a number of semi-public performances of this work, and recorded parts of it at the Abbey Road studios of the Columbia Gramophone Company, London, on June 12 1933. The first major performance of the sonata was given by John Kirkpatrick, at Town Hall, New York, on January 30 1939.

I wish William Masselos would record the work. The one recorded version that impresses me is by Aloys Kontarsky, with Willy Schwegler,

flute, recorded in Cologne in November 1961, and released in this country the following year (Time 58005/S–8005). One major reason why
I prefer this recording is that it uses the off-stage flute at the end of
the Thoreau movement. I know that Henry Bellamann thought that
its introduction broke the mood, both of the movement and the entire
sonata—that John Kirkpatrick thinks the same—that it was better to
let the *idea* of Thoreau's flute remain an abstraction. But the disembodied
flute sound, coming as Ives wrote it, seems to me to be a symbol, not
only of Thoreau himself, but of the spirit of Transcendentalist Concord, of New England Transcendentalism as a whole. To dispense with
the off-stage flute, and use Ives's *ossia* (only consider his other *ossias*,
intended for "Mus Docks, dear & nice"), is surely to miss the entire
point of the sonata—the entire point of Ives's music, really. And to
dispense with the flute is to lose the transcendental calm that descends
over the final measures, over the remembrance of the whole work, after
the flute sounds die away.

## 5. ORCHESTRAL MUSIC

### Robert Browning Overture

The first recorded performance of this work was by Leopold Stokowski at a public concert in New York, October 1963, followed by
the two commercially recorded versions that interest me: (1) by Leopold Stokowski and the American Symphony Orchestra, recorded in
December 1966 and released the following year (Columbia ML–6415/
MS–7015); and (2) by Morton Gould and the Chicago Symphony
Orchestra, recorded in February 1967 and released the same year (RCA
Victor LM–2959/LSC–2959). Stokowski's interpretation is the more
luminous, and charged with the sense of overpowering alchemy that
the work demands. The record is unfortunate for the performances,
by two other conductors of two other orchestras, that appear on the
reverse side. The Chicago Symphony performance is wonderfully clean-
cut and hard-driving—wonderfully played, too, with never a sense of
flagging in the cruelly exposed brass writing. The string-tone is un-
pleasantly thin, and intonation faulty, in the extreme upper register—
something that is not at all in evidence with the much younger American
Symphony Orchestra. The Morton Gould record has the advantage of
having the 2nd Orchestral Set, and *Putnam's Camp*, from the 1st Orchestral Set, on its reverse side.

*Orchestral Set No 1  "Three New England Places"*

Apart from Morton Gould's performance of the second movement, mentioned above, the only recording that appeals to me is by Howard Hanson and the Eastman-Rochester Orchestra, recorded in May 1957 and released in 1958 (Mercury MG–50149), Stereo version in 1959 (SR–90149). This is a conductor who could bring a passionate conviction to the interpretation of works he believed in, and *Three New England Places* is one of those works. The Eastman-Rochester Orchestra is made to sound very much finer than it deserves to sound. Frankly, I am waiting for someone to resurrect the original version, for full orchestra and organ.

*Orchestral Set No 2*

The version by Morton Gould and the Chicago Symphony Orchestra (RCA Victor LM–2959/LSC–2959) is the only one so far in existence, and nothing could be finer than this performance of a work of tremendous eloquence and subtlety, and enormous complexity.

*Four New England Holidays*

Incredibly, there are still no satisfactory recordings of any of these pieces—each a separate entity, and two of them (*Decoration Day, 4th Of July*) among Ives's greatest writing. There are a number of recorded versions available, but there is something in each and every one of them which mars them ineradicably for me.

*Symphony No 1*

The Chicago Symphony Orchestra, under Morton Gould, again, is the only performance I can recommend. It is an unequal work, but the second movement is hauntingly beautiful early Ives, and a clue to his later command of vast arches of sustained melody. Recorded, with the *America* variations and *The Unanswered Question,* in November 1965 and released in 1966 (RCA Victor LM–2893/LSC–2893).

*Symphony No 2*

There is no recording of the authentic version. In the spurious version, the best performance I have heard was the BBC recording made by Bernard Herrman with the London Symphony Orchestra in April 1956, and broadcast on May 25 of that year.

*Symphony No 3*

Even more than *3 New England Places,* Howard Hanson's performance with the Eastman-Rochester Orchestra—conveniently on the

reverse of the 1st Orchestral Set (Mercury MG–50149/SR–90149)—
gets to the core of a work that is Ives's private and personal testament
to Evangelical Christianity. It is one of the very few Ives works that
requires, nay, demands, and even vindicates, the convictions of an
Anglo-Saxon Protestant mind. Technically by far the least demanding
of Ives's orchestral works, Hanson gives a reading that radiates gentle-
ness and simplicity. And, withal, a passionate sincerity that recalled
his early years with the Eastman School. But I am scandalized by the
arrogant, insensitive, careless playing of this symphony in other recordings I have heard, by famous orchestras—so-called—and famous
conductors.

> It is tragic that the original MS is still lost, because there are
> things in all the available recordings—even Bernard Her-
> mann's recordings for WCBS, which incorporate Ives's cor-
> rections—that Ives himself added, or left out, or changed,
> or tampered with, when he had to rewrite the score, virtually
> from memory, at Elk Lake in 1911. The original score *must*
> be found.

### Symphony No 4

Still the only version for me—and the only version that follows
Ives's express direction for at least 2 or 3 conductors—is the recording
by Leopold Stokowski, with David Katz, José Serebrier, and the American Symphony Orchestra, recorded on April 29/30 1965 and released
the following month (Columbia ML–6175/MS–6775). The interpretation—like any interpretation of character—is open to criticism: wrong
tempi (for some), wrong dynamics (for some), changes in instrumentation (for some), willful distortions of the music (for some), &c, &c.
But Stokowski's most virulent critics are not his peers—and he has
many of them—but accomplished little musicians who are dedicated
to the art of triviality. The man remains an enigma. The sound he
produces from an orchestra—recorded or live—has always been im-
maculate. At worst—and that can be very bad indeed—he offends
against the accepted tenets of "good taste." At best, all the eccentricities
of his readings are swept aside in performances that are so convincing,
only the most bitterly prejudiced can take exception to them. And
what of them ?  What tenets of "good taste" do they observe in their
own performances of Ives's music—if they have the ability to perform
it at all ?

The recording of the 4th Symphony was made under the direction of Columbia's chief recording engineer, John McClure, a few days after the symphony's first complete public performance, at Carnegie Hall. The labor of deciphering the abysmal copying, both of the score and the orchestra parts, was accomplished during the first two rehearsals for that performance, so that most of the time at the recording sessions could be spent making music, or at least trying it out for the benefit of Mr McClure. The final recorded performance has a rarity of distinction that places it among the greatest recorded performances of all time.

# INDEX

*(Herein all musical and literary works have been italicized for greater clarity.)*